Cross Country Dreams
and the Journey to a Championship Season

CHRIS QUICK

BREAKAWAY BOOKS
HALCOTTSVILLE, NEW YORK
2013

One Way, Uphill Only: Cross Country Dreams and the Journey to a Championship Season

Copyright © 2013 by Chris Quick

ISBN: 978-1-62124-008-2
Library of Congress Control Number: 2013945593

Published by Breakaway Books
P.O. Box 24
Halcottsville, NY 12438
www.breakawaybooks.com

Palatine team website: PalatineCC.net
(Twitter @PalatineXC)

Chris Quick's personal author site: QuickTakes.net
(Twitter @cquicktakes).

FIRST EDITION

This book is dedicated to my wife, Meredith,
my three crazy children—Madeline, Christopher, and J. J.—
my parents and brother,
and all the Palatine boys, coaches, and parents
who helped make my dreams come true.

To Marcus, Tony, Peter, Timmy J, and Monkey,
thanks for the thrill of a lifetime.

CONTENTS

PREFACE

Each year thousands of high school athletes embark on the journey of their seasons. From the highest varsity level to the freshmen "B Bombers," high school sports are an integral part of how young people define themselves. All athletes join their high school sports teams for a reason. Some might seek individual excellence or team glory. Others might search for self-improvement or a sense of belonging. Hopefully, playing sports is still fun and gratifying, no matter the level of aspiration.

In that tradition, high school cross country athletes begin their season's odyssey in the sweltering heat of summer training and end in the crisp beauty of the fall racing season. Whether they run on a powerhouse team or are just conditioning for another sport, cross country athletes have more that unites them than divides them. They all understand the trials of miles, the searing fire in their lungs during a race, and the day-to-day commitment it takes to find that magical improvement. Each runner who toes the line in a race—whether a local dual meet, a major invitational, or the state finals—comes to the starting line with a goal. It might be to win the race. It might be to run a new personal best. It might be a simple desire to beat an old rival. Whatever the reason, each person toes that starting line running toward something.

This book is aimed at all those young men and women who step to the line looking for something deeper. Unlike football, baseball, or basketball —sports played with a ball and in concert with others—cross country racing begins with an individual dilemma. *How much am I willing to hurt myself today?* Team play only begins when each individual answers that question and accepts the pain. All sports require sacrifice of their own varieties. The unique aspect of running a three-mile race is that the primary opponent is you. After all, you can stop at any time. No 250-pound behemoth is going to inflict pain on you. No six-foot-six dream of a shooting guard is going after your jugular each time down the court. In cross country racing, the attack comes from within.

As a longtime athlete, fan, and coach, I have always wanted to read a book that captured the uniqueness of high school training and racing. I've read numerous books about training, running history, and collegiate cross country, but I've never found one about high school running that sated my thirst. Chris Lear's *Running with the Buffaloes* comes closest to expressing the insular and tight bond of a championship-level cross country team, but it does so only for the collegiate level. The University of Colorado at Boulder is located in rarefied air. Adam Goucher went on to be an Olympian. Mark Wetmore is one of the greatest distance coaches in the United States. What I wanted to read was something more common, something about the roots of that greatness.

Since I couldn't find such a book, I decided to write it. An Advanced Placement English-Language and Composition teacher, I had sadly let my own writing lapse even as I taught others to write. After a while, that felt a lot like driving alongside my boys when they were out on a hard twelve-mile run.

I found my inspiration to write again from an amazing group of thirteen sophomore students in my critical thinking–gifted class. Three of those students—Michael Nowicki, Jenny Ripka, and Faith Hollander—pursued writing for their semester-length independent study projects, and they challenged me to complete a project as well. Writing seemed only natural. It is an old rule of thumb to "write what you know," so the Palatine boys cross country team became appropriate fodder.

After finishing fourth in the state of Illinois and returning most of my varsity team, I knew that we were going to be good in the coming year. But I had no idea where the journey would go. So I started to document the daily happenings of the team in journal form, usually for one free period per day in the English computer lab in Room 217. My first journal documented a long run I did with the boys the Monday after the

Nike Cross Country National meet. After nearly qualifying as a team, a number of my juniors went to Portland and ran the open race. When they returned, it was their belief that we could win the national meet the following year.

I immediately had my idea for this book. From beginning to end, I wanted to document—for them—the year we spent trying to reach this goal. While winning nationals was a worthy goal, our more important mission was to win the first boys cross country state championship in Palatine history. Five times previously we had finished second to Elmhurst York, the greatest high school powerhouse in American cross country history. I promised them that I would write this narrative as their graduation gift.

I am happy to say that I finished the week after they graduated, and they now have a memento of the incredible ride we went on together in quest of state and national championships. Some may think this book a self-righteous declaration from a solid, but not entirely great, cross country program from a random suburb of Chicago. There are certainly programs with better reputations and better credentials. The intent was never to boast. Instead, I aim to offer glimpses into the journey toward our ambitions. I would guess that we share much with all athletic strivers at the high school level. The gap between aspiration and end result is often daunting. But the teams that win decide to try anyway. We stated the goal and went after it with everything we had for an entire year.

This narrative centers on the relationships among me, Peter Tomkiewicz, Marcus Garcia, Tim Johnson, Anthony Gregorio, and Tim Meincke as we tried to make our common dreams come true. Many more athletes and coaches were central in the season, but their roles are diminished here for the sake of a cleaner narrative. I hope that everyone involved with the Palatine distance team knows how vital they were to our success. I'd like to thank all of the athletes, parents, alumni, and coaches who helped us along the way. Many of the instrumental players are mentioned if not fully fleshed out. I would never have been in position to coach our team toward a state championship without the help of hundreds of Palatine loyalists.

In the end I hope this book reads like what it is: a love letter to my team and to running itself. It was written piece by piece, event by event, through the ups and downs that all coaches and athletes experience as the dramas of our seasons unfold. As I wrote, I had no idea how our journey would end or who would be proven the hero or the goat. At times it spares no punches.

Characterizing developing young men of seventeen and eighteen years of age is never easy. I tried to render both myself and the boys as faithfully as possible. If that offends, I apologize. We are all flawed people seeking to do our best in an athletic pursuit—nothing more, nothing less. I hope that any coach would be able to empathize with the trials and tribulations of this narrative. Disappointment and elation are constant companions in any career spent guiding young people. Whenever our seasons are all said and done, I hope we all realize that the journeys we take and the memories we make are the true successes, whether we win state championships or not.

I knew back in December 2010 that the coming year might be the best one of my life. Already blessed with two healthy kids, my wife and I learned she was pregnant soon after I began writing, and the story of my family runs in parallel to our athletic quest. The book is thus part narrative and part memoir. I understand that the writing of such a personal experience could come off as self-serving, but I invite you to meet the young people I worked with and see for yourself. "The Fab Five" and I spent three and a half years rendering this one three-month season into being. I hope you enjoy the ride as much as we did.

Chris Quick

BEGINNINGS

The men arrayed themselves across the starting line and prepared for the firing of the starter's pistol. Down the long line earnest youths performed their final rituals before entering the fieriest crucibles of their lives. Some milled around, nervously shaking out their arms and slapping their quads. Others prayed. Still others huddled with their friends and teammates. In a few short moments the men of Palatine, twenty-four other teams, and the best individuals from the state of Illinois would thunder down the broad incline of Detweiller Park to battle for the 2010 Illinois state title in cross country.

The crowds had built throughout the day, watching the title races in the smaller classes as they waited for the main event—the Class AAA boys. Lukas Verzbicas of Carl Sandburg, defending Foot Locker national champion, was about to take on Craig Virgin's immortal course record of 13:50.6 for three miles. Jack Driggs, the erstwhile champion from the legendary Dukes of York, was set to challenge. The men from Neuqua Valley laced up their spikes and prepared to defend their state title. The year before, they had run the perfect team race to win it all. Upstart programs such as O'Fallon and Lake Zurich knew that today might be their time to ascend the podium. Each team had arrived with a dream.

The race would be contested under the brilliant finery of a perfect November day. Temperatures hovered in the high fifties, and crisp sunshine cascaded over the open field. The crowning bluffs surrounding the park resounded with the crisp yellows and burnt oranges of oak and maple trees. Near the finish line one maple tree had shed most of its yellow leaves the night before. Only a few brave stragglers held on. To the east the Illinois River slinked easily through the landscape. Another dry

Illinois autumn had firmed up the course and dust rose in the air as fans and athletes scrambled to their final places.

By late afternoon comfort displaced the early nippiness. The assembled throngs eschewed their hats and winter jackets in favor of one more stolen moment in their summer regalia. Frantic teenagers ran their school flags across the starting field while others casually tossed Frisbees or applied face and body paint. The York pep band, ensconced among the denizens of the Long Green Line three hundred meters from the finish, played with its usual gusto. More than five thousand people awaited the furious action of the fastest race of the day. The giant crowd, though, was oblivious to the storming tempests inside the stomachs of the men.

In Box 18, seven young men from Palatine prepared to take their shot at a state title. Anthony Gregorio wore his usual mask of anger and focused grumpiness. Slightly built and small of stature, he did not look the part of a champion. He shifted his weight nervously from foot to foot, cracking his neck and preparing to marshal his speed. Reuben Frey and A. J. Laskowske, the senior leaders, inhabited their silent resilience. Marcus Garcia furrowed his thick eyebrows into a race-day scowl. With his sweat up, Ryan McGough's Irish cheeks betrayed their ruddiness. A half-miler by trade, the nervousness gripped him harder than the rest. Stoic as usual, Tim Johnson held the fence and swung his leg nervously to and fro, trying vainly to loosen his hips and his nerves. But there was nothing loose about these final moments. Even Tim Meincke, the team joker, a man who rarely bent a serious thought anyone's way, wore a mask of concentration. As each wiggled in the starting box, the whistle called the field to attention. Slowly the men tightened their formation in the close confines, steadied themselves, and bent their knees into a starting crouch.

As the starter ascended his ladder, a deafening quiet descended over Detweiller Park. The once buzzing crowd found solace in its quiet, and the men . . . well, the men found no solace at all. The empty stomachs gnawed at each, anxiety incarnate. The sudden quiet drained the air from the surrounding atmosphere. Even the muttered mingling of relatives and friends in the crowd dwindled away. The starter scanned up and down the line. Each athlete grabbed his last gasp of calm breath. The orange-sleeved arm went up in the air. Then, the long cry of the whistle. Sometime in the next thirty seconds, the gun would be fired. The starter waited for all to be still. Previously twitching muscles reached for impossible bits of calm as each man anticipated the imminent explosion. For a moment everything in the world receded to zero. The coming action held no value. Past action held no value. Man by man they all reached the deadly space between the whistle and the gun.

Five hundred meters away I stood with Matt Sheehan and my assistants, pointer finger taut on the start button of my wristwatch. Once started, I would probably not look at the watch until long after the race's conclusion. Such rituals brought comfort in nervous moments. We tried to chatter away the hopes and fears that might be exposed in the next fifteen minutes. We tried to pretend that this all did not matter as much as it did. We tried to pretend that an entire year of work was not on the line. We had poured our energy into dreams that could only be fulfilled by the seven teenagers who would carry the burden. Finally, it all came down to a simple matter of physics. First, the speed of light. The assembled throng exploded into action headlong down the beginning incline. Then, the speed of sound. The whip-crack of the starter's pistol hummed over the now driving young men. From afar it looked like a grand cavalry charge, the Light Brigade once more descending into the valley of death. In some respects that is what it would be. An act of self-destruction.

Finely wired with taut muscles and sleek as a gazelle, Verzbicas effortlessly bounded to the lead. The opening descent underscored the beauty of his galloping rhythm. In his wake followed Driggs in the legendary green and white of the Dukes of York. After shadowboxing for an entire season, the two heavyweights now became conjoined. Close on their heels came the men of Palatine.

Leading the charge, Tim Meincke embraced his desperate audacity, possibly for the first time. Stuck as the seventh man on the Palatine var-

sity, he had spent most of his season fending off challenges from his teammates. In all respects he was not supposed to be near the lead. Bending
around the congested open curve at the north end of the course, the field
turned left and completed the hairpin back toward the finish line and
the crowd. A shock of red shot to the front as Meincke's irrational turn
of speed sparked his teammates to action. Reuben Frey moved up to join
him as Gregorio rode his shoulder. As they approached the half-mile
mark, Marcus Garcia and Tim Johnson joined the trio to create a desperate cordon of five across the front of the main field. Verzbicas and
Driggs bolted by the massive pine at the famous "zigzag" and felt the full
energy of the crowd for the first time. The cheers from the Long Green
Line buoyed their champion, and he ran with the force and aura of the
hundreds who had preceded him. Next through the turn came the entire
scoring five from Palatine.

Photo by VIP Photography

The Palatine boys charge to the lead at the 2010 Illinois state meet.
From the left, Marcus Garcia (1809), Tim Meincke (1812), Reuben
Frey (1804), and Anthony Gregorio (1807). Tim Johnson is also vis-
ible on the far right.

Two months before on this course, the same group of runners had placed eighth in the Peoria Notre Dame Invitational. Their mistake that day had been passivity. They had forgotten what happens to men who do not run with a severe want. Determined not to relive that moment, Tim Meincke bundled up the considerable ocean of irrationality at his disposal and unleashed it with his full force. Seventh men do not lead the state meet. Not for long anyway. But there was something inspirational in his running. I felt it leaning over the ropes as I screamed out, "2:13!" when they passed the half mile. Years of experience told me we had just committed the cardinal sin. Lesser runners do not open at that pace at Detweiller. The opening decline had seduced many across the years. To open at that pace a man would have to be anything but a lesser runner.

We'd created our own trap the night before in our final team meeting. All week long, we'd fed the guys newspaper clippings about men from Palatine who had unleashed legendary performances in this race. We told them about Bob Watson's drive for home to win the 1988 state title, and Steve Finley's desperate surge in the final meters to do the same in 2005. We told them of nobodies who had found their stride and men who had given their all in the service of the team. Mostly, we told them about Mags. In the lead-up to the 1980 state meet, Mark Magnussen had been injured and in Coach Joe Johnson's doghouse. Coach Johnson even held Mags out of the varsity lineup at the conference meet, forcing him to prove his worth at a JV invitational. Mags survived the test and then led his team to a sectional title and a berth in the state finals. After a ripping speech from Coach Johnson, Mags silently reached a conclusion: He was going to run as hard as he could for as long as he could. That line of thinking saw him run the first mile of the 1980 state meet faster than he had ever run one single mile. At the exit of the back loop, Mags and teammate Lou Guerra were first and second in the state.

The picture of that duo adorned our bulletin board all week. Mags went on to finish thirtieth as Palatine won its first-ever state trophy. Only 18 points separated them from Elmhurst York and the top of the podium. It would be the first of five times that Palatine claimed the runner-up trophy in a year when York won.

Tim Meincke was our Mags. I sprinted away with desperate hope in my legs, but concerned. I half expected all of them to fade badly heading into the back loop. I ran full-bore across the field to my normal spot at the loop's entrance and listened to the roar from the top of the course. Thousands of fans lined both sides of the running lane before the field took a tight left-hand turn at the top of the hill and ran behind the starting line. As the runners passed the fans, the wave began. First from the lower reaches of the course and then proceeding toward the finish line, people turned and began their frenzied migrations to the highway side. Crazed fans streamed across the opening field in frantic flight. As a youth I had performed this ritual year after year in support of my dad's teams. Now I could only watch as the race came my way.

Illinois Highway 29 runs parallel to the park on its east side, and casual travelers must stare in befuddlement at this odd spectacle each year as they unknowingly enter its chaos. Now running downhill again, the field descended toward the mile mark, ignoring the stray cars that slowly passed on their right. The growing swell of sound indicated their imminent arrival. The roar built steadily from buzz to cacophony and then crescendo. Spectators lined the ropes three- and four-deep all around. Through the tunnel of noise only the heads of the athletes and flashes of school colors could be seen in the small gaps between the fans. Flashes of jerseys and elbows sparked hopes and fears as I awaited our fate. The rational side knew what was coming. They could not hold that pace. We had blown it. How could we be so stupid? All that work . . .

And then the field popped around the corner and came parallel to the woods. And there they were. Six of them. Tim Meincke took the right-hand turn across the bridge at full tilt and dove into the back loop in sixth place. Still locked to his hip were Reuben and Tony. A. J., Timmy J, and Marcus followed through right on their heels. If this was to be an act of self-immolation, it would at least be a delayed burn. Later, I would look at the unofficial scores recorded by the timing chips at the one-mile mark. We led our closest competitor, Oak Park–River Forest, by a score of 57 to 138. In cross country the scoring is simple. You take the top five guys, add up their places, and the low score wins. Our entire scoring five was in the top twenty at the mile.

After watching seventh man, Ryan McGough, hammer into the back loop, I crossed the second bridge nearby to watch the race unfold in "the Triangle." Although the triangular section ceased to exist after the course's revision in 2003, the name stuck. Everyone involved with Illinois cross country knows that the Triangle sorts out the early speed from the true players. Far from the roaring crowd, the men come back to earth. When they exit the loop, the real race begins.

I darted into the loop at full speed and hauled to the halfway mark. I was having the time of my life. I'd always wanted to coach a team that was in the thick of it. We were. Gregorio looked strong and comfortable in his lead position, but the others had begun to fade, first slightly and then badly. I crossed the path at the halfway mark moments before Verzbicas arrived. His split was ungodly. He covered the first half of the race in 6:50, well ahead of Virgin's record pace. Stuck in the mire now, Driggs broke from the leader and looked content to hold second place. His dreams of an individual title were over, but the team title still hung in the balance. Behind the lead duo, no hierarchy had been established.

Our men wore their distress all over their bodies. While more responsible runners paced in rhythm up on the balls of their feet, I could see our leg and arm action slacken. Gregorio's chin waved ever so slightly side-to-side while Reuben took the bellowing breaths of a fading man. His quads produced less and less lift with each stride. I chided each man in turn to relax. I implored them to compete. I also gave them a message that might spark a rally: "We're winning! We're winning! We're winning!" As usual Marcus looked me in the eye and gave me a look that said, *We got this.* I was far from sure. Meincke's early spirit crumbled under the weight of the start as his previously flowing stride disintegrated. Each stride shortened, and his action became more vertical. He foundered like a sinking ship at sea as runners swarmed by on each side. It was the last time I saw him until after the race. He had inspired his teammates to bold action, but his race was over.

As the guys exited the loop, our odds were getting smaller, but I would have taken fifty-to-one before the race. Maybe this was our one. I tore off down the entry road with a posse of crazed Palatine fans and alums to get to the inside of the course at the mile-and-three-quarters mark. Someone had finally stirred up the hornet's nest at the front of the race. Malachy Schrobilgen and Jack Stapleton, the powerful Oak Park duo, hammered by with Cody Webster, the sensational miler from East Moline, just adrift. Guys who had run more conservatively started the drive for home while our front five struggled to maintain composure.

Our goal was to be winning at the two-mile mark and then find a way to bring it home. At the halfway point we clung to a narrowing 115–148 lead over Lake Zurich, but the climb to the two-mile mark knocked us out. The scoring runners from the two great powers in the state—York and Neuqua Valley—ate us alive from behind. The drums of the band and the waves of green fans urged the Dukes on, and their five seniors, friends across the years and all of Coach Joe Newton's miles, answered the call. After executing their patient race plan yet again, the men from Neuqua Valley also responded. Coach Paul Vandersteen's winning plan from the year before had convinced them that they owned the last mile of this race. From the bottom of the course I could see our guys running up the course's inside line and fading. Now there was a mile to go and nothing but seven bankrupt men. Former Palatine coach Fred Miller calls the uncharted waters of the final mile "the moment of truth." He believes there is no physiology that can prepare a man to answer the call. He has to own a spirit capable of fighting the pain.

As the race made its way down the highway one final time, I hoped for one last rally. Tony had established himself inside the All-State top twenty-five and was clearly running great. He came by in eighteenth place, struggling to maintain composure, but sturdy. A. J. and Timmy J passed in thirty-fifth and thirty-seventh, fading but united. Reuben held on just adrift, desperately now, vainly managing to keep his poise. Despite the fade, we were still in it big. Just down the crowd line, Vandersteen urged his men forward. They were charging, up on the balls of their feet. Running with only one shoe, junior star Mark Derrick moved right into the thick of our pack. His junior teammate Taylor Soltys had already passed, charging headlong toward the top fifteen. In the early fifties, Marcus Garcia tangled with the middle of the Neuqua Valley pack. He looked sublimely melted. His cheeks and eyes drooped from the strain. His lifeless quads struggled to find the power to fight the good fight in the deep hurt of the race. I gave him the best advice I had, hands beating on the ground, voice cracking, my battered Cal hat sweat-stained and adrift: "Marcus! Marcus! Marcus! Marcus!" I hoped the vocal electric shock would serve as resuscitation. As the fifth man, his spot would matter the most in the scoring.

I hooked it up the incline as best I could, hoping to get to the finish line before Verzbicas. Craig Virgin's 13:50.6 is the standard for greatness in Illinois cross country. Until Chris Derrick from Neuqua Valley ran 13:51 in 2007, I had never seen anyone remotely approach it. In full flight behind the crowd line I followed the great champion as he strained up the final incline. His long brown locks bounced above the crowd line, but his stride's earlier grace faded amid the agony of the uphill finish. Desperately he tried to hold form and summon more speed. The announcer counted down the seconds to the record over the public address system, but Verzbicas's early speed came back to haunt him, too. Later he would describe his narrow miss of the record as the consequence of a divine wind. He won in 13:54. Driggs finished second in 14:15, but had done his job. The Dukes of York had a two-point stick in their battle for a twenty-seventh state championship.

Plowing into the coaches' area at the finish line, I saw the top two cross while frantically searching for my parents and brother. Afflicted with cerebral palsy since birth, my brother, Chad, is a legendary fan. He and his wheelchair have been fixtures on the finish line at state since 1980. I found him with his electric wheelchair pulled up to the fence, standing on his foot pedals and screaming maniacally at East Moline's Cody Webster as he kicked home in third place. Even though my dad used to coach their crosstown rivals—the Moline Maroons—blood runs thick in the western part of Illinois. My father had coached Webster's mother as a prep and Cody's coach, Chris Wallaert, had been a captain for my dad. My brother wore his battle face. His cheeks flushed to a deep crimson as his frantic voice implored my boys to move. He screamed at no one in particular. He just implored them all to "GO!" I stood on the battery pack of his wheelchair and grabbed my dad's shoulders to steady myself for the final view.

Outside our state, people would probably laugh if told that the Illinois state meet finishes up a hill. The final three hundred meters of the race certainly go up an incline, but only in Illinois would anyone call it a hill. Still, after nearly three miles of racing, each man must face the ultimate test of Illinois cross country. Three hundred meters out the course zigzags ever so slightly around a pine tree and then comes face-to-face with the finish line for the first time. There comes a point in the state meet when everyone's cards are on the table, when the athletes have been flat-out for so long that nothing remains. Utter emptiness. When each runner gets to that point, he will hit the zigzag and then see who he really is. These three hundred meters—a distance runnable in under a minute—separate the glorified from the also-rans. I knew that our race strategy left us ill equipped for the finish, but every now and then in racing you place a bet and go all-in. The boys had risked everything. We had agreed that we were a single-outcome unit. There had been no discussion about second or third. We only toed the line to win.

With Driggs safely in with low points, that prospect darkened, but I still held out hope as I watched Tony Gregorio slide his tongue sideways out of his mouth and fight up the inside line for every last spot. His habit of chewing on his tongue in desperate moments betrayed just how far into the well he had gone. A thicket of five guys caught him just before the finish line, and even one last surge couldn't get him around. He crossed the line in twentieth, safely All-State for the first time. Unfortunately three young men from Lake Zurich passed just in front of him. I had hoped that our area rival would find the bright lights of the state meet too hot, but they had risen to the occasion.

I looked desperately for the rest of our men. I could see them hammering up the inside line in close contact, but they were no longer in the mid-thirties. Derrick and his single shoe had gotten by three of them in the final drive and so had York's sophomore star, Alex Mimlitz. A. J. Laskowske burst to the line close on their heels, mouth agape and arms driving like pistons. The week before he had run a disappointing race. This one was far from it, a forty-fifth-place capstone effort for one of the toughest runners of my career. The rest of the scoring then came in a frantic blur. Five more York runners and two from Neuqua mixed in with two more from Palatine. The long-held dreams of so many young men came down to slivers and fractions of seconds in the final desperate moments. Neuqua's Vincenzo dal Pozzo drove past Reuben to close right on the heels of his teammate Josh Ferguson, who caught Tim Johnson fifty meters from the line. The York seniors and their sophomore wingman refused to lose on this day—Hedman, Hedman, Simo, Gornick, and Milling all finished in the space of five seconds. My heart sank. York had all seven men in the chute. Where was Marcus?

With Palatine and Neuqua Valley in a virtual tie, the fifth man would decide it. I finally spotted Marcus heaving his body up the incline, but he was no longer hanging out in the mid-fifties. Runners streamed around him as he clawed for the line. Then I saw them bearing down. Three Neuqua Valley guys right on his tail and closing. We did not need minute differences. We needed a gap in the scoring, but Marcus Garcia had run himself out. His body looked washed out, like a photo overexposed to the light. The anaerobic demons shredded him up the final hill. He would get home somehow in seventy-sixth place, but my stomach sank. The fifth scorers from both Neuqua Valley and Lake Zurich had closed the gap.

I turned to my dad and got our count. He writes the raw scores on a tiny sheet of paper for me at all big meets, and it looked good. One guy in the twenties, three more in the forties and fifties, one more in the seventies. That was usually good enough for the podium, but was it enough this year? The times were astonishing. He had our fifth runner at 15:14

with the rest near or under 15:00 for three miles. It had been the fastest state meet since 1976, with forty-seven men running 15:00 or better in our class alone. Once official, our times would stand as the third-best effort in school history. We had accomplished our first goal. We had run our best when it mattered the most. But standing there watching the times and places of the top forty come across the scoreboard, I had the sinking feeling that our best had not been enough. I put that aside and cast out through the crowd to find my boys.

I searched vainly at first. As the runners released from the finish corral, there were the usual series of emotions. Exhaustion and happiness. Exhaustion and desolation. Mothers hugged sons and friends surrounded their teammates to begin the process of making the memories, turning the experience into narrative, relishing the finale of their season's drama. Looking frantically about, I finally spied our guys standing in the parking lot behind the finish area. They were celebrating with all their might, circled up, laughing. Tim Meincke stood in the middle, a ringleader, regaling the collected group of parents, alums, and teammates with the newly minted story of his audacious charge. I burst in, hugging each young man in turn, swelling with pride. To a man they described it as the most fun they'd ever had while racing. We had been winning deep into the race for the first time in school history, and each guy behaved as if we had won.

In my own irrational way I agreed. I knew that we had probably given away a top-three podium finish by running the way we had, but the feeling in the huddle was not one of regret. Instead, it was an embrace of the act, a celebration of a style of racing that fit nicely with romanticized notions about what it meant to be a runner. Each man had run with the Mags mantra, pure of heart and pure of purpose: We had gone as fast as we could for as long as we could. In a picture that ran in the *Daily Herald* the next day, Meincke stands mouth agape, infused with joy. With his 135th place finish cast aside, he celebrates. Christened "Monkey" long before by his teammates, Tim is all playful glee and unburnished happiness. Another patron of risk, Marcus stares at him with a giddy smile on his face, reveling in the ludicrousness of it all. The effort had been inspi-rational, crowning, unforgettable. It had also gotten us fourth place.

The athletes and coaches of the 2010 Palatine cross country team celebrate their great race and their "invisible" fourth-place state trophy.

Photo by Cindi Johnson

I waited nearly forty-five minutes to confirm that cold hard fact. Run-ning with more discipline, the men of Neuqua Valley took a state trophy from our grasp inside the last hundred meters. They beat us by 9 points, roughly one to two seconds per scoring runner. In one of the closest and fastest state meets ever, Elmhurst York grabbed the title by a mere 2 points over Lake Zurich. The final scores: York 162, Lake Zurich 164, Neuqua Valley 180, Palatine 189, O'Fallon 200. Admirable as it was, our effort had not been enough. The results dampened our spirits, but the essence of the day remained. No one walked around with outward regret. That was all stored somewhere inside our recesses, an unspoken thought that mixed with all the "what-ifs" of competitive sports: *What if we had played it safe? What if we had shown more discipline? What if we had not risked so much?* Those thoughts would come to the fore in everyone later, but they stayed safely buried in the moment.

Reuben Frey and I celebrated the beauty of what we had just done. As we looked at the results, another glaring fact came to bear. We had placed fourth and off the podium, but missed winning the state meet by only 27 points. No Palatine team had been that close since Mags and the 1980 crew. In 2004 and 2005 we had earned runner-up trophies, but each time we had been more than 100 points from the team title. Now here we were with nothing.

In the end the proximity to ultimate glory proved intoxicating. For the first ten minutes of the 2010 state cross country final, we held the race in our hands. No Palatine team had ever gone that deep into the race in the lead. The door to a state title would remain shut for another year, but the young men who left Detweiller Park on that gorgeous afternoon left it mangled on its hinges. They had kicked and kicked and kicked with all of their force and collective will. They'd taken the ultimate racer's risk. They had clung to one another with their fingernails and been bested. We took no trophy back home. But everyone heading home in those vans took away something greater, something beyond tangibility. After so many years of striving we all smiled at one basic truth. We could win the Illinois state meet.

ROLLING MEADOWS

The end of a cross country season is always a time of mourning. Whether we win or lose the big meets, whether we walk away edified or angry, the bald, honest truth is simply that it is over. No more races to live for. No more journey. Just space and time and reflection.

The journey to that fateful fourth-place finish began long before, seeded in a meeting with the boys the previous January and centered on a forty-page dissertation I had written on how to win a state championship. I called it "The Cross Country Manifesto," and into it I poured every idea I had about how to make the program great. For three months I thought about every fraction of advantage to be gained. Could we hydrate better? Could we recruit better? Could we improve our workouts? Could we improve our marketing and fund-raising? Could we employ better nutrition? Could we improve tactically?

Notwithstanding our finish in the IHSA State meet, the manifesto quickened the pulse of all involved. The difference between victory and defeat in that race had been eyelashes, slivers of execution. On the right day we could have won. We had been winning. Even more, the Manifesto had laid out a two-year plan. Year two still lay before us. It centered on five young men who had dominated as a group ever since they were freshmen. Five times before men from Palatine had placed second in the Illinois state final, but we had never won. Sooner or later, it would be someone's time. Unbeknownst to them, I had written the plan to win on the backs of Anthony Gregorio, Tim Johnson, Marcus Garcia, Tim Meincke, and Peter Tomkiewicz. The first four had nearly run us to glory in the 2010 state final as juniors. Peter had been beaten out for a spot by Meincke and watched the race from the sidelines. After watching the first four run and perform admirably, he had a gigantic itch to scratch.

Throughout his career, Peter Tomkiewicz had been the awkward man with one foot in and one foot out. Already tall as a freshman, he grew tremendously as a sophomore. His frame filled out to six foot four, but he couldn't shake the gawkiness that growth occasioned. He couldn't seem to find a comfortable home within the team, either. The indomitable foursome of Gregorio, Johnson, Garcia, and Meincke bonded easily as freshmen and stuck together like glue in practice and races. But Peter flitted around the margins, uncomfortable in his own skin and failing to fit tightly into the group. His penchant for talking smack on road runs and then disappearing for summer training also failed to endear him to his teammates. Throughout his junior year, he ran well but remained on the outside.

No one can be exactly sure where his metamorphosis began. I like to point to a couple of track workouts in late October heading toward the 2010 state meet. He was an alternate at that point, but I took him aside and preached the value of comfort and relaxation. An athlete without much speed and few fast-twitch muscles has limited options when running on a track. He can desperately reach for speed and power that will never be there. Or he can relax. At some point I realized that Peter needed to accept who he was. He needed to find an internal rhythm, an easy manner of running. Watching him run tall and relaxed in those October workouts, I marveled at what he could do when he started to inhabit his skin more fully.

With this image in mind, I asked Steve Johnson, our club coach, to give Peter a shot in the Nike Midwest Regional meet the week after the Illinois state final. Comprising teams from Indiana, Ohio, Missouri, and Illinois, the regional meet served as a gateway to the Nike Cross Country National (NXN) meet. Only the top two teams would automatically advance to the biggest stage in American high school cross country.

Steve had noticed that the meet organizers were allowing more than seven entries per club into the championship race, so he added Peter the day the team arrived in Terre Haute, Indiana. Little did we know the controversy this would cause. Unseen and unheard of throughout the season, Peter experienced a moment of transition that few runners ever witness. Early in the race, I saw him running tall, gracefully even, moving rhythmically through the field. By halfway he had passed Marcus and taken aim at the front end of our team. It was more than a good race. The entire effort was a study in personal discovery. For the first time Peter Tomkiewicz understood who he was and embraced it. In the space of sixteen minutes he discovered the easy-to-inhabit self he would carry into adulthood.

He finished that race as our fifth man. The problems began from there. He had been a late addition to the race and thus was not one of the "designated" seven runners. It mattered. His finish flipped the Palatine XC Club into third place overall, installing the boys as a likely at-large selection into the NXN meet. It was not to be. A couple of weeks later, Nike changed the result and threw Peter's finish out of the scoring. The change moved our boys to fourth. Our Illinois rivals Neuqua Valley moved into third place and went on to place twelfth in the nation.

It was a bitter pill for all involved. Despite the setback, a number of our boys still flew to Portland for the NXN meet and ran the open race. Peter was one of them. He placed sixth. In the process he defeated his teammate Tim Johnson for the first time since freshman year. His time also dominated most of the other runners from Illinois who later participated in the championship race. They could take away his spot in the race, but no one could send him back to the junior varsity. Peter Tomkiewicz had become the man he wanted to be.

As an online spectator to the NXN meet, I was eager to talk with the boys about their experiences. During the club cross country season after the state meet, Illinois High School Association (IHSA) rules no longer allow me to coach my varsity. They meet with Steve Johnson and Fred Miller, our volunteer club coaches, while I spend my afternoons jogging with alums or our girls coach, Joe Parks. It is a relaxed time of year, but also one of constant yearning. To be left out of the battle is more than I can bear. I constantly bite my tongue and bide my time as the varsity works its way through the Nike Regional and National meets. Finally the interregnum comes to an end, and I am free to run with our guys in our voluntary open gym runs over the winter.

Normally, I dread winter running. As a year-round runner, I am usually devastated by the first snowfall. The snow blankets the sidewalks and cuts our normally large repertoire of runs in half. Gone are the halcyon days of summer, running through Deer Grove West in short shorts, sweating but happy under the humid July sun. The summertime is pregnant with the possibilities of the coming cross country season. It is a natural time of purpose and accumulating passion.

Winter represents the opposite. We are well removed from any imminent competition, and the struggle to find the motivation to train hard overwhelms even the most stalwart athletes. The wind howls and bites. On some days it blows right through whatever you are wearing and goes straight to your core—a heart-stopping, stand-up wind that declares victory over those who challenge its bite. Winter wind wills itself into your skull, freezing the nostrils and numbing the brain.

On Mondays throughout the winter the boys keep up with our weekly long runs, yet the routes are limited to three rather boring out-and-back runs to rival schools: Hersey, Fremd, and Rolling Meadows. These routes not only allow a convenient turnaround point with a bathroom, water, and heat, but they are also part of a larger gamesmanship that goes on within the Mid-Suburban League. Every now and then, a Fremd runner or two shows up and gets a drink in our athletic hallway. We make it a point to go back with twenty guys the next week. The next week I might see Jay Renaud and Tim Phillips heading over from Hersey with ten or fifteen guys. We always make a mental note to go back soon with more.

This Monday at least promised some good conversation since our girls and guys had recently returned from the national meet in Portland. Still, no one wanted to run Meadows. It's ten and a half miles straight out and back with much of the route on a rather bleak frontage road. It is always dark when we return on these winter jaunts, and this one promised to be embittering as we all noticed the wind howling from the north. It would blow into our uncovered faces during the entire return. Ryan McGough, our senior 800 meter ace, joked that he would kill himself if we went to Meadows. Ten seconds later the team leaders announced that we were going to Meadows. Groans ensued.

I had dreaded this run all day long as well, but I immediately shifted my attitude when the trek began. I quickly found myself moving up alongside Peter. He was awash in confidence after his string of break-out races. Without much tact, he made sure the group knew that he had beaten Johnson, and he also noted that his time surpassed Neuqua Valley's best man by twenty seconds. Time and place aside, it was the kind of declaration that had failed to endear him to his teammates. Always a man on the make, he hadn't yet learned the dignity that comes with success.

Even Nike could not take away his newfound confidence. Running with him now, into the cold of a December night, I knew I was witnessing one of those miraculous changes that coaches in all sports see. We live for the moment of transition, the moment when a kid arrives, when he gets it, when he accelerates from a participant into the "exceptional man." If Peter could succeed in these Nike Regional and National races and was only our eighth-best man, then how many other potential heroes did we have on our hands? Running beside him I saw his growing rhythm. I marveled at how he generated any speed. His size-fourteen feet landed with a glacial thwop on each stride. He was all limbs and awkwardness—like a newborn colt first released from its mother's womb with limbs intact, but no neural ability to control them.

Peter's lack of obvious physical assets actually hid other strengths that were far more important in the distance running world. He had heart, and when a distance coach says that, he means it in both metaphysical and physical ways. Sure, he possessed the inner toughness to meet the extreme moments of truth that our sport requires. But inside his chest sat one of those monster hearts, the kind that made do with thirty-eight beats a minute throughout the night and powered the engine past the point of exhaustion. He had a natural gift that you couldn't see or teach, but his teammates didn't recognize it. To them, Peter was still the pesky kid with the slows who talked too much, and none of his teammates liked to lose to him.

It didn't help that Peter needled Tim Johnson throughout the run. Johnson had run 4:21 for 1600 meters the year before as a sophomore and was a Division I–level recruit, but Peter managed to put ten seconds into him the previous weekend in Portland. Tim said that he let Peter win (in typically apathetic teenage fashion), but the remark scalded. Was my most talented guy tough enough for the year ahead? In the hyper-competitive world of Illinois cross country, any small chink in the armor might be exposed. We needed Johnson to be good. Actually, we needed Johnson to be superlative, to challenge for the state title.

Past Kirchoff Road, I jogged up alongside Anthony Gregorio and gave him the business about how Peter was on a mission and would get him next. Such friendly rivalries drive all training groups, and I hoped to fester this one into a beautiful symbiosis. Peter didn't back down. He made a half-serious crack about moving up to number one. It was all said in the awkward way that teenage boys talk, but Gregorio took it seriously. Even on this cold winter night, you could feel his burning heat. The massive chip he carried on his shoulder kept us warm on these runs, and nothing burned Tony Gregorio more than losing. When we had run terribly in Peoria the previous September, I exiled the guys into the huge hills that overlooked the Detweiller course for an hour of soul searching. Tony then came home and ran four more miles in the dark for a total of twenty miles on the day. His All-State showing was a product of such inner drives. Even that success couldn't stop his burn. He still felt insulted by the world and ran to keep it off his back, to show a doubting crowd that he could shape it on his terms. Everyone knew Peter was joking except Tony. Tony filed it away and vowed never to let Peter beat him in anything—a finish, a rep, a race, a brisk walk to the bathroom.

We ended up at Meadows with a group of twelve stalwart souls and bundled up for the tough return journey back to Palatine in the cold, dark night. Two freshmen, Eddie Graham and Marco Chilelli, made it to

Meadows for the first time, and we gave them some props for the feat before dropping them on the return. They made it back chilled and tired ten minutes after us, but they could see the standard. There was a lot of work to be done between the two of them and us.

On our run home, Tony looked over at me and simply declared, "Wow. This run wasn't nearly as bad as I thought it would be." At some point on Rohlwing Road, I ran in the cold and the dark for eons just focusing on A. J. Laskowske's feet hitting the ground. Such was my trance that I literally lost my place. I bundled up into a zone of physicality where I no longer conceived of my running as a conscious act. I just let it happen. Before I knew it, we were firing past the bike path near the school in full motion, racing one another through the darkness and into our future.

The topic on the last half of the run had been the NXN meet. Enlivened by Peter's brazen race, the five juniors looked around and agreed that we should just go ahead and win the whole thing next year. Peter said it first with a sly giggle and a sideways glance, but then the conversation turned. They were serious. I didn't disagree. Jogging on through the night so far away from the next test, it all seemed so possible. Even as the flurries started to descend and the darkness grew ever blacker, we ran with that impossible hope in all of our chests. Once spoken it became part of the larger drive bubbling inside each of us.

For the first time ever, all our goals seemed touchable. The Illinois state title. The NXN meet. The college scholarships. Surrounded by our incubating confidence, the moment seemed right. The year ahead would be our time. By run's end, this common sense of purpose enlivened the pace. Heading past the stop sign at Carpenter Drive with a half mile to go, Peter told me that he was all-in to what we were about to attempt. Right then I saw the end of the marginal man. From then on he was at the center, driver rather than passenger.

To connect with the boys in that way, to join with one another in the kind of boundary crossing we were enacting, meant a great deal. As we winged on through the night, fighting the cold and the gripping darkness and the speeding headlights of cars that drove too near, all of us felt a pregnant sense of possibility. Our visions and dreams involved competitive acclaim, no doubt, but they also seemed achievable through commitment to common action. To be there that night with those boys hammering away toward a goal eleven months, three weeks, and five days into the future was the signal pleasure of my day. Who could fail to enjoy such clear purpose?

FIVE GUYS

A month after our run to Rolling Meadows, the five juniors, my assistant coach, Matt Sheehan, and I gathered at my house to write the plan for our year. A year before I had done the same, taping a massive piece of butcher paper to a wall in my old town house and sketching out a time line. The plan outlined it all. Our rivals, their returnees, their track times. The eighty-mile weeks. The major workouts. The key meets of the season. At the end of the time line I had circled in giant red letters ILLINOIS STATE CHAMPS 2010. That vision had not come to pass, but the rest had. We had done the mileage. We suffered and struggled and dry-heaved our way up Blue Ridge Road in Winter Park, Colorado. We had run ourselves into oblivion in the state final. In the end all we got was a glimpse. That glimpse became our starting point.

Cross country teams are made up of many men. At powerhouse Illinois programs like York, Neuqua Valley, and New Trier, more than 150 boys join each year. In its own way each program offers a lot more than competition. All the best offer a species of camaraderie, inclusion, and athletic opportunity that many of the young men would never get in other sports. The typical cross country athlete has been rejected more often than not. Tony Gregorio had played baseball and basketball. Neither sport had much use for a short young man with limited speed. Almost all of my runners used to play soccer. Somewhere along the line, most realized that their lack of height, their lack of quickness, or their lean musculature was going to leave them on the margins of the major sports. So they came to our programs, organizations that thrive on the downtrodden and the second chance, to scratch an athletic itch. We take them in and then begin the search that dominates every cross country coach's season: Who are my five guys?

It takes five to score. In a varsity cross country race, each team gets seven entries, but only five make up the team score. The sixth and seventh guys can "bump" runners from other teams to lower places in a race, but they become useful only in tight situations or as emergency scorers if one of the top five falters. Most good programs have ten to fifteen quality athletes vying for the varsity, but the eternal search is for the magic five.

Ever since they were freshmen and sophomores, Gregorio, Johnson, Meincke, Garcia, and Tomkiewicz had been dubbed "The Fab Five," an homage to the Michigan freshmen who nearly won the NCAA basketball title in 1992. In under-level races where all five competed, they had never lost. Coach Sheehan and I knew from early on that single classes with five dominant runners were few and far between. Usually, a varsity cross country team is a mix of grizzled veterans and electric young talent. This team was different. All five men had grown up together. They had been injured and rehabbed together. They had trained together, moderately at first and then viciously. As we prepared to draw up our plan, they also brought something more spiritual to the table than other groups. The years of training had made them a family. Prone to the spats that brothers have, they fought at times, but the blood had become thick.

I invited the whole crew to my new house near the school. Still in the process of moving in, I arranged some plastic totes and my ragged old couch in my new living room for the meeting. While the accoutrements weren't fine, the stark setup mirrored the task ahead. In front of my faded blue couch was this year's empty tapestry, a massive sheet of paper taped to my empty wall. We were here to fill it with aspirations.

Marcus Garcia and Tony Gregorio showed up first. Both guys were nursing injuries and neither had been on the group's run out in Barrington earlier that morning. A full-blooded hater of cold weather, Marcus had been nursing an iliotibial band injury, but I doubted his leg hurt as badly as he let on. Tony, of course, would die before missing a day of work, so I immediately worried that the ache in his shin was something more. The boys deposited their shoes at the door. Or at least Tony did.

From left, Peter Tomkiewicz, Tim Johnson, Anthony Gregorio, and Tim Meincke prepare to start the Hinsdale Hornet–Red Devil freshman race. Marcus Garcia was absent due to injury.

Marcus had to pause for a moment to pull off his brand-new cowboy boots. Ever the scammer, Marcus had accepted $100 from his mom to buy new clothes at the mall. Instead he paid $30 for the boots and pocketed the rest.

In many ways the fate of these five guys was sealed the day Marcus Garcia dedicated himself to the cause. I first noticed him at the start of freshman year. To my surprise, an early interval workout with our freshmen was dominated, and utterly so, by this groovy-looking Nicaraguan kid with a strong rhythm and a need to burn himself to smithereens rep after rep. I recognized early on the tools of a great runner. When he ran, he burned just to feel the burn. Coming from a small Catholic school, he was eager to please, to make friends and earn security in a big new place, but the need to punish himself with the power of the run was stark.

Marcus always had the tools to run with a powerful rhythm, but the hardest task was taming the beast. The day after dominating the workout, his hip was shot. He spent most of the rest of his freshman year on the bench, alternately healing and destroying himself. But I had seen enough. The animal inside had reared its head. Few athletes have enough passion to make the run hurt to its fullest. In him I sensed something primal, beyond basic humanity, something that wanted to inch closer to the brink of the abyss. If properly motivated, he would jump just to see how deep it could get.

From there Marcus grew in fits and starts. He would show moments of maximum engagement and then disappear for weeks at a time, especially when the weather got cold. During the spring of his freshman year he participated in gymnastics rather than track, spending time with his older brother and flipping cool tricks for the girls. Still, he would often be spied up on the East Gym shelf at odd times of day pounding out laps barefoot.

As a sophomore Marcus went through the normal series of events— skip large swaths of off-season work, come in early with bravado and fire, blow himself to pieces, rehab, repeat. Halfway through sophomore cross country, he took the bait. He and his teammates went down to the York F/S Invite and dominated the sophomore race, winning for the first time in school history. When an odd series of events—a case of swine flu, a temperature at an inopportune time, a mental collapse by a senior— occurred during the 2009 post-season, Marcus was thrust into the heat of battle. His first varsity race ever was the 2009 IHSA State meet. He placed 148th with a time of 16:03 for three miles. That race set the hook.

Something about racing at the highest level tweaked Marcus's vanity and excited his ambition. Underneath his cool demeanor, the myriad bracelets, and the flirty moments with girls lay a true competitor. From then on he committed with all his force. Don't get me wrong. The growth came in fits and starts. Gaining trust took time. Asking Marcus to subsume his considerable charisma for the good of the unit took time. Getting Marcus to attach himself to a routine of training schedules and monotonous work took time. At heart he is a wild man, and breaking him in order to train him would have been counterproductive. I gave him the space to figure it out, let him miss more days than I would have liked, and paused before giving the sharp remonstrance I would have delivered to most. Marcus is a man you want on your side, a man full of vital energy, but you only want him at your side on his terms. The free spirit had to reconcile himself to an intentional subjugation.

So he persevered. He quit gymnastics and ran track, hating the training and the cold and the length of it all, even as he found his stride. After a summer of improved dedication, he ran throughout his junior season as our fifth man. His teammates felt his burn in training and, even more important, in those vital moments before a race. Marcus wears a look of determination on his face that cannot be taught. In moments of intense concentration, he will lock eyes on me or a teammate. His nostrils twitch and flair like he's a bull pawing the ground. His thick black eyebrows lean in as his eyes crease and narrow. The look inspires concerted action.

It also reels you in to Marcus's magnetic nature. Unlike many of my athletes, Marcus has other options. He is athletic enough to be a gymnast. He makes short films and fiddles around with playing bass and being a photographer. He listens to psychotic screamo music or fragile atmospheric jams or whatever trendsetting piece of musical art you might hear about six months from now. Marcus merely lends his gift to this activity. The difference between Marcus and a masquerading impostor is that he lends it with the fullness of his heart. Marcus cares. He could have been a master of irony but he gave all that up for this genuine search, this two-year-long quest to win it all. The power of Marcus is that he chose to be with us.

Marcus transformed our team from a collection of well-meaning, diligent workers into a crew with swagger and an ironclad belief that we could win it all. Who else could grow a mustache inside of a week? Who else could shave his hair into a Mohawk with a dangly mullet and still look good? Who else would buy a blanket with his own picture on it? For the most part our runners are sedate, well meaning, orderly, and committed. Marcus can be that but he always approaches it with an edge. When we preach modesty, he can do it. But he bought that blanket when he was a junior for one purpose: If we won the state title, he was wearing that damn thing on stage. In the end the blanket is all. It shows Marcus in full mama's-boy smile, arms crossed as he politely kneels for the photographer, trees radiant in the background. Just a normal picture except it is blown up to four feet wide and three feet tall and worn as a cape. He may follow directions and do your bidding, but inside he is always four feet wide and three feet tall, always bigger in self-concept than reality. He wears that love of himself on his sleeve just to remind you how great he knows he is. The reason I love him is simple. I agree.

After showing off his new boots, Marcus and Tony plopped on the couch and waited for the rest. Coach Sheehan arrived soon after in his Duke sweatshirt with Tim Johnson, Peter Tomkiewicz, and Tim Meincke on his heels. "Wrong Way" Meincke had gotten lost even though my new house is three blocks from the school, and he had already been there. They all shucked off their shoes and had a seat on the shabby blue couch. At one end of the paper I had written JANUARY 1. At the opposite end I had written NOVEMBER 5, the date of the 2011 IHSA State meet. The month before I had dreamed about our guys running and winning the national meet. I awoke with a phrase in my head and wrote it in the journal I keep by my bed. In the morning, I turned to the final page and read the phrase, *The Architecture of a National Championship*. That became our title.

I picked up my black marker and began to set a bold agenda on the blank canvas. As the marker squeaked briskly across the paper, I first detailed our competition. Generations of Palatine runners had come up against York, the immovable force of Illinois cross country, and found themselves lacking. Still, with a suspect senior class and a bevy of inexperienced newcomers, the Dukes looked vulnerable. The feeling in the room was that our time had come. The emergence of Neuqua Valley to state and national prominence complicated matters, and I warned the guys against overconfidence, noting that Naperville North also returned a core of young and talented runners. All three teams had finished in the top four at the NXN meet in the past six years. They had been where we wanted to go so the aim was simple. Knock off the best in Illinois. Then compete for the national title.

The ambition was certainly presumptuous for a program that had never even qualified to the NXN meet. Neuqua Valley and York had placed twelfth and fourteenth in December, but we had beaten Neuqua twice—once early in the season and once with our "illegal" lineup of eight guys at NXN Midwest Regional. Looking at these results, our aspiration ceased to be a fantasy. It was a tangible statement of possibility. Peter and Timmy J echoed that sentiment, reminding me how well their times from the NXN Open race had stacked up against the best in the nation. All five concurred that our solid race would have placed us tenth to fifteenth in the national race the past season, and we had five of our best eight runners coming back. No one flinched at the grandiosity of the vision.

With the concrete objectives set, we turned to the spiritual dimension. The year before I molded our season around a dream I experienced while taking an afternoon nap. In the dream, I saw the Palatine varsity and I running up a mountain and chanting "soul glue" over and over at the mountain's peak. We formed a circle and swayed rhythmically back and forth, repeating the "soul glue" mantra in unison. At first I passed the dream off as an afternoon delusion inspired by a great race Reuben Frey had run earlier that morning. Upon further thought, *soul glue* seemed an apt descriptor of cross country team racing at its finest. Only by embracing their "soulful" connections to one another can a racing unit become more than the sum of its parts. Down the path of the soul lay the potential for elevation.

In Colorado we reenacted the soul glue vision (minus the swaying and chanting) when we ran a grueling five miles up a mountain to ten thousand feet. When we jogged back down, our connections had hardened. The coming varsity would need to find similar unity, a task made more difficult by the existing divisions between the Fab Five and the rest of the team.

As we reminisced about the previous year's mountain run, Meincke brought up just how sad it would be when the current seniors graduated.

Forged on mountainsides and the fires of heated competition, their bonds had hardened into stone. I told them that I visualized a similar relationship between them and the upcoming team. In my mind, the relationship was like the chicken and the egg. You couldn't have a winning varsity without the support of the rest of the team and vice versa.

We certainly could go it alone. Between the two coaches and the five juniors we would stand a good chance of running to a state championship. In some ways an intense focus on just these five could even pay dividends. But there was also a danger in such a limited focus. What if one of them got hurt? Or sick? What if one of them contracted mono or incurred a stress fracture? Where would we be then? Even more important, what kind of legacy would such a limited focus leave? What would happen the next year?

I argued that every man had to matter, regardless of his talent level. A committed man at any speed was better than a talented one who did not care. I told them of my duty to commit these five to the spiritual magic and physical potential of the broader team. As talented athletes these five had mainly trained with their senior friends and the graduates from the past two years. Those bonds had yielded performances far beyond what any of them could have achieved alone. But much to my chagrin, a few of the five hardly even knew the freshmen and sophomores. Marcus and Meincke would have failed a name quiz had I given it that morning. I knew there would come a time when these five would need the rest. They could be great as a self-contained unit, but they could only reach a magical level of performance—the championship synergy—by working in close alliance with everyone else.

To win a state title every man in the organization, from Anthony Gregorio to Will Padilla (a 7:41 miler), would need to put his full weight behind the team for an entire year. The focus would be on developing the common spirit to train hard and race fast. The five would create the team. The team would create the five.

With that vision set, we discussed process. I challenged them to find meaning in the daily burden of year-round training. As team leaders they would need enthusiasm for the daily pursuit; it would be their job to help the group accrue the miles across the many months between then and next November. Sitting near my window and gazing into the teeth of a frigid January day, Marcus looked less than enthused. Unlike Tony and Peter, he could never just button up and become a slave to the daily run.

I asked them to be the captains of this process and enjoy it for its own rewards. We were certainly aspiring to lofty goals, but often as not runners failed to reach those goals. If that happened, then we would have to be content with the joys of laboring together, the emotional connections we formed with one another, the lifelong value we created in the pursuit. They had to believe that perfect process could create the perfect race.

We ended the meeting after a couple of hours with the paper full of ideas and aspirations, hopes and dreams, processes and purchases. If I have learned anything from coaching, it is that you must be willing to state the impossible dream before making it reality. State titles are not won with rhetoric, but the quest can only begin with concrete affirmation that the goal is in play. When Caesar crossed the Rubicon, the point of no return in his invasion of Italy, he famously uttered, "The die has been cast." At the end of our year's plan, the words 2011 IHSA STATE CHAMPIONS and NXN CHAMPIONS stood out in big black marker. The dates had been circled.

As the boys left and I watched them walk to their cars, I recalled one of my favorite passages from *On the Road* by Jack Kerouac. He writes, "The only people for me are the mad ones, the ones who are mad to live, mad to talk, mad to be saved, desirous of everything at the same time, the ones who never yawn or say a commonplace thing, but burn, burn, burn, like fabulous yellow roman candles exploding like spiders across the stars . . ." To surround myself with the "mad ones" was enough for me. Tony Gregorio was a madman. So were Marcus Garcia, Peter Tomkiewicz, Tim Johnson, and Tim Meincke. And so was I. Finding these people was enough. To pursue a year of life with them, with the type of vigor and purpose we had outlined, was enough. Come a November win or loss, nothing could diminish the value of the mad pursuit.

SNOW

If our grand meeting to set the year's agenda had been inspiring, then that feeling quickly gave way to the torpor of winter training. Unable to meet officially for practice, the boys lumbered through the maintenance part of our year. In a program where the hard-core athletes train year-round, there is little time off. What does exist is emotional vacation. The winter is that time. Each man has a chart with his suggested mileage. The group meets on its own, policing itself, ambling through the long runs and chugging out the miles at a steady but less-than-prodigious rate.

Winter is filled with normal teenage rites of passage: Friday-night basketball games, semester finals, indoor boredom. While most students remain cooped up inside during the winter, distance runners face the most difficult tests of the year. The run is always there, no matter the temperature or the wind. With no coach, no required runs, and nothing but the voice of ambition in his ear, each man must look at his chart and figure out how to put up the miles across the desolation. That difficulty abates some when official track practice starts in late January, but all of us would carry the daily burden of the frigid winter run until spring brought the thaw.

On the morning of Tuesday, February 1, everyone in the Chicago area awoke with the same ominous feeling: snow coming. As midwesterners we are used to seeing weathermen gird for the unbelievable and the volatile. Most of us take it in stride and wonder whether the sensational stories of local weather are anything more than a consequence of our collective boredom. Other than sports and weather not a lot happens in the Midwest, but this story grew legs. Forecasters spread word of a biblical apocalypse. In Palatine, we all knew it would be bad when District 211 canceled school for the next day at two thirty on Monday afternoon.

The weather interruption cast an irrational pall of disappointment over my workout plans. Canceling school meant canceling practice. We had only started our official track season the day before, and this meant an interruption in our aerobic buildup. Nothing ruins a distance coach's day like a break in the routine. As usual, I searched through my extensive catalog of rationalizations, intent on finding a way to meet and run. Then I went outside.

Stepping into the blizzard after school on that Tuesday, it was obvious that running—at least doing it for physiological gain—was a moot point. Even though I live only three blocks from Palatine High School, I drove that morning in anticipation of some true weather fireworks. As I sat in the ensuing traffic jam, snow enveloped my car in sheets, flinging itself in wave after wave of spiky crystals. The wind whipped in a frenzy, whistling ever so slightly through my barely cracked window. I felt safe in my car, but half wished that I had walked. What kind of distance runner drives three blocks?

This shameful feeling compounded when I saw Tim Johnson stumble out of a snowdrift at the entrance to the student parking lot. Timmy J lives two blocks from school, and it is a running joke on our team that he is always the last guy to arrive for morning practice (or any other official meeting). Usually, he and his mom pull up to the school about twelve seconds before practice begins, and he manically strides in the school doors just before roll is called. The team joke is that practice can finally start when Timmy J arrives. So it was a bit ironic that he was walking home in the worst blizzard we had seen in years.

Watching him stumble through the growing drifts, I thought about the year that lay ahead. That past fall Tim's junior cross country season had been derailed by a case of mono. From late July to mid-August, he ran nary a step and then struggled to meet expectations during the regular season. He rallied with great races at the Illinois state meet and the Nike Midwest Regional, but the entire exercise had been difficult.

Tim's running career had been one of the most dissected entities of my coaching career. His father, Steve Johnson, ran for Hersey in the late 1970s and used to hold that school's record in the two-mile run. An enthusiastic runner with a child-like love of life, Steve had been a great addition to our program. He ran with the boys on weekends, brought granola bars and Gatorades on hot days, and shared with our team his life-long love of running. When we needed to find a club coach for the post-season meets, Steve filled the void and organized the club for both the boys and girls. He submerged himself into coaching the athletes and helped our girls team qualify to the Nike National meet twice. They had placed eighth in the nation that past November.

I wondered what impact his dad's presence had on Tim. A son of a great runner myself, I understood the implicit pressures. My dad ran 1:51 for the 880-yard run in college and was an All-State athlete in the mile run in 1966. It's not always easy to reconcile those stats to your own when you have a bad race (especially in my case, where my dad was my coach). Steve sensed this pressure enough never to lay it on Tim, but we all knew from watching Tim early on that he had much the same talent. The comparisons were never direct. But Tim felt them just the same—probably more from the coaches than his father, yet always there.

Early on a bifurcation emerged between Tim Johnson, the person, and Tim Johnson, the runner. Sometimes I wondered about the separation. As a person Tim is gentle and kind, quiet and respectful to a fault. Those who know him well see his sly sense of humor and his easy-going affability. Not much bothers him outwardly. In comparison with other champion athletes I had coached, Tim was refreshingly ego-free. Countless times he had performed with great vigor in service of the team. I watched often at practice as Tim complimented teammates or quietly took a freshman striver under his wing. Genuinely quiet, he usually melted into the tableau.

That was exactly his problem. Star athletes, especially in track and field, cannot just be part of the scenery. During his freshman cross country season, we had an early meeting with Tim where we told him that it was okay to pass his teammates. For a coach the subject of the meeting was patently absurd. But it was necessary. In his first few races he worried about showing them up, of losing their friendship if he became the top dog. Call it naive or sweet, but that impression certainly didn't jibe with the prevailing team ethic. Already a striver, Tony Gregorio would've given his eyeballs to beat Tim Johnson. I was more used to counseling my stars to pay attention to the rest of the team or approach the sport with greater humility. I had never met a young man so afraid. Maybe he feared the expectations that would come along with success. Maybe he actually did fear insulting his teammates. The situation started to resolve itself after that meeting. Tim scored a dominant victory in the Palatine Invite freshman race and ran away with top freshman honors on our team.

That's when the trouble started. Over the winter of his freshman year, Tim was diagnosed with Osgood-Schlatter disease, a painful knee condition related to rapid growth. Although not uncommon in young runners, the reaction from his parents was difficult to deal with. Used to pushing hard, I suddenly had to be careful both with Tim and with the politics of training Tim. He struggled to run ten miles a week. He still raced fast—4:48 for 1600 meters as a frosh—but you could see the weight of expectations on his shoulders. That difficult season culminated in June with a Tim Johnson summit meeting in my living room with his parents. They were concerned, as they should be. I felt lost and pressured, not quite sure how to deal with Tim's injury or the intense scrutiny of my training program.

We agreed on a plan for the summer, but the meeting set a larger construct. Here we all were meeting about Tim, but Tim was not there. For this one young man, there was a world of negotiation above and beyond the coach–athlete relationship. Unlike the other four, Tim existed as a concept. His outsized talent, his father's running history, his mother's involved care, my sky-high expectations, and the needs of his teammates all hovered above him from the beginning. We all wanted the best for Tim, but the enduring question with him had always been: What did Tim want?

He told me he wanted greatness. He told me he wanted to be the school record holder in the 1600 meter run. He told me he wanted to be state cross country champion. But these utterances were difficult to parse. Was this Tim talking? Was it his father? Was it his teammates? Was it me talking back to me? When things went well, it was glorious. Tim ran 4:21 as a sophomore and qualified individually to the state track meet. His sectional qualifying race was a piece of redemption from the preceding spring, a manic drive to the line in the wake of soon-to-be state champion Alec Bollman. As the two embraced on the Palatine track after a one–two finish, I thought I saw both the current and the future champion. Tim ran great the next week at the state track meet, briefly taking the lead in his heat before fading. I thought he had arrived.

That trajectory was not the one he would run. After that there was mono, more difficulty, and more negotiation. As I watched Timmy J stumble and slide through the growing snow piles, he nearly lost his balance and crashed to the sidewalk. His backpack full of books weighed like an anchor. Sometimes he trained and raced with a similar burden. Whether we had asked him to carry it or he had taken it of his own accord, no one knew. In the coming year it would only get heavier. The least I could do was ensure that it was his decision to carry it.

It also struck me at that moment that we could have run. The snow bulldozed through Tim's layers as he frantically scanned the traffic and tried to cross the street to his house. Running would have served no physical purpose, but there was probably some edge to be gained by braving such absurd elements. I saw Tim's burdens as outsized, but maybe they were just more magnified versions of the burdens we all carried. Competitive runners feel the pressure each and every day. For many the races are the vacations, the momentary glimpses of action in a lifelong sea of training.

The shame I felt as I slowly idled and accelerated through blizzard traffic was due to a violation of the unspoken codes of distance running. Runners have to be tough, and you are taught that bending to outside influence is only for the weak. The only true struggle is the one between the man and his pain. Everything else is tangential ephemera, temporary

49

blockades. I once saw Dan Iverson, the girls coach at Naperville North, insist that distance running is a countercultural sport. He couldn't be more right. To run long distance you need to go against most of the prevailing trends in our culture. We have drivers in the neighborhood who call the school each winter to complain that our runners are outside in cold temperatures. They see our work as an affront to normality.

I finally made it back to my house, steaming with the realization that practice and school would be canceled for a couple of days, mad that our softened culture had once again shut us down. I like snow days as much as the next guy, but they force me to embrace someone else's arbitrary limits rather than my own skewed version of possibility. Sure, I can rationally understand why running in one of the worst blizzards in Chicagoland history on unsafe roads is a bad idea. That still does not change my sense that someone else—possibly one of our competitors—is out there living the distance runner's code more courageously than us.

To coach or compete in the distance world is to measure oneself against a common lunacy. To cancel practice is to court the possibility that Joe Newton is out there somewhere with the York varsity tied up as sled dogs pulling him to another state title. It's to irrationally believe that Paul Vandersteen and his Neuqua Valley men are out there running a long run to the North Pole at easy on the way out and tempo on the way back. It's to know that somewhere, somehow, someone else is gaining on you.

Call that paranoia. Call it competitiveness. Call it stupidity. But living by this countercultural code involves embracing the outer fringes. If Johnson could walk home from school, we probably could have run. If I could shovel my entire driveway by 10:30 AM the next day and dig my family out, we could have run. If we wore enough layers, we could have braved the extreme cold of the following Thursday. Most of us had participated in enough tough runs in ridiculous conditions that we became collectors of these absurd experiences anyway. Never run up a mountain before? Check it off. Never run in the worst blizzard in ten years? Check it off. Never risked heat exhaustion to complete an eighteen-mile run? Check it off. Never run 10 x mile repeats just because an alum said it was her favorite workout? Check it off.

In the end we are all competitors, but there is more that unites us than divides us. That is why you see distance coaches and athletes sharing workouts and having an instant bond. Opposing football players and coaches often want to kill each other out on the field, directing the violence like it's a personal vendetta. Distance runners only want to kill themselves with pain and then bond with one another afterward. We all checked into the same asylum long ago. All our doctors and family members diagnosed our countercultural sickness long ago, but we all look at them like they are the mad ones. Who wouldn't want to run in a blizzard?

When we finally returned to practice, I knew the winter would be long. We would head outside to run each day unless someone told us otherwise. Motorists would call and complain. Parents would sit at home and fret. Administrators would worry. We would run our miles and get in shape for the long track season. Tim Johnson would continue to wage the training wars with his teammates and carry his burdens toward unknown conclusions. Much of February would be joyless outdoor running where we wore too much gear to really run fast. Pervasive cold would lock up our muscles. The north winds would chop down our wills, and snowstorm after snowstorm would lead us off the sidewalks into the narrow gutters of the streets. February is the cruelest month, but it is also the shortest for a reason. Distance runners know we can only take so much to keep the code alive.

The good news is that March lies just around the corner. Soon enough, the temperatures would rise. When they got to forty-five degrees, it would feel like seventy to us, and we would go for our annual "Buns and Guns" run to celebrate the coming of spring and the thawing of our muscles. The shirts would come off. The spandex and short shorts would be the only layers separating us from a state of nature. The speed would start to bloom with the spring, and all would be right with the world. Well, there would probably be rain and then extreme humidity and then a sad return to the first frosted morning. But none of it would matter. It's all part of the code. The only faith we needed was that inside all the torment there would be one seventy-degree day with no wind. We would step out onto the track among our brethren, give each other a knowing nod, and set off as fast as we could, embracing the pain like only we knew how. Afterward we would shake hands and go for a long cool-down.

SYMPHONY

After the cancellations and anxiety of the blizzard, it was time to get back to work. The midweek storm left us with a legacy of piled snow, unsafe roads with creeping drifts, and no sidewalks. The winds swept in from the north and replaced the hazy whiteout of snow with the frigid sting of February air. Days unfolded in a juxtaposition of bright sunlight and soul-defeating cold. Still, there was no fitness to be gained by jogging in the hallways. We had to go outside.

The forecasters predicted eight degrees for a high on Tuesday, February 8. Windchills would fluctuate between zero and ten below, and I debated the sanity of running our first interval workout in such conditions. I half expected a rebellion. Even though Palatine runners consistently step up, I still wonder whether one day they will just stop showing up. I met the guys by the cross country bulletin board just after school, and it quickly became obvious that they shared the same mettle as their forebears. No one complained. They just put on the layers, grinned, and bore it. Some "double-bagged" it and put on two layers of spandex tights. Others wore ski masks and ski goggles. We looked like an armored band of nerdy misfits.

We ambled up the stairs to the second floor for attendance, and it was already a great day because everyone was at practice. The plan was to run one of three tough "interval" workouts in the Mill Valley neighborhood. Interval workouts stress the body's ability to process oxygen and help athletes get used to the intensity of race pace. Intervals are simple. Run hard for a specific amount of time or distance. Then rest for a period of time and do it again. Gradually, they get harder and harder. A good interval workout puts a man face-to-face with his limits. The gains thus become mental as well as physical.

The day's session was divided into three simple workouts. Four repeats of one mile for the two-milers. Six repeats of half a mile for the milers. Twelve quarter-mile repeats for the half-milers. For the veterans these workouts were old hat, a simple introduction to the more difficult workouts to come. Early workouts provided the scaffolding to reach greater heights. We ran one every two weeks in the early season and today mattered in a big way. Run amid difficulty, this workout would set the tone for the season.

Before heading out we got a boost from two alumni who were working with us. James Macatangay (aka Jimmy Mac) had been with us nearly every practice since the previous summer, and his impact had been immeasurable. Jimmy Mac was one of my original heroes, rising from seventh man on the freshman team to an All-State thirteenth by his senior season. He scored in the top five on two state runner-up teams in 2003 and 2004, and more than anyone I knew, James loved to run. He ran high mileage throughout college even after being cut from the University of Illinois track team his freshman year. By senior year, he competed with the scholarship athletes on the Illinois cross country team even though he was training himself. After taking a job in the area after college, I convinced him to come back and help. He trained with our varsity throughout the summer and fall of 2010 and was a prime reason we had run so fast in the state meet. His hard work also led to a 2:36 clocking in his Chicago Marathon debut. Our varsity loved to run with Jimmy, and I knew that Tony Gregorio salivated at the opportunity to turn the screws on him.

My second alumni assistant, Mike Nigliaccio, was another story entirely. Niggles (as we fondly called him in high school) was the original worst-to-first guy of my coaching career. When Fred Miller and I started coaching together in 2001, we had twenty-five guys on the entire team. Niggles was by far the worst. His form was wretched. He hadn't lost any of his baby fat, and he talked too much for his own good. Slowly but surely, he dropped weight, grew taller, and dropped time. By senior year he challenged for varsity on a team that placed second in the state. Mike gave me the essential faith that all cross country coaches must carry— every man or woman can be a great one. These stories of faith and achievement were the lifeblood of our program, and Niggles reminded everyone of the incredible heart that lies within each runner.

After announcing the workout and each runner's appropriate group, we bundled up and prepared for the cold. With our track under three feet of solid snow, we were forced into an annual Palatine rite of passage: workouts on Mill Valley.

This neighborhood just to the southwest of Palatine High School had seen more than its share of misery. Few of our runners hold a positive association with its cracked and whitewashed streets. Mill Valley is where you go when you have nowhere else to go, the purgatory of workout venues. It has none of the scenic beauty and tranquility of Deer Grove West or the plush sod of Hamilton Reservoir. Mill Valley gives no aesthetic rewards and bestows no easy laurels. Few leave a workout on Mill with anything more than frozen fingers and blank soreness. On especially bad days in purgatory—like a winter snowstorm or a driving rain—we are not allowed to practice far from school so we run what is fondly known as "the Weave." The Weave is simple: Run all of the cross streets between Mill Valley and Monterey repetitively until the coaches relent. A full Weave is around four miles. Down Hedgewood. Up Saratoga. Down Ventura. Up Stark. Down Carmel. Up Arrowhead. Repeat.

Many of the Mill Valley workouts are steeped in team lore. Veterans watch the newcomers' faces grip with pain as they eat it while running the gradual ascent of Mill Valley. They know that Monterey's corresponding decline never quite pays back what Mill's opening incline takes away. Newbies expect it to even out. It rarely does. Veterans also know that dodging cars is one of the more dangerous games out on Mill. Ironically, no one in the neighborhood ever complains. I hope that our toughness has become some sort of neighborly badge of honor. They know to look for us, and we manage to keep a cordial if not entirely gracious relationship.

The workout was a first-time experience for our freshmen, and we jogged into the warm-up with silent resolve. I am never sure whether to label this pre-workout attitude as concentration or a sense of impending doom, but I always like it. I hope it's concentration, but I remember trudging into more than a few workouts during high school with a deep foreboding. Winter weather only accentuates this pre-workout despondency. The day's ration of stiff subzero wind would turn everyone's cheeks red and freeze the hairs in their nostrils. It would multiply the normal pain of running by an unseen exponent. Once the workout began all those thoughts of pain and privation usually floated away, but I could see the doubt creeping on our slow jog out to Mill. More than a few faces wondered, *What am I doing here? This is insane!*

On cold days we go right from warm-up into workout. Everyone was already grouped up, and the coaches and volunteers dispersed to their respective loops. I jumped in with the varsity 800 meter group, which was running a fairly easy rhythm workout of quarter-mile repeats. The intent was to lay a base of rhythmic running at faster and faster paces before we got to the real speed endurance work in late March and early April. I tagged on as we went through the motions, quietly relaxing on the downhill and pushing intensely on the uphill. Uphill, the wind bit on any pieces of exposed skin. Downhill, we rode the scary breeze as best we could. Back and forth they went: seventy-five seconds uphill, sixty-second jog, seventy seconds downhill. I ran every other one to save my hamstrings. It gave me time to watch the symphony play.

I stood in a snowdrift, freezing as the sweat froze on my temples, and watched the synchronicity of all the players. The brand-new guys and those returning to fitness were strung out, but working hard. I heard them "passing the ball" back and forth. "Passing the ball" entails shouting out words of encouragement to your teammates throughout a workout. Sometimes a man only needs to hear his name called to get through the difficulty. Senior captain Erik Bethke was returning to form from some medical issues, and I watched him prop up our freshmen and fill them with positive reinforcement. He was another in a long line of great Palatine leaders, selfless to a fault and absolutely devoted.

The varsity passed Bethke's group on their way up the incline. Long-time friends Tim Johnson and Tim Meincke embarked on the first of a season-long series of interval workouts designed to make them elite milers. They attacked their half-mile repeats with vigor, rhythmically mimicking each other with Coach Sheehan in tow. Tony Gregorio, Peter Tomkiewicz, and A. J. Laskowske attacked each mile repeat with stoic intensity, and word spread quickly that Tony was nailing the workout. Jimmy Mac was clearly not on his game yet, flailing far back of the leaders, as Tony breezed through the first two reps in 5:04 and 4:58. On such a cold day his burn to be the best kept him warm.

Few athletes in my career have burned hotter on a daily basis than Anthony Gregorio. I first met him in passing at a junior high cross country meet. His sister, Olivia, ran for the Palatine girls team so I was excited to see if he had any potential. My first impressions were less than spectacular. Barely above five feet and more pudgy than lean, he certainly fought hard in the race but remained far adrift of the leaders. I pride myself on being able to pick out runners from a young age. I usually sense some combination of mechanics, desire, competitiveness, or natural aerobic ability. On first watching Anthony run, I felt nothing but limits.

The process of developing great runners has two benchmarks. The first is the epiphany when I realize their potential exists. Sometimes it is a hint of perfection in their stride. Sometimes it'll be ten seconds of fight they show at a crucial moment in a race, even if they turn up a loser. With Tony, I had to cut through the small size and see the beauty in his motion. He flowed. No hitches in his stride, odd arm carriages, or biomechanical infighting between his limbs. Just straight-ahead flow.

The second benchmark occurs when the athlete does something that makes him believe. In between my recognition and his, there often lies a long expanse of time and a wide gulf of differing opinions. It is my job to show the athlete how far he can go if only he would put his toe in the water and swim. I still remember the exact moment Tony put his toe in the water. In the 2008 Palatine Invite freshman race, Tony took a "shot."

A "shot" is an irrational moment for a runner, a desperate and unfounded attempt to do something that there is no physical evidence he can actually do. Most shots end in failure by traditional estimations—a weak place, an inability to finish strong—but almost all shots are valuable.

Tony Gregorio's shot was his decision to try to win the Palatine Invite. He irrationally bolted to the lead and opened a fifteen-meter gap on the field. At the halfway mark he was still winning. Then the suffering began. The wheels came off. The monkey jumped on his back. Choose your favorite running cliché. Tony's teammate Tim Johnson came from off the pace to catch him and win the race in spectacular fashion. We ended up having two glimpses of potential in one race.

That race became a metaphor for two of the most talented athletes I would ever coach. Timmy J was talented, reserved, and rational. He bided his time until the moment was right. Tony was gritty, stubborn, and audacious. He also approached the world with a big chip on his shoulder. The chip could derive from a classic Napoleon complex, but I ascribe it more to Tony as the product of a semi-charmed life. His parents divorced when he was young, and it was never easy for him, his sister, or them. He divides his time between two parents and loves them both, but his road to adulthood was not necessarily easy. It feels like Tony is out to prove himself every moment of every day. He just can't take his foot off the gas.

Like many runners, he had also been underestimated in every sport he ever tried. He was too small to be great at basketball or baseball, and even his divided Italian and Puerto Rican heritage put him on the outside of the beaten path. Chips take a long time to form, and I'm not sure a person ever gets rid of that default stance, that "me against the world" mentality. It's both a blessing and a burden.

Tony acts like he doesn't approach the world from a spot of perceived inferiority. He acts like it doesn't mean a ton if a teammate beats him in a repetition or in a race, but everyone knows that to be an utter falsehood. No one kicks a fence or betrays the sadness deep in his eyes if every little competition doesn't matter in an outsized way. Tony boils when he loses, and he boils even hotter when he outworks someone but still comes

Coach Quick and Anthony Gregorio talk prior to his first indoor race of the 2011 track season.

in second. Since he perceives nearly all runners and students to have more talent than he does, he puts that chip to good use.

He also fools himself about his perceived lack of talent. His heart pumps blood at abnormal rates, and his mechanics are fluid and poetic. He moves with ease where others find only struggle. It was in this combination of physical gift and mental derangement that his greatness as a runner came to fruition. Running is the ascetic's burden. You must be willing to whip and flog yourself, and it helps if you already find reasons to whip and flog yourself anyway. Whether Tony whips out of devotion to the cause or out of some deep-seated sense of inferiority, I've never been quite sure. The point is that he can crack the whip, and the pain is his pleasant embrace of his full potential. The only moment he likes more than whipping himself is cracking it on someone else.

And crack the whip he did on this day. He closed the workout with mile repetitions of 4:56 and 4:58. I didn't have the heart to tell him that each rep was probably thirty meters short since they had used the wrong mark on the street. That truth would have ruined his day. As he finished the final repetition, he declared victory by looking back at his dragging teammates and Jimmy Mac struggling down the final decline. He assumed the winner's pose, gracious and encouraging on the outside, but implicitly dominant. After all, he was already half recovered and cheering while they still labored through the final spasms of the toughest rep. The declaration was not lost on anyone.

Beyond Tony's varsity group, the entire practice unfolded like a symphony of beautiful parts. As we cooled down back to the school, I reveled in my deep admiration of the boys. Something intrinsic, something buried deep inside was unleashed in our workouts. I marveled at how each man played his part. I marveled also at their willingness to do it all with me. In a smaller squad, each man has to put in just as much effort as the fastest man. Some freshmen had just played their parts—six quarter-mile repetitions—because the symphony could not reach its full potential without all its players. So Will Padilla ran his 100-second quarters, striving to get better, while Tim Johnson passed him with visions of a 4:15 mile in his head.

For the most part the symphony played without any goading or chiding from me. I remained just as amazed by its kinesthetic beauty as I was when listening to a full orchestra. They mostly worked in silence through the desolation of the cold, but I felt their energy. The synergy of all the parts—fast and slow, young and old—to create a beautiful whole was what we strived for each day. We didn't always nail the parts, but on this bitterly cold day, stuck in the purgatory of our workout year, we had. Today had been perfect process. We all hoped that we would grasp a state champion's glory in the coming year, but for now the feeling of satisfaction on the chilly cool-down back through the darkness to the school would have to suffice.

THE YORK INVITE

As I walked to school on the morning of the York Indoor Invite, I found myself striding with more vigor. The pervasive gray gloom offered little promise of abating, so I was glad that the day's races would be held indoors. The early-March weather reminded me just how much winter still clung to its shrinking foothold. Coming up the eastern sidewalk to the school, the gray tranquility was deafening, a thunderclap of quiet before the fury of the day. I had called a 7:45 AM meeting for the varsity distance guys, and I was walking in there with something to say. The last couple of weeks had been a brutal slog through one of the coldest and snowiest winters in Illinois history. I hoped that today would remind us why we had braved those elements.

Every year the York Indoor Invite offers our first tests of the track season. After opening with two low-key dual meets versus St. Charles East and Bolingbrook, we headed straight into the lion's den of Illinois distance running. It was a trap meet in so many ways. York and its West Suburban Conference rivals started their season in mid-January while our conference made us wait two weeks past the official start date. Schools like York, Lyons Township, and Oak Park–River Forest also have the benefit of training in posh indoor facilities. At Palatine we had touched our snow-encased track for the first time the Tuesday preceding the meet.

With York superstar Jack Driggs running the 4 x 800 meter relay and the 600 meter dash, the entry sheets had us as the top seeds in all three distance races. I wasn't sure we were that ready, but I liked the drift of those expectations. It was time for our emerging junior class to put its feet into the fire. We always looked like we were running in army boots in the mud next to sharper athletes at this meet, but that hadn't stopped us from delivering great performances in the past.

The guys usually welcomed my talks before big races. Sometimes I aimed for fire and sent them out the door screaming, but this was no Palatine Invite. Sometimes the seniors talked and there were tears and closeness, but this was no Mid-Suburban League conference meet. Today was just one in a series of important tests. I aimed for gratitude, competitive fire, and perspective.

The night before, I had read a great *Sports Illustrated* article about Lance Mackey, the four-time defending champion of the Iditarod. Mackey's story is a wild one—replete with cocaine addiction and cancer before his dog racing triumphs—but that wasn't what drew my eye. Instead, I loved the bond that Mackey had with his sled dogs. Many of them were bred from down-and-out dogs he collected when he was at his lowest point. The part I loved most was a small ritual he did each year. No matter whether he was winning or losing, Mackey stopped five miles from the finish line to thank his dogs. He wanted to make sure that they got the attention and respect they deserved. Sled dogs are some of the finest endurance athletes in the world, and Mackey had spent most of his life trying to answer the question, *What makes a sled dog pull down a trail?* I often wondered the same about high school distance runners. After reading the article, I decided that it was time to "thank my dogs."

I am famous for crying in these meetings, especially when I become overwhelmed by the sacrifices of my athletes. It was too early for tears, but the quiet resolve in the room was there. I thanked the varsity for putting up with the difficult training of the first four weeks. Almost every man in the room had suffered a nagging start-up injury, illness, or the simple boredom of rigorous winter training. I pointed out that our seeds for the meet were good, but I also reminded them that, like the Iditarod, the track season was a long journey full of peaks and valleys. Today was for learning. Everyone knew that our first attempts at York would be races of discovery. I encouraged risk taking and mistake making early in the season and reminded everyone that fast times or not, we were going to York to win races. I also ended with a favorite reminder: We needed to have some fun. Early-season races are blessedly pressure-free, and I wanted everyone to remember to laugh. We broke on that idea and headed for the bus.

As the bus pulled up to York Community High School, I was reminded that this place had been the center of high school running excellence for a half century. Even the green shades in the classroom windows have an aura, as if the pervasive green acculturates youngsters into their future greatness as distance runners. You also half expect to see the mystical ghosts of Dukes past roaming the hallways, stuck in some kind of purgatory where they just can't let go of the greatness. You might run into Ron Craker and Jim White racing in the PE hallway or see the ghost of Donald Sage mopping the floor. In truth, much of that is hyperbole for me now, but my kids are still turned on by the mystique of York. In talking to York guys over the years, I have been struck by both their politeness and their nerdiness. Distance guys are distance guys. Only when we began seeing them as men rather than myths could we beat them.

Walking into the field house, everyone got that rush of adrenal excitement. I looked over at Tony Gregorio and told him, "Oh, it's on today, baby!" After training outside for five straight weeks on Mill Valley and in the gutters of Palatine's streets, entering York's palatial indoor facility reminded everyone that the true track season was upon us. This meet was a welcome gateway back into the world of competitive distance running after our winter sojourn.

York's field house is pristine and fancy, a collegiate environment more than a high school one. Plaques for the various sports deck the walls, declaring how many conference, regional, sectional, and state trophies each program has won. Predictably, the boys track and cross country placards burst with greatness, but I am always more disturbed by the lack of excellence in girls golf. It's simply bare, devoid of any titles whatsoever. For some reason the first hope I have every year is that girls golf has finally reversed its half century of misfortune and turned the corner. Alas, I was disappointed again. I would have to wait for next year.

As a distance running aficionado, I find York's field house to be the closest thing Illinois distance running has to a museum. You have to love their audacity. They only display the state championship trophies in their front hallway. There are trophies from other sports sprinkled in, but it is mostly a trip down Joe Newton Memory Lane. Coach Newton took over the program in 1960 and quickly drove it toward state and national greatness. Under his leadership, the Dukes had won twenty-seven state championships. Anything less was failure. They are the single greatest dynasty in any high school sport in American history. In the fifty-two years of Newton's tenure, the Dukes have placed in the top three a staggering forty-three times. Still coaching cross country at age eighty-two, Coach Newton and his boys would once again be our primary obstacle come the fall cross country season. We had never beaten them in the state final. My five junior stars and I walked into the field house believing this was our first step toward changing that fact.

As we awaited the meet's start, Marcus, Tony, and I toured the trophy cabinets. It was a thrill to see the state championship trophies of many of the greatest teams in Illinois history. You actually have to walk down a side hallway and find some old dustbin trophy cabinet with the second- and third-place trophies, sadly convalescing with all the other "failures." Even these trophies gave me a thrill as I recalled some of the great Illinois teams that rose up and pushed the Dukes off the top step of the podium. Whether we liked it or not, York history was Illinois cross country history, and I relished the opportunity to do battle with their excellence. Nothing gave me more of a charge than raising young men up to challenge the mighty Dukes. That exercise is the essence of Illinois distance running.

After releasing the boys to warm up for their races, I ran into my family on their way into the meet. My pregnant wife had blessedly gotten the day off when my mom, dad, and brother came in from western Illinois and absconded with Madeline and Christopher, my two older kids. A coach for more than thirty years at Geneseo and Moline High Schools, my dad is a member of the Illinois Track and Cross Country Coaches Association (ITCCCA) Hall of Fame. More than anyone, he understands the obstacle that is York. On this day he was content just to be "Grandpa," but he was here supporting me for another reason.

Together, we had shared the quest to win a state cross country title throughout our lives. In 1988 his greatest team ever at Moline placed third to incredible teams from York and Schaumburg. It was the only time he would ever step on the podium and hold a state trophy in his hands.

A few years later, my friends and I came of age and ran for him. In 1991, a late fall from one of our scoring runners relegated us to a disappointing fifth-place finish. We were sophomores then, full of ambition, and we vowed that we would win it for him by the end of our careers. Those dreams went up in smoke our senior year. The best we could do in 1993 was another fifth-place finish. Although he coached for thirteen more years, he never again took a team inside the top ten.

My dad was a scholarship runner in his day, a speedy half-miler for Western Illinois University in the late 1960s. He possessed 49-second quarter speed and the lean, snappy build of a great long-distance runner. My favorite picture of him shows his leg planted as he takes a turn around a flag on a cross country course. He is poised and graceful, his quadriceps muscles bulging with the tension of his stride. The power of his youth astonished me. Used to seeing him stopwatch in hand, I always wished I could have seen him race in his prime.

I inherited little of his natural ability. In high school he only ran for two seasons. His junior year in track he ran 5:00 for the mile. The next year he ran 4:20 and was All-State. Entering high school, I was more scrawny than imposing. Like Tony Gregorio, I barely topped five feet and was much more talented in the classroom. I wanted to be good, but I just didn't have the body of my friends. My best friend in high school, Jamie Verstraete, was All-State three times for my dad. He was the natural. I was the made man.

With little talent to speak of, I started to work. Like most other kids coached by a parent, I knew the fundamentals and had the motivating force inside my home each day. My dad never pushed me to run until I told him I wanted to be good. After that, we worked together closely, setting reachable goals and building for the future. My breakout races occurred junior year during track. I ran 4:43 for 1600 meters and pushed pace deep into the sectional qualifying race. Over the following summer, I ran nearly nine hundred miles, filling my days with long runs and longing. We all worked—seven seniors, all best friends—to win the big one for my dad.

Halfway through the season, shooting pains started screaming down my right leg. The doctors found a pinched nerve in my back. The pain was a result of extreme sciatica. Every time I put my right foot down, I could feel the electric shocks all the way down into my toes. Mid-season I ran 16:00 and was our fifth runner in our major invites. By October I couldn't race effectively, but my dad still made me run in the state series. Injured and embarrassed, I lobbied for my frosh-soph teammates to run in my place. He wouldn't have it. If we won it all, it would have to be together. He made me run in the state final where I placed two hundredth in a time of 16:38. The pictures from that day show us in the gym at Peoria High School, eyes ablaze with tears. We had failed.

I couldn't take it. After that disappointment, I gave up on running. For the next seven years I focused on schoolwork and ran nary a step. I finished Bronze Tablet at the University of Illinois and won a fellowship to Northwestern University for PhD study in history. Even while serving as manager under Gary Wieneke at Illinois for both the cross country and track teams, I knew that something was missing. Good grades were edifying, but they lacked the rush of competition and the purpose of the quest.

My need for that animating quest hit me square in the jaw in April of my first year at Northwestern. I was sitting in my studio apartment in Rogers Park, bathed in afternoon sunlight and reading a boring book of historiography on my couch. I remember sitting the book down and staring up at the ceiling. I had only one thought: *I am not happy.* And in that split second, I knew what I wanted out of my life. I called my mom later that day and told her the news: "Mom, I'm giving up my PhD fellowship and coming home to marry that girl I've been dating. I want to be a cross country coach. If I have to teach high school, I will." I finished out the year and started to walk the path that was meant for me.

Actually, I started to run it. Many years removed from my last jog, I bought a pair of running shoes and started to train. It took me two years to earn my MAT degree from Western Illinois University, but all along I was plotting. I wanted to build a cross country program that could win it all. For two years, I wrote about it, plotting and scheming for the day when I'd get a chance to coach. I picked up experience by helping my dad coach two Moline teams to the state cross country meet. In the spring of 2001, I landed my dream job when I was hired to teach English at Palatine and coach cross country with Fred Miller (a hall of fame coach in his own right).

From day one I was after the business my dad and I had left unfinished. Our entire life together had been spent on the journey to this championship. Call it misguided, but the goal and the process were interchangeable. What we really wanted was to do it together. Winning would be the icing on the cake. He had driven across the state not just to see his grandkids or watch some great races. Both of us sensed that this was the group. These guys could be the ones who took us where we had wanted to go for over thirty years—even longer in my dad's case. From now until next November, he was all-in. Just like me. Just like the boys. Every training idea, every potential injury, every race plan was filtered through our near-daily phone conversations.

My mom sensed this as well, and she gave my dad and me the space to do it. An experienced cross country junkie herself, she had long since lost interest in track races, but her grandkids were a powerful enough pull to get her across the state on a Saturday morning. Mads and Christopher couldn't have cared less that they were at a track meet. As four- and two-year-olds, respectively, they just wanted to be where the action was and see something new. They would spend most of the afternoon coloring in the bleachers and running around the school hallways with "Papa" Quick.

My parents also made sure to bring my brother, Chad, who is known all around the state as a cross country and track fan. Chad has cerebral palsy and cannot run himself, but he had been there through it all with my dad and me. Same goals. Same desires. This yearly journey, the buildup through track, the summer miles, the fall season, was what we had done our entire lives. All three of us lived for it. Chad has seen much of Illinois cross country and track history unfold right before his eyes. At state track he sits on the finish line each year. At state cross country he is a fixture in the coaches' box near the finish. All the best coaches in the state know him. I knew that it would be the thrill of his life to see us win it all.

Waiting for the meet to get under way, we chatted in the foyer of York's field house and looked at the state trophies. We marveled not just at the number, but also at the greatness. Standing in front of the 1999 state championship trophy, we tossed around memories of what most consider the greatest team in Illinois history. York had scored 24 points in the state final, placing six runners in the top twenty-four. Many fans believed that this was the greatest team in national history. Standing there looking at it all, my dad turned to me and stated the obvious: "Wouldn't you just love to win one?"

The loudspeakers blaring first call for the 4 x 800 meter relay snapped us out of our reverie and back to the task at hand. For many years our theoretical hopes and dreams had washed ashore on the hard banks of reality. Thinking and saying you want to win is one thing. Forging concrete reality on the backs of five teenage boys is another thing entirely. The gap between concept and reality is vast.

Our philosophy in that day's meet was to stick our varsity guys into their best races for the first time all season. Tony Gregorio intended to qualify to the Illinois Prep Top Times indoor meet in the 3200 meter run by running at least 9:43. He ran a solid race, recording a 9:37 and finishing second, but his "finish" also provoked the day's greatest bit of hilarity. St. Charles North's Ryan Senci took off with eight hundred meters to go and ran away to win. Tony chased gamely. As he came to the close of his race, I clicked my watch and then looked up to see him continuing. I started yelling, but he was lost in the zone, accelerating down the backstretch into his final kick. The judges at the finish line were bewildered. Suddenly scared, Senci asked me if he had another lap. I smiled broadly, turned to my varsity, and declared that Tony would never live this down. With the entire crowd yelling at him to stop, he ran an extra lap. So there it was: 10:10.7—the best 3400 meter run of the indoor season in Illinois.

The rest of the meet was full of normal first-invite successes and failures. Our senior half-miler, Ryan McGough, trotted through a slow four-hundred-meter split before getting unboxed and letting his speed go. Prospect's Kellan Strobel caught him with a hundred meters to go and motored to the win. The 1600 meter run was thrilling as usual. Without Driggs to power it along, Johnson and Meincke looked like scared little kittens as they cowered in fear of the lead. They ambled through halfway and fell like suckers into a sit-and-kick race that neither was prepared to win. St. Charles North's Billy Clink lit up his speed at the quarter to go and took it away. Both ran inspired races late in the game, but left only with some powerful lessons learned.

It is never easy to compartmentalize an early-season meet. If the goal was to win races, then we went zero for three. In another sense, humbling losses and peaks at potential greatness are powerful motivators. Everyone walked out of the gym knowing they were in the thick of it and could hang with the state's best. There would certainly be more rounds to fight. The boys from St. Charles North showed that they were ready to play at the elite level. Kellan Strobel's monster speed and competitive heart would be waiting for us come the MSL conference meet. Jack Driggs wouldn't hide for much longer in the 4 x 800 relay and the 600 meter dash. Everyone was learning, training, and biding their time.

I concluded the meet with one final goal in mind. My dad had wanted to see if Christopher, my two-year-old, could run an entire lap. So we all took off down the backstretch, dodging in and out of the departing kids. Christopher wore his red Palatine hoodie and ran wildly, driving his arms with exaggerated motion. At home he runs around our house and asks my wife and me to yell, "Go Pirate boys!" as he runs in circles. We rounded the south curve and hit the straightaway and little man showed no signs of letting up.

So we jogged to the line, three generations of Quicks, and I thought suddenly of all the joy I still got from running. Here I was with my dad, my high school coach and hero, and here we were showing my son something that both of us loved so intensely. As we hit the finish line, I leaned and looked over my shoulder just in time to see my little guy throw his arms back, thrust his chest forward, and lean for the line. Perfect finish.

We slowed to a walk, and I paused for a second to shake Jack Driggs's hand on a job well done. If our goals on the day were to compete hard, have fun, and keep perspective, then I considered it mission accomplished. I got to see someone as gracious and great as Jack Driggs run. I got to see my own boys compete their hearts out and run with the passion that Palatine men should. And I got to run a victory lap with my dad and my son. Track meets are about many things—the greatness of Driggs, the speed of young men, the mystique of York, the fun times and friends—but they are also about fathers and sons, coaches and athletes, and the bonds we forge one lap at a time.

THE MID-SUBURBAN LEAGUE

Although the York Invite was a stern competitive test, it held no special emotional place in the racing season. Like most meets, it gave opportunities and provided competition. But it was not the kind of meet that stirred your soul or kindled your better nature. At most track invites the races are just races. Hard-fought, for sure. But just races.

All that changed the morning we arrived at North Central College for the Mid-Suburban League Invitational. With one team of the twelve missing, it wasn't quite the "indoor conference" meet, but for all intents and purposes it was. North Central's new indoor facility was a slice of magic. The spongy two-hundred-meter track had a gorgeous bounce to it, like you were walking on springy pillows of marshmallow. You could smell its newness and feel the grooves in the brand-new surface. When I walked in with the boys and smelled the air, it felt like MSL time.

An MSL meet can be felt in the air. It's a buzz of anticipation, a tense rush of excitement. All athletes need do is sip from this cup and they can transform into a greater manifestation of themselves than they ever thought possible. I've seen it happen one too many times to discount the effect. MSL meets are summative, transformative, and ecstatic. To run at York was to engage with the deepest myths about Illinois distance running. To run our MSL rivals was to come face-to-face with ourselves. These were runners from communities like ours. The rivalries had been spawned long ago in frosh-soph races that later migrated to the varsity level. The athletes could look one another in the eyes and read the old battle scars. The glances and hushed hellos were cordial, but steely. We would battle each other for berths in the state finals, for spots on our résumés, and for simple pride. The rivalries here ran across the years and across the generations. These were races that mattered.

The legacy of our conference had been written across the years not just in the state record books, but also in weekday dual meets and in the wide-open spaces of Chicago's northwest suburbs. Populated mostly by well-to-do suburbanites and up-and-coming American dreamers, the twelve schools that make up the Mid-Suburban League are in the wheelhouse of distance running demographics. Their generous pay schedules also ensure that more than a few expert coaches have made the conference their home. A couple of years into my tenure at Palatine, I went to the MSL post-season cross country meeting and realized just what we were up against.

I looked around the room. Outside of Joe Newton, Jim Macnider at Schaumburg was the most successful boys coach in state history with nine state cross country trophies, including three state titles. His brother, Jon, had won three state titles in his own right at the helm of the Schaumburg girls program. Debbie Revolta had coached team state champions in both cross country and track at Barrington. John Powers of Conant coached Jeffrey Thode to the state championship in cross country and the state record in the 1600 meter run. The list went on and on: Jamie Klotz of Buffalo Grove, state champion 4 x 800 meter relay, Tim Phillips of Hersey, state champion in the 3200 meter run, Mike Stokes of Prospect, state champion in both the 1600 meter run and the 4 x 800 relay. Those were just the state champions. The list of All-State athletes, top ten teams, and conference champions was practically bottomless.

Even my colleagues at Palatine had intimidating résumés. Steve Currins took over the Palatine girls program a year after its first cross country state title in 1989 and drove the program to five more. He had helmed so many trophy teams in cross country and track that I couldn't even count them. He'd even coached the Beecher boys to a Class A state runner-up trophy in the 1970s and guided Shelly McBride to a state record in the 1600 meter run while at Crete-Monee High School. Joe Parks, my partner in crime at Palatine, had been one of my biggest rivals when he helped lead St. Charles North to consecutive boys state trophies in the mid-2000s. He then transferred to Palatine and took our 2009 girls team to their first state cross country title since 1996. He and I had vowed to maintain the programs' standards of excellence.

This endless list of accomplishments surely rests on the backs of fine athletes, but year after year these cordial rivals of mine were the motors of such achievement. In my earlier years their résumés had been a source of intimidation. Now our relationships carried a respectful collegiality tinged with competitive madness. In many cases these were the finest programs in the state, and the men and women who helmed them were at the top of the profession.

Such meetings were stern reminders that if you didn't eat your Wheaties in the MSL, then someone else was going to have you for breakfast. One of my favorite aspects of being in this fraternity—and this extends to the kids as well—is the basic collegiality. Coaches in our conference know that getting to the top of our league means getting to the top of the state. Sometimes a post-season meeting is more victory celebration than grim meeting of rivals. No one begrudges anyone else's success. I know how competitive the conference can be, and I knew then that certain people in the room couldn't stand one another. But in the end we are each other's greatest assets. Neither my kids nor I could earn anything without them. Those pesky competitors from Schaumburg, Prospect, Conant, Barrington, and the rest drove us crazy, but they were the engine that made our team go. When Fred Miller and I started coaching together at Palatine, we made one basic agreement. If we could be the best in the MSL, then we could be the best in the state.

One of the first things I did upon arriving was find Jamie Klotz. As head coach of Buffalo Grove's cross country and track teams, he is one of the true characters in Illinois sports. To know him and love him, you must be anesthetized to an endless stream of filthy language. He's not the kind of guy you take your mother to meet. My mom has met him. All she could say afterward was, "Who is this guy? I've never heard anyone say f*** in so many creative ways." On MSL days, he goes straight into barbarian mode. With his bright red goatee, shaved head, and numerous tattoos, he coaches with the ferocity of a medieval Viking. The man should be decked out with a battle-ax and an ancient helm scarred with the blows of former foes. When I hear the first "Attack! Attack!" of the meet, I know it is time to go. Klotz and I always look each other in the eye and think the same thing: *Are you ready to bang today, brother?*

This battlefield ethos permeates MSL competition. Sometimes the winners and losers are not the most important part of an MSL meet. What matters is the size and intensity of the battle. If enough of us come together and decide to go at it, we can create a race worth seeing, one fought with a singular intensity and beauty, one fought to the purest depths of exhaustion. The end result is glory for all.

Our conference has certainly seen its share of incredible athletes in all the events, but the real heat of an MSL track meet lies in the distance races. Many of the guys and girls spend much of the season training for this meet and avoiding one another. The effect is a lot like two prize-fighters who beat up on lesser opponents, but keep ducking the title shot until the time is right. Each season has a shadowboxing period that works slowly toward culmination.

The other dynamic that drives the conference is an odd system of leads and understudies, masters and apprentices. Each class of MSL athletes defines itself against the classes above it. As with most conferences, the seniors dominate. Often the usurper has to unseat an All-State senior or even a state champion to take the throne. In the most exciting races a young usurper gains the throne and a new champion is crowned.

My favorite example of this is Conant's Jeff Thode. Track fans now know Jeffrey as the 2008 state cross country champion, the state record holder in the 1600 meter run, and a 3:58 miler at the University of Iowa. If you are from the MSL, you probably remember Jeffrey as a solid young athlete who kept running up against two seemingly immoveable rivals: Hersey's Kevin Havel and Palatine's Mat Smoody. Jeffrey improved to an All-State finish as a junior in cross country, but he could never quite touch Havel and Smoody, who both finished in the top five. Early in his junior year of track the two seniors kept serving notice that they were still in charge. On one beautiful night at the outdoor MSL meet, Jeff Thode usurped the throne. He hung with Smoody and Havel deep into the conference 1600 meter run, looked at them out the corner of his eye at 300 meters to go, and then threw down the gauntlet. All those years of struggle and difficulty vanished. He demolished the MSL outdoor record with a sensational 4:10 clocking. From that moment on, Jeffrey Thode was a champion.

This dynamic was a perfect one for my five juniors. Still too slow to make the lineup, Peter was relegated to the 4 x 800 meter relay, but the other four had earned entry into the prime races of the day—the 800, 1600, and 3200 meter runs. Foremost in my mind was the emergence of Tim Meincke. After his fantastic flameout in the state cross country final, Tim had rededicated himself. His training through the winter months had been focused and dynamic. Slowly, he challenged up the ladder of the team, mirroring Tim Johnson in workouts and taking it to Tony Gregorio whenever he could. As we walked in and saw the heat sheets, I smelled a fresh opportunity. So did Tim.

Ever since I watched him run a 5:35 mile at his eighth-grade track meet, I had pegged Tim Meincke as a star. He did not win the race or run an unbelievable time. What I noticed were his legs. He passed what I call the "Kenyan ankle test." It is not hard to miss the sleek musculature of the Kenyan athletes. In contrast with the calf muscles of our bulked-up American football players, the Kenyan calf is sleek—close to non-existent. They run on twig legs, feathering the track, gliding along like apparitions chasing shadows out of the mist. Ankles come in many shapes and sizes, but what I usually look for is a man who can wrap his thumb and pointer finger around his ankle and have the two fingers touch. Tim Meincke has gorgeous runner legs, long twiggy pins with sleek muscles and skinny ankles. He looks like he jumped out of a running catalog.

Aside from his physical gifts, Tim is a true original. He is beloved within the team for his competitiveness, his intense attitude, and just how outrageously weird he can be. Everyone called him "Monkey" from day one. It's one of those rare instances when a nickname captures the essence of a man. Monkey has a bit of a screw loose, and it makes him one of the most sincere and endearing people you could ever meet. In junior high, Keith Janosch and the Sundling coaches called him "Wrong Way" Meincke in tribute to the countless number of times he got lost during road runs and cross country races.

The guys could also write a book of "Monkey-isms" culled from years of Tim's weirdness. He might chide the entire team to run "like Seabiscuit" during a hard tempo run or instruct us about the necessity for well-thought-out plot lines in . . . ahem . . . adult features. The week before the MSL meet Marcus was lying on the floor at 6:02 AM when he farted loudly. Monkey rushed over, lay on the ground, and spooned him before Marcus stood up aghast and aflame with laughter.

Monkey is also a fitting nickname for a man whose racing instincts are often detached from appropriate reality. His primal instincts have often served him well. There is something brutal about the way Monkey competes. He simply has no methodology. He reacts with such emotion and force, especially in varsity races, that I fear taming him. The utter wildness of his racing spirit is the source of his greatest triumphs and his most humbling defeats. Trying to teach Monkey pace is like asking a championship basketball player to stay in the offense. You might get something more fluid, but the constraints also might cost the individual his burning brilliance. The extra flammable ingredients always threaten to burn him to pieces, but he just might catch everyone else on fire before that moment of self-immolation.

As proven by his flameout at the state cross country meet, Tim's irrational exuberance had both inspired and burned the rest of us before. He's like the early speed in the Kentucky Derby—determined to go out fast and take the race even though the mile-and-a-quarter distance might break him in the end. Heading into a cross country season where he would carry the load of the fifth scorer, we were ill equipped to handle any more late-race fades spun off from early attempts at glory. Maybe Tim Meincke was too fiery to be saddled. But all of us knew that someday his ferocious wind would have to meet the calm turbulence of the rational world. In the future we would need the grimly predictable more often than erratic brilliance.

Looking at the heat sheets for the 1600 meter run, I smiled at his opportunity. Both Tony and Monkey would go head-to-head with Prospect's Kellan Strobel. Neither had ever beaten the senior in a track race, and it was prime time for them to take the throne. We drew up an aggressive race plan centered on trading leads off the front of the race in order to drain Strobel's kick. Our exuberance would have to wait though, balled up and alive, since the 1600 meter run would be contested at the end of the racing day. We first had to sit back and enjoy Marcus Garcia's bid to challenge the conference's other top dog—Barrington's Erik Peterson.

Avoiding winter running per usual habit, Marcus started the indoor season at the bottom of the varsity totem pole. Just three months before he had run 5:05 pace for three consecutive miles on grass. By February he could not even manage that pace for a single mile. The climb upward had been slow, but steady, and Marcus still possessed his most charming asset. He believed he was the fastest guy in the building.

As he left our final meeting and jogged to the starting line, I left him with one last piece of advice: Don't lead the race. Marcus is a notorious pace-pusher, a "one-stepper." On road runs or workouts, no matter how hard the group runs he always pushes one step ahead. The result had been a career-long string of runs and races where the pace increased exponentially. He often behaved like a caged beast, scratching and clawing at the cage of rational pace, wanting to run free and push it from hook to crook. He and Monkey were bred the same way.

A pace-pushing philosophy was sheer doom for Marcus in a race of this caliber. Both Peterson and Schaumburg's sophomore star Evan Prizy were major kickers. Ever since finishing fourth at the MSL cross country meet as a sophomore, Peterson had become the MSL's alpha male. His sixth-place finish at the state cross country meet the previous fall had further painted the mark on his back. Prizy and Marcus came ready to steal his throne, relishing their underdog roles. Before the race

I asked Ty Gorman, Peterson's coach at Barrington, how fast Erik wanted to run. He looked at me with a wry grin and said, "He'll probably run about one-tenth of a second faster than whoever gets second." Peterson wouldn't hammer from the gun. He loved the late-race fights. If Marcus went for it, he would be sacrificed on the altar of the early pace when the racing got hot in the second mile. Because he was weak in fitness already, I advised him to relax in the pack and marshal his energy for a late challenge.

He led it anyway. Right from the gun, he broke away and took the lead. He held it through the mile before fading badly, suffering on his way to a personal best of 9:52. It was another in a long series of romantic-hero runs that yielded only moral victory. After a solid opening mile, Prizy and Peterson separated themselves from Marcus and took off with Buffalo Grove's Jereme Atchison in tow. Each lap got faster and faster as the three rolled negative splits. Atchison dropped with four laps to go as Prizy brought his filthy speed to bear against Peterson's wry toughness. Peterson is a gamer, though, and no mere pretender was going to beat him. Whoever took him down would have to be a champion. The two battled into the last four hundred meters before, out of nowhere, Atchison came kicking by both.

The move goosed the two leaders, and from three hundred meters out they dropped Atchison and contested each other side by side. If Peterson gave in, Prizy would not just win the race. He would win a confidence that far outweighed the 10 team points and whatever paltry medal was awarded. The race wasn't about winning. It was about keeping the sophomore where he belonged. Prizy threw everything he could at Peterson on the last lap. He kicked at the gun, he kicked down the backstretch, and he kicked again at fifty meters to go. It was to no avail. Peterson maintained his throne. He cruised away to win in 9:27.5, but young Prizy walked away with a glaring new personal best of 9:27.9. He knew then that only minute margins separated him from the top.

A similar spectacle unfolded later that afternoon in the 1600 meter run. The table was set for a great boys mile. On the backstretch during the girls races, I stopped to talk with Prospect's Mike Stokes. He had entered both of his senior stars, Kellan Strobel and Greg Netols, fresh in this race. I saw Fremd's Andy Mack and two Schaumburg stars, Travis Morrison and Pat Swiech, intensely striding and readying for battle. Both Gregorio and Meincke sensed the potential of the moment. Most of the conference's best were there and fresh.

As they stepped to the line, the crowd reduced its volume to a slight hum, and then—for one beautiful instant—the entire field house went quiet. The assembled field stood upright, heard the command for "Set," stepped to the line, and then—released. The field house erupted. We planned to send Gregorio through the four hundred meters in sixty-five seconds to get the pace moving, but Strobel immediately took the lead. He looked to stamp his dominance on the field from the gun. After improving to twenty-seventh in state cross country, he was back in his more natural habitat: the tight oval, the storehouse of speed. The previous May, Strobel had nearly anchored Prospect to a state title in the 4 x 800 meter relay. The narrow loss had been a powerful motivator, and he had competed with an edge throughout the year. This distance had never been his forte, but he now meant to erase that illusion.

He hit the quarter mile in sixty-three seconds and kept the hammer down. I was yelling furiously at my junior tandem to ride in Strobel's wake and relax. Quickly the cord started to cut from the main field. By halfway Strobel, Gregorio, Meincke, and Swiech were clear. The stage was set for the three juniors to challenge for the throne. Swiech was running well, but he started to lose form and drop ground heading into the final two laps. By then Strobel was well clear and cruising as Tony and Monkey vainly gave chase toward the stocky, powerful senior. Just when it appeared that he would run away with it, just at the moment when he was about to force a concession, I saw the first glimpse. Even from the far curve, I saw his shoulders rise. His chin tilted back ever so slightly. He reached up and gasped for air. His impeccable form started to deteriorate. His arms lost all fluidity. I threw a glance at Jimmy Mac, and both of us thought the same thing. *He's done.*

At 150 meters to go, Gregorio and Meincke hit the top of the backstretch and smelled blood in the water. Remembering all the countless long runs and intervals they had run together, the two best friends put their heads down and charged. Like two expert fisherman, they slowly reeled in the leader down the backstretch. By this point, the north side of the track was a furious tunnel of noise, awash in the frenzied cries of competitors and fans who knew just what a great MSL race looked like. The frenzy reached its peak into the west curve as Meincke got to Strobel's shoulder with Gregorio in tow.

But it was not to be. Strobel had earned his laurels through too many years of struggle to fold in the last fifty meters. He gutted it out to the line and took the victory by less than a second. Like Peterson, he carried too much pride in himself and in his colors to give in. Prospect trumped Palatine, but the result was anything but bitter. Everyone involved crushed their lifetime bests. While they might not have inherited the champion's throne, my two juniors finished with new personal bests of 4:22 each. Strobel defended his turf by only the slightest of margins.

After the meet, the coaches and athletes reverted to collegiality. I congratulated Kellan on a race well run and looked forward to the next time we would all get together to create races worth watching and winning. The existing order—Peterson and Strobel—survived to fight another day. Each knew, though, that the challengers were breathing down their necks. Outdoor season now loomed, and its surprises were always the best of all. What new talent would emerge? Who would be crowned champion come May? In the MSL the impossible often became real, and I knew that all of the coaches and athletes exiting the field house would relish the next time we got together and fought it out like each race meant everything.

My juniors had run new personal bests, yet failed to subvert the existing order. For the first time in their careers, they would be counted on to carry the distance side of the track team. Tim Johnson placed second in the 800 meter run in a new best. Marcus ran with his usual mania and was subdued. Both Gregorio and Meincke had performed admirably.

Tony had expected to do well, but Meincke's race was different. He delivered the unexpected shot. It had been heard around the conference by an array of coaches and athletes. Next time around he would be the hunted rather than the hunter. With that newfound status came the burden of being the best. To become a state champion both he and the rest would have to survive the imminent trials of the outdoor season.

THE MORNING LOOP

Two weeks removed from the MSL Indoor Invite, we began to ready for the rigors of the outdoor racing season. Before we could challenge the best runners from other schools, we first had to sort out who would earn the spots on our own team. Many boys within the squad were in heated competitions for coveted spots in the MSL Outdoor Conference and IHSA Sectional meets. In these meets only two runners were allowed in each of the cardinal distance events—the 800, 1600, and 3200 meter runs. The rest would either ride the bench or fight for a spot on the 4 x 800 meter relay. On a team where multiple men were capable of running the state qualifying standards, competition began in practice.

The workouts between the end of the indoor season and the big invites in late April began the transition toward greatness. On good teams full of ambitious and competitive young men, these workouts too often trend toward racing. No workout in our program generates this sentiment more than our tempo runs on "the Morning Loop." Whereas track workouts are conducted near or below the athletes' race paces, a tempo run involves running extended distances at a hard rhythm. The pace will never touch what an athlete could perform on the track. But the tempo gets you nonetheless. The lactic acid creeps slowly into the muscles. The burn comes on, languidly at first, then like a rush of sickness somewhere deep in the run. Only a certain type of man can master the tempo. The half-milers possess neither the patience nor the oxygen capacity to master it. The Morning Loop is the playground of the strong men, the hard-core distance fanatics.

It was early morning and dark as I walked quietly to the school for the first Morning Loop tempo of the track season. The moon glistened overhead as a beautiful reminder of early stillness. It was one of those split moons, not quite full, and the clouds interspersed beautifully with the darkness. I paused for a second in the middle of the east fields. I listened to the quiet and felt the gentle wind on my face. These calm moments were priceless. I took them because I knew that the run to come would be anything but patient and calm. Morning Loop tempo never was.

The training group's usual habit was to run our long run every Monday and incorporate a fast twenty-minute tempo finish at the end. These runs often involved savage accelerations on the back end of twelve- or thirteen-mile runs. I had borrowed this idea from Neuqua Valley's Paul Vandersteen after one too many classes of his guys looked stronger than mine in the middle of cross country races. Still, the extra distance numbed the intensity of the effort. When we got halfway through the track season, we returned each Monday morning to a Palatine standard: the five-mile Morning Loop tempo.

There's something about the demands of this workout, the insanity of it, the repetitive mythology of it that kindles your fire and fills you with trepidation. Waking up, putting your feet on the floor, dressing quietly, and getting to school is never the same when everyone knows we'll hammer the Loop. I usually set my racing flats out the night before and run through my anticipated splits as I beg myself to fall asleep. Now that I'm older, Morning Loop tempo is more race than workout, and I know that I will charge headlong until I get dropped. It's like driving a car without brakes, but it also has the exhilaration and speed of the moments before the crash. Morning Loop tempo is victory and insanity, love and loss, pain and breakthrough, straight-up grip-it-and-rip-it running. It's a mainline rush of pace.

We had track team pictures on this particular day so I wanted to make sure we replaced our normal long run with the tempo workout in the morning and another easy seven- to ten-mile road run after school. Most of the varsity would run twelve to fifteen miles on the day. I called all the guys on Sunday afternoon to deliver the news. Some took it in stride. Others betrayed their fear with a slight sinking of the voice. Everyone had been dropped on this run at some point. Everyone also knew their personal best time and believed in the loop's fitness promise.

When I came to Palatine ten years ago, the Morning Loop was a seldom-used road run that I helped bring out of obscurity. In a manic bit of youthful zealousness, I walked the entire route with my measuring wheel and spray-painted the half-mile marks on the ground. I started at the light pole in front of Palatine's athletic doors and headed west up Cunningham Drive. The loop proceeds from there down Hicks Road to Northwest Highway and then bends north up Rohlwing Road back to Palatine High School. More funky trapezoid than loop, the loop runs exactly five miles from the light pole to the light pole. The distance came out to the foot on the measuring wheel. A piece of perfection was born.

Everyone in our group knows the half-mile marks: ten to fifteen yards before the telephone pole preceding Carpenter Drive, end of the sidewalk by the old Kmart, the sidewalk in front of Popeye's Chicken, the streetlight at Hicks and Northwest Highway, the middle section of the split-rail fence on Rohlwing, the bush at the entrance to Winston Campus, thirty meters past the creek bridge. Then it's time to drive for home, last half mile from Carpenter Drive in.

The mythology of the Morning Loop built early on. When we started running it regularly in 2002, no one on the team could break thirty minutes. We struggled Monday after Monday to master 6:00 mile pace over the five-mile distance. That fall, we trained with discipline and precision, and the loop was our test track. Senior leaders Jorge Calvillo and Nate McPherson called out the same pile of glass on the sidewalk every day for a season. We ran into the exact same white PT Cruiser with wood paneling at the exact same stoplight every Monday morning. An unknown jogger, known to this day simply as "Morning Loop Guy," ran the exact same route as us. No matter how fast we went he would pass us on the opposite side of the street, presumably the best runner in all of Palatine. He ran with bounce and beauty, a perfect representation of what we wanted to become. He runs earlier now, but if you watch you can still find him jogging through the early-morning mist, passing us at a glide. Then he is gone. A shade in the night, a running ghost, a phantasm of the Loop.

To know the Loop is to know its simple geography. It is to wait for the beautiful smell of Spunky Dunkers doughnut shop and know that you can never stop. It is to eternally wonder why anyone would open a store that is half antiques shop and half accounting agency. It is to wonder who stays at the Bel Air and The Haven, two decrepit motel relics of the 1950s. It is to know that there is a hydrant to dodge and a pole to slap every time you run down Northwest Highway. It is to accept that stopping at the Palatine Road stoplights might save you oxygen, but will kill your rhythm. It is to know how to peek through the bushes in the dark so a wayward car doesn't run you over. It is to know how to jump the puddles that form on Reseda when it rains and that we only cross Rohlwing diagonally at the stop sign.

Much of our love lies within the speed the Loop guarantees. Its subtle terrain and history find their way into your bloodstream through an odd species of diffusion. To run the Loop is to engage its history of speed, its legacy of darkness and unfettered aerobic horsepower. Guys might amble through other five-mile runs in thirty-six or thirty-seven minutes, but that never happens on the Loop. Usually, guys run thirty-two or thirty-three minutes and have no idea why. When Steve Finley was in quest of a state cross country title, we rarely ran it in over thirty-three minutes. One day Big Fin decided to test the Loop's limits. He hit the mile in 5:17 and never looked back. Not to be outdone, fellow senior Glenn Morris ran him down in the final quarter mile. His 27:20 clocking was still the Loop record.

On this crisp April morning, Tony Gregorio decided that he would make his bid. He didn't announce to the group that he intended to run fast. No one ever did. An attempt at a historic time was usually preceded by one of two things—a terrible race or a glorious one. The best Loops are either redemptive or declarative. Tony had just run 9:23 for 3200 meters the Saturday previous at the Illinois Prep Top Times meet so everyone in the group knew that he would test the loop soon. The week before Tony had freaked out in the Palatine circle drive because I led the group out too slowly on an easy run. He obviously had Morning Loop greatness on the brain. Who was I to stand in his way? Knowing it would be far past my ability, I took splits from the heated safety of my Chrysler.

To run 27:20 a man needs to average just under 5:30 per mile. Most attempts at the loop record are undone by one simple fact—the first mile is usually a warm-up before the tempo progresses. Tony hit the mile mark just before Carpenter in 5:57 with Marcus Garcia and Reuben Frey in tow so I figured the mark was out of reach. Then he moved. By a mile and a half, he was gone, with Marcus, Timmy J, Reuben, and Monkey churning in his wake and gasping for air. All of them were great runners in their own right. Tony was making a bid to be more than great.

Coach Sheehan and I marveled at Tony's economy as he plowed through the second mile in a 5:24 split. Usually we exalted if anyone ran that for their finishing mile. Tony glided on past the faded light of the Popeye's Chicken sign and disappeared into the darkness, sliding gracefully through the first glimmers of the dawn. Behind him was the normal clutter of the Loop. Everyone was tasked to run his own tempo pace rather than race, but that often was not the case. On this morning the back end was destroyed, asphyxiated by the early pace. Peter had just returned from a weeklong trip to Florida. He had run fast during indoor season, but his time on the beach had dulled his ability and his spirit. He was getting throttled. Lots of darkness, but nowhere to hide.

Sheehan and I knew something special was afoot when Tony came through the third mile in a split of 5:14. He had the resolved look that great distance guys get when they push the pain threshold. His look betrayed a sick relaxation, a slight fear of the unknown, a careful glimpse into a potent intermixing of pain and pleasure. The great ones always look the calmest when their muscles boil hottest. The rest of the varsity hung on gamely, but they were strung out after a sub-11:00 run through the second and third miles. They would all finish under 30:00, but that time was a brutal slog on this gorgeous morning. Each man continued through the solitary darkness wondering, as usual, *Why am I doing this, why am I putting myself through this pain, will anyone notice if I quit, how can I finish at this pace, gotta keep going, gotta stick with my teammates, gotta love the hurt.* The Morning Loop invited the savage interior monologues all distance runners endure. In a run where no one could hide, even your head offered little solace.

Tony started to flag as he approached the school, but he still managed 5:20 for the fourth mile and was squarely on record pace. Just behind him Reuben Frey threw his hands on his head and began walking. Even during tough workouts this was rare, and Sheehan and I quickly pulled over. We sat him down in a driveway in a near-blackout state before he recovered and jogged it in. Probably a potent mix of dehydration and asphyxiation. We tended to Reuben and then sped home to see Tony's finish.

He came up the slight rise on Rohlwing Road with glaring concentration and a bounce in his stride. This was no longer a workout. It was a test against a myth. The Morning Loop had vanquished many men in our program. It certainly had beaten Tony before, but he went full guns into the last half mile, beating the sidewalk to a pulp, forcing the Loop to yield beneath his grotesque desire. The last half is where Palatine champions are born. Prior to winning our state trophy in 2003, we used to run all-out on the last eight hundred meters every day. Senior captain Tim Larson would yell, "Finishing is what?" We'd respond in unison, "A habit!" That team reached the moment of truth in the 2003 IHSA State meet—the zigzag through the trees at three hundred meters to go—and responded with joyful flight. The best teams finish because they care for one another. Palatine guys learned to care by sharing the pain and sweat uphill in the closing stretch of the Loop. If you can beat the Loop, then you can beat Detweiller, too.

Tony rounded into the circle in full gear, but the time was not meant to be. He ran a stunning 27:30 after flagging in the final mile, but the record would stand for another day. Afterward he reacted with his usual mix of anger and stupefaction. Too often he built his self-concept through comparison, and taking down records from alumni had become his means of elevation. Vanquishing a record set by Morris and Finley—two of the All-Time Greats—would validate all his hard work. Knowing how hard he had run, he simply quipped that "those guys had to be monsters to run that time" and stalked off to cheer his teammates into the finishing stretch.

Guy after guy broke 30:00, and I remembered back to those early days when a 6:00 pace was such a burden. Since then we had endured through state trophy ecstasy and humiliating defeat, but the one thing we always had in common across the generations was the Loop. It was always there for us, beckoning the guys to run faster, to reach farther, and—someday—to conquer.

We walked out to the track for our post-run sprints with a gorgeous red sun just cresting the horizon. We all stopped in the early-morning light to enjoy the few moments when the human eye can look directly into the sun. For a brief time it was quiet. Then Erik Bethke walked up from behind and declared, "So guys, I accidentally kicked a bird on the Loop." From there the exhaustion put itself away, and we were back to our normal selves. The sacrifice of the morning was over, and we returned to our workaday lives. We pondered the big questions: "Can you accidentally kick a bird?" "Why isn't Marcus Garcia featured more in the columns I write for *ESPN Rise*?" "Why is Tim Meincke so weird?" "Why would a bird sit on the sidewalk?"

Our practice descended into its usual pattern of jolly fraternity and aggressive banter. The guys ran strides on the turf field, and Sheehan and I stood and talked about the greatness of Tony's run. We wondered what fruits such fitness would yield come the state track meet and his senior cross country season. Even better, Tony's burn for greatness had enlivened his teammates. Marcus, Timmy J, Monkey, and Reuben had all been pulled to personal best efforts. He had taken on the mantle of leader and never once looked back.

Once again everyone had woken up, put their feet on the floor, and attacked the Loop. The overwhelming feeling afterward was relief. The hard part was over. Marcus would go and sleep through a bunch of classes. Meincke would pretend he knew what was going on in math class. Tony would pretend to have read his AP English homework. I would pretend that grading papers while sleepy was something other than drudgery. But really, everything spanks of anticlimax after a Morning Loop tempo. The sense of challenge is already over for the day, and nothing else can provide that rush. The boys would amble through the rest of the day, tired to the core and bored to the max, steeling themselves against the next early dawn when they would get to see who they really were down deep in their cores.

PLATEAU

In the weeks following that epic tempo run, we sank into the malaise that looms over every track season. The dreaded plateau. The calm before the storm. At some shifting point each year, the outdoor track season vanishes into a quagmire of bad weather, wind, and necessary patience. After enduring the daily deprivations of winter running, the only hope most have is that one day—in April—it will finally be warm and the real track season will arrive.

But most of our days were spent in a miasma of rain, wind, and dashed hopes. When we did compete, my varsity fretted about their slow times and lack of punch. Tony Gregorio couldn't understand why his personal bests now seemed so far out of reach. Bit by bit, his confidence eroded. Peter and Marcus staggered under the weight of the wind and the chill of the rain. Fresh off the successes of his indoor campaign, Tim Meincke developed tendinitis in his knee. As a couple of days piled into two weeks, his confidence vanished. Nothing came easily.

Days of goodness popped up, but the weather debilitated even the most optimistic. Meets were canceled due to snow, rain, wind, or all of the above. Opportunities to cash in on the long promises of training were abandoned and unrecoverable. The only choice was to keep on, but that was tough when the boys had worked for an entire winter only to have Mother Nature hang tooth and nail on to her frosty foothold. Even the sunny days had highs in the forties. All we could do was train and hope. The workouts continued, transitioning toward real speed work, brutal repetitive reminders that we were still putting money in the bank.

In mid-April we had three meets in one week canceled due to weather.

For all intents and purposes the seasons of our junior varsity and frosh-soph were over. All of their hard work had been gauged toward peaking in these meets. Now they were left with nothing. Even a disappointing race result was preferable to no race at all. We compensated with time trials, but these manufactured race situations had nothing on actual competition. How could you manufacture the fight inside a competitor from another school, a man in a Prospect, Schaumburg, or York jersey? Time trials might lead to personal bests, but they lacked soul.

I had seen all of this before. Track season is always a long journey, and we spend weeks every year stuck on the plateau, wandering in the wilderness of the early outdoor season. Each year we manage to find our way home and scale the mountain to the IHSA State track meet. The plateau was part of the test. Many fail and cannot transition from the heights of their indoor season to the big meets in May. Some of my own competitors would fail. Only the stalwart few would make it to the end fully fit and brimming with that magical late-season momentum.

For those fortunate few, the perseverant souls, track season would pay off. There would be a time when the temperatures failed to fall at night. The clinging heat would envelop them in its moist embrace. At that moment all the months of deprivation and wandering would disappear. Suddenly everything would be right in the track universe.

Mother Nature has a way of paying us all back. Sometimes she wraps a track meet in such poetic grace that the beauty consumes you. The sun fades slowly as the stadium lights come on. The crowd is there in force to enjoy the plastic stillness of a gorgeous spring night. All of the pent-up anxiety and despair from the plateau is then so beautifully channeled into fit moments of explosion that it can bring you down with its ancestral power. If you love track and field, then you are willing to bear any burden, to push through the howling rain and biting wind to reach such a moment. If we persevere, that glimpse will give us the feed to last through any number of wintry and rainy days. The moment sustains like an echoing guitar droning on an empty stage, just waiting to be picked up again by its master.

Reuben Frey and Anthony Gregorio race near the lead in the 3200 meter run at the MSL West division championship.

In most track seasons my first inkling that the tide has turned comes at the Wheaton Warrenville South "Red Grange" Invite. Run in mid-April each year, this meet organizes competitors into A, B, and C flights with each team's top competitors matched against one another in the A flight. From there the meet becomes a test of depth as each team lines up its second and third best in the lower flights. Each year we face some of the best distance runners in the state from Prospect, Waubonsie Valley, Wheaton North and South, and Naperville North. For many of our athletes it is the final opportunity to make a mark against top-flight competition and gain entry into the championship meets to come.

We talked throughout the season about sweeping all three levels of the 3200 and 1600 meter runs. The conversations had been both presumptuous and ambitious. They were also colored by an inner voice that reminded me of past problems. It's a tried-and-true maxim that one time a season we will eat "humble pie." I'm experienced enough now to digest these moments for what they are. I'm still not able to enjoy them. Every humble pie tastes as bitter as the last.

Humility is not always a virtue that serves racers well. Racing is inherently a self-serving activity. After all, the individual only has himself to control. He must survey the terrain and judge the weakness in others. At some point he must declare himself better than the rest and take his shot. He must believe that he alone has what it takes to sustain that move and win the race. Humility doesn't help in that moment. Only a man who is full of himself gets to the finish first. We thus have an unfortunate paradox. It takes a self-centered, ambitious man to win track races. But it takes a humble man to prepare for them.

In the gap between ambition and humility lies an entire universe of human frailty. When Palatine guys do not race with a "humble ambition," we get into trouble. The most humbling moments occur when we start to count past laurels—last year, last season, last week—as determinants of future success. We had throttled all of these teams in the fall cross country season when we reached our racing peak. The week before the race, I noticed a flippant cockiness as we talked about the races. It was as if the races had already been run, and we had easily flipped the switch and shuffled our competition aside. The easy talk obscured the dawning reality—only actual effort can win a race.

This brooding sense of trouble crept in at first, a lackadaisical workout the Wednesday before, a cocky attitude when I revealed the heat sheets, a general whiff of entitlement as they went through the motions during Thursday-morning practice. All too often when dealing with young people, the thrill of victory converts awfully quickly into hubris. Nothing is more destructive than excessive pride. Nothing athletes did in a race yesterday has anything to do with the race they are about to run. Losing sight of humble preparation is the biggest faux pas in athletics.

There was nothing wrong with our aspirations, but watching the kids practice set my intuition aflame. Guys seemed to be going through the motions rather than putting their full weight into the work. Track is a seventeen-week season. Moments of torpor are common in "the plateau," but it was alarming that we were nearing our championship phase in such a blank stupor. A Wednesday time trial with the junior varsity resulted in zero personal bests and zero enthusiasm. Everyone ran awful, and I left the track ranting like a lunatic and hoping that my varsity's performances at Wheaton would correct this attitude.

They didn't. They ran much worse. We won two largely uncontested sections of the 3200 meter run before Mike Lederhouse from Glenbard West ate Tony's lunch in the fastest section of that event. Tony's late-race bid to win was more whimper than bang. He made edge move after edge move, pushing gently away and then relaxing. He never once tried to go for it. It was like watching a person try to drop a grown man with a BB gun. To run a man off your hip requires something monumental. Lederhouse simply shadowed him, biding his time and relaxing as Tony took the brunt of the wind. His feeble attempts to drop the pace bore little resemblance to the monstrous doses of courage he had shown at the end of the indoor season. Even worse, when I looked in his eyes during the race I could see the fear.

No matter how hard he worked, Tony still expected the worst. Even he was not convinced that he could be a champion. Lederhouse put the hammer down with a lap to go and blew him off the track. Afterward, Tony sat on the infield, eyes boring into the turf field, searching for answers.

At the end of the night, we came to our bread and butter: the 1600 meter run. I looked at the 1600 meter field of the A division on paper and wondered just how much Tim Johnson would win by. After all, hubris is contagious. I asked Timmy J to go out hard and stress the field from the gun. He did that, but immediately let the field back in by relaxing on the second lap. After that it was all downhill. When the race hit with a lap to go, he had no response. Either the early lead, the overconfidence, or some bad advice from his coach got him to that point with nothing left. He settled for a 4:27 clocking and a non-competitive fourth-place finish. Tim Meincke followed suit in the B division, letting Prospect's Matt Ashton destroy him by seven seconds in the final two hundred meters. In the last curve, he dropped his arms ever so slightly, and I saw the universal sign.

He quit. Peter certainly gave full effort all the way to the line in the C division, but he was annihilated in the kick by another Prospect athlete. Three races. Three last-lap capitulations.

Bad races always engender a blizzard of questions. Were the athletes properly conditioned? Did they have the skills or experience to execute the race plan? Were they tired from recent workouts? Was the race strategy flawed? Or did they fail to prepare properly? To warm up? To eat and sleep right? The final question was the toughest: Did they really want to win? I usually let the emotions prompted by a race rest before addressing the athletes. Nothing is less fair than blaming an athlete for something that was my fault. I usually wait to see if my reaction mediates, whether wisdom takes the place of anger. So I waited for them to put on their sweats. I walked a lap in the frigid darkness. I searched for the positives. I found none.

I wanted them to see my disappointment. Charging straight toward the visitors bleachers and our team camp, I barked at Johnson and Meincke to meet me by the back fence. They knew it was coming. I stormed up the stairs of the west bleachers and ordered both to follow me. Eyes downcast, they slowly trudged out of the stands. We stopped in the dusty gravel behind the visitors bleachers. I ordered both to get their eyes off the floor and look at me. Carefully away from the crowd and the rest of the teams, I let them have it. I told them I could handle tired races, weak race tactics, or losing to a better man, but I knew what a runner looked like when he quit. In my estimation, both guys had quit.

Meincke snapped back that he had not quit, that he had run all-out to the finish. His defiance got my dander up. I showed him the splits from the final two hundred meters and wondered aloud just when Matt Ashton from Prospect had gotten that much better than him. Feeling attacked, he started to talk back, but then thought better of it. Disappointed and stunned, Johnson just stared straight ahead and took my criticism in stride. My admonitions were impassioned and honest, perhaps too much so. My athletes know when I am mad that I mean it. Whether they had quit or not, they at least knew my disappointment.

Both men possessed uncommon talent. Both had run sub-4:23 for the 1600 meter distance, but neither had come close to touching his best.

As I sent them off into the night on a long cool-down, I wondered whether the problem was one of will. Men bequeathed the gift of talent often rely on it from an early age. When they meet others of a similar ilk, they realize that the time to cruise has passed. From then on, they have to develop the champion's iron will, the crushing desire to never let up, to go full guns blazing each time out because letting your guard down only invites the demons. Tony Gregorio knew those demons well, and I hoped that some of his everyday toughness would start to rub off on my underachieving milers.

Before we got on the bus I took the whole distance crew aside. Every track season has a turning point, and I hoped this was ours. We needed to snap out of the plateau and start climbing. With the varsity assembled in a semicircle, I called guys out one by one on recent breakdowns during training and racing. I vowed that we would get back to racing and training with reckless abandon. The guys who would run in the big meets would be the ones who fought from starting line to finish line. I could tell by the concerned looks in their eyes that the message was received. We walked quietly to the bus, tails between our legs. Our MSL rivals from Prospect had beaten us soundly across the board. This was only one round of a long fight, and I hoped that we would scratch and fight every tenth of a second the next time we met.

Riding the bus home, I stared out the window into the blank darkness. The long, quiet bus rides home at late hours always left me longing for home and hearth. When I opened my front door quietly after 11 PM, Meredith, Madeline, and Christopher were all sleeping soundly in their beds. I skulked in and checked on every one, but sleep did not come easily. The wheels were still spinning. In such moments alone after midnight I come face-to-face with the indefinable search. What inner compulsion led me so far adrift? What was I out there seeking while my wife and kids wiled away the hours? Did my hopes and dreams really hang on the string of teenage performance? If they did, what did that mean?

The darkness always provokes the toughest questions. Around 1 AM, I put my latest existential crisis to bed and went upstairs to attempt sleep. Something inside was still restless, though, and I stared at the ceiling and looked for the answers. I knew not what mystical race I was looking for or what solace I would find in these boys and a life lived by the run. All I knew was that I still sought the pearl of great price, and it was out there somewhere, elusive but alive.

THE PALATINE RELAYS

After a series of hard knocks at the Wheaton ABC meet, we continued to search for answers. Some of those answers lay within the individual nature of track and field. The gap between team cross country success and individual track greatness is always acute. In cross country the boys run as a unit. In track they are often left to their own devices, prey to the individual speed and whims of others. In cross country the outcome can be greater than the sum of its parts. In track the parts are all. With the Palatine Relays looming on the horizon, we needed some recalibration.

Every year for the past seventy-nine years, the Palatine community has hosted an annual track meet. Two early track proponents—Carl Megel and G. A. McElroy—started the meet in 1933, and the event wove its way into the fabric of Palatine. The Relays is both a competition and a community touchstone, a beautiful mixture of memory and present power. Each year, I am tasked with coaching the young men to victory in the present even as I am reminded of all that has passed. The guys can feel it, too. I'm not exactly sure how emotional exuberance translates into performance, but I know that our guys put the fire on the track each year to try to win this meet. We went after our twenty-fourth Palatine Relays title with all guns blazing, hoping to ride the ghosts of Palatine past even as we gave the returning alumni another taste of glory through our fresh eyes. This dichotomy is the life of the event.

The emotionality of the Relays was further accented by the enormous gathering of alumni to honor Coach Joe Johnson. A hall of fame coach in Illinois, Coach Johnson had died on the Christmas Eve just past, and the seventy-ninth edition of the Palatine Relays was a clarion call to those whose lives he had touched. The funeral was held just after Christmas in

Volunteer coach James Macatangay prepares for the Palatine Relays alumni mile. In 2004, James placed thirteenth in the IHSA State meet to earn All-State honors.

Photo by MaryAnn Graham

Arizona, and many of Joe's favorite people and alumni had been unable to attend. Fred Miller, my former coaching partner and one of Joe's best runners, organized the festivities with a goal of having a hundred alumni participate in the annual Alumni Mile. The turnout was incredible. Men from all eras of the program showed up to put their feet on the track one last time for the man who turned the Palatine distance program into a state contender. The waistlines may have grown and the times may have slowed, but the pride remained.

During the intermission, alums Chris Wheaton and Mark Visk said a few words to the assembled group of family and friends. These ceremonies always look quaint and inconsequential from the outside. Had you not known the man or understood his impact, you might have passed it off as just another tribute in a world that offers far too many tributes. But when Wheatie and Visk spoke, you could see and hear the passion in their eyes and voices. The encircled alums surely grasped the consequence of the moment. Many had flown in from other states or driven long distances to be together once again. As someone who is more caretaker than progenitor, I watched and listened. I heard the quavering voices. I saw the stifled tears. I saw the meaning of the man in the eyes of the men. When Mark Visk reminded everyone how Joe Johnson "spoke belief into our lives," I reflected on the man who had done that for me. I never would have found any force in my life had my father not challenged me. Joe had done a similar service for these men, and they were here to pay him back through the smallest of gestures: one last interval.

I could give credentials, times, and All-State finishes of all the great ones who showed up to honor Joe. I won't do that because it would miss the point. At Palatine any man who puts his full heart into the team is an All-Time Great. Joe introduced alums to the current team by that moniker, and being an All-Time Great meant far more than being a fast runner. Speed does not make the man. The men make the speed, and Joe grasped that from early on. He knew the simplest truth in distance running. If you coach the right kind of men, you will find ones that are fast. The greatest homage to Joe's coaching is that the men who showed up to remember him and honor his legacy were the right kind of men—hardworking, gracious, successful, and caring. Some of Joe's best teams only had twenty-five or thirty guys. He discovered that winning at Palatine took a collection of the right men, all equally dedicated. It was humbling to meet so many who took time out of their lives to honor a man who helped them. To run the Alumni Mile with these men was an honor.

Afterward I got a chance to speak with a ton of alums and introduce them to my current athletes. We had called on the spirit of Mark Magnussen in the previous fall's state meet, so it was a real treat to introduce him to our current crew. Watching Tim Meincke shake his hand unified our efforts across the generations. Our performances later that day did the same.

In a fitting hour of action to end the morning session, we experienced the rare momentum of a track team finding its full force. Watching a

Photo by MaryAnn Graham

More than a hundred Palatine alums and friends of the program start
the Alumni Mile in honor of the late Joe Johnson.

track team in full flight is a lot like watching a stupendous rally in a baseball game. For a brief moment in time, something so difficult—like hitting a baseball—becomes easy. Each man feeds off the energy and focus
of the others. The hits start to flow. One here. One there. Then the big
one. In a track meet the performances come right on top of each other,
minute by minute, and work exactly like a baseball rally. Sooner or later,
someone feels all that energy, steps to the plate, and hits a home run.

Our rally started with a brazen declaration of greatness from Ryan
McGough. Like Johnson and Gregorio, he had been a victim of the
plateau. For weeks he had been running not to lose, starting conservatively and getting hammered in the final stretch. Now he took it to the
field from the gun. His red cheeks and bouncy blond hair framed the
determination in his eyes. At the hundred-meter mark, he was gone, the
field left in his wake. Howling wind be damned. His wire-to-wire win was
the catalyst.

Tim Johnson toed the line next in the 3200 meter run. We advised him to bide his time and stay in the group rather than riding the gusty winds alone for the entire race. We asked him to find a spot, somewhere in the second mile, to show the mettle of a champion. That spirit had been lacking in his disappointing race at Wheaton. Nothing about the day suggested conditions were ripe for a brilliant showing. There was too much cold, too much wind.

Somehow Timmy J gave everyone a glimpse of his true power. You could see it building as he entered the top of the straightaway with two laps remaining. His cadence picked up. Rather than carrying his arms high in rhythm, he started to swing them, gathering steam, building impulse for the long drive home. Into the teeth of the wind he moved with a ferocity that stunned the still-crowded field. Shocked and chagrined, they quickly fell apart. Timmy J flew home, burying himself into his work and destroying the field. His time of 9:33.7 was his best by more than 15 seconds. It was the race of a champion.

Photo by Cindi Johnson

Tim Johnson prepares to make his move in the 3200 meter run at the Palatine Relays.

That win left only the distance medley relay (DMR) in the morning session. Already rolling, we now moved into our bread and butter. The DMR is a test of distance depth. The relay begins with a 1200 meter leg, sandwiches the speed of the 400 and 800 meter distances into the middle, and then gives way to the 1600 meter anchor leg. Senior leader Reuben Frey had been assigned one job all day, and it was to get us the lead after the first leg. He ran fearlessly and passionately, riding the lead group for two laps before exploding to the lead. We held it through the next two legs and dropped a twenty-meter advantage into Tony's lap for the anchor leg.

He knew what to do with it. St. Ignatius's sophomore star Jack Keelan, thirteenth in the state cross country meet, exploded from behind in feverish pursuit. Tony knew he would need a special run to get it done. So he did what he does best. He just went for it. To that point Tony had never broken sixty seconds for four hundred meters in his life. He ran the first lap in his personal best. It was both suicidal and glorious. It also broke the opposition. By the end of the first lap, the gap was forty meters. All his competitors saw was an ocean of track and the blank sea of wind in between them and the lead. He suffered for his early speed, but his audacity ended the race before it ever started.

On a day when we paid homage to the racing and coaching spirit of Joe Johnson, our guys showed that what Joe had built was stronger even than his own life. It had endured. With the full community of Joe's All-Time Greats looking on, the boys proved the power of his legacy. The Palatine Relays is about accessing performance through community pride. Boys at Palatine have reached into the well at this meet for nearly eighty years to pull up water and drink. It is impossible to quantify, but the call of tradition usually precedes the reality of performance. To perform well at the Palatine Relays is to commune with the ghosts, to recognize one's own place in a vaster panorama. Modern science has figured out a great deal with regard to human athletic performance. But what does it have to say about people using the energy and emotion of a moment—purely intangible variables—to enhance physicality itself?

Of course, our boys had more than ghosts to chase. The tangible men were there in service to their mentor, and we all felt Joe Johnson's spirit. I'm absolutely convinced it was why we won the meet. His spirit lived in the men he coached and continued to live in the young men I coached. Sometimes a man's life matters so much and is so perfectly hewn to the place he spent his time that it is woven into its fabric, its DNA, its guts. Sometimes I have no idea why boys and girls come out for cross country at Palatine. Sometimes I have no idea why they train so hard and race so meanly. Sometimes none of it makes any rational sense.

The answer has to be mystical. We all call on our ghosts—whether it be to get through tough times, to celebrate life, or to run faster and jump higher. In Palatine the ghosts are everywhere—in the trees surrounding Ost Field, in the air at Chic Anderson Stadium, in the grass roots out at Hamilton Reservoir and Deer Grove East, up on that dirt hill at Riemer Reservoir. If you have the will and the need, the ghosts will talk to you. Their voices are always one step away, and you can call on them when the moment is right.

THE CHAMPIONSHIP PHASE

With the Palatine Relays safely behind us, we turned—finally—to the "white-knuckle" phase of the track season. At Palatine this phase comprises the Mid-Suburban League outdoor conference meet and the IHSA Sectional and State meets. Throughout the state young men run fast and improve through the season, but few will ever shine in the championship phase. Running fast is one thing. Becoming a champion when it matters the most is another.

In track and field men and women are defined by their marks. Ever shifting, these marks symbolize each athlete's fullest measurable potential. The key conceit is that once a mark has been performed, it can be performed again. As such, athletes work through various tiers of identity in the same season. Their names become synonymous with their best performances. Meincke and Johnson were now "4:22 guys." Peter and Marcus were "9:40 guys." Only Tony was an All-Stater.

Only the lesser men peg their identities to their marks. The real greats peg theirs to the laurels. Each year in track, there were only eighteen state champions, nine All-State berths in each event, eight All-Conference spots. Winning a championship brings a whole new level of discovery. The résumé of the champion is replete with titles, not times. Of course most great champions possess the marks to win, but not always. Many can run fast. But only a select few possess the will to win and the savvy to run their best when it matters the most.

Few remember the man who ran fast in the mid-season but couldn't get it done at the end. Years later he'll be the "old baseball player" from Bruce Springsteen's "Glory Days." He'll have his story about how fast he ran. He'll regale you with spectacular stories about his prime fitness and winning an early-season race in the Such-and-Such Memorial Invite. He'll also have his excuse—why he didn't qualify, why he didn't make the final, the illness he contracted that shot it all to hell, the minor injury that robbed him of his confidence, the lifetime of regret he feels from not timing it right. No one will remember. His memory will be etched outside the bright lights. Only the champions retain their identities. The marks melt away into inconsequentiality.

For most of our juniors the championship phase was a first opportunity to earn the laurels that mattered most. All season long we had struggled to win against good fields. All five young men had made progress, scoring points in big invites and challenging the existing hierarchy, but none had scored a signature win. Despite our best efforts, the existing order held firm. The challenges as May rolled around were twofold: earn entry into the state championship meet and then find a way to get in the medals.

The qualifying challenge became tougher when the IHSA revised the qualifying standards for the state meet. Milers would now have to run 4:21.6; the 800 meters (1:56.6) and 3200 meters (9:28.8) had also been reduced. These weighty standards loomed overhead the entire season. As contestants in one of the most loaded distance sectionals in the state, the only safe and secure route was to run the time. The first and second finishers in each event at the sectional qualified automatically, but no one—not even the best of the best—ever counted on that route.

As our men prepared to run in our own Palatine Sectional, the anxiety became palpable. The fight to make the lineup had been hotly contested. Tony, Marcus, and Peter all threw their hats in the ring alongside senior Reuben Frey for the two spots in the 3200 meter run. In practices Tony and Reuben were the strong men, but both Marcus and Peter threatened after going one–two at the Carlin Nalley Lisle Invite in early May. Their times of 9:38 and 9:40 were declarations of new identity, but neither man had moved the needle.

Tony and Reuben took the line at the MSL Outdoor meet and solidified their credentials. On a windy day they showed the guts and desire that champions possess. With the winds howling over twenty miles per hour, they attacked the field from the gun on a suicidal pace. Reuben paid for his early urgency and finished seventh, but his strong pacing set it up for Tony to take third. Only Barrington's Erik Peterson and Buffalo Grove's Jereme Atchison could best him. After the race it was obvious that Tony and Reuben had the right synergy. Marcus and Peter were out, relegated to the bench for the season's biggest meet.

It stung both. Marcus earned a cursory reward, making the sectional meet as a throw-in for the 800 meter run, but that race was well outside his strengths. Even as that race loomed, he asked to attempt the 3200 meter qualifying standard in a time trial. The day before the sectional, he and Peter brought their spikes out to the track and gave it a go. The weather cooperated, and I sensed a new level of seriousness in both. Jimmy Mac offered to pace them through the sixteen-hundred-meter mark under state qualifying pace. Racing in an old John Paxson jersey, he still looked the part of a champion runner. He had been as responsible as anyone else for Marcus's and Peter's improvements so it was fitting that all three took the line together. As the flag dipped limply above the scoreboard, I gave my customary "barbarian yell" start command and sent them on their way.

Slowly but surely both Marcus and Peter had found more powerful rhythms. Marcus ran with a new and more upright style than before. His physical gifts had finally blossomed as full complements to his raging self-confidence. Peter's discovery had occurred in the cross country post-season, but now he fully inhabited the track. In earlier years he would lurch and pull for his speed. The consequence was a draining inefficiency. The more he struggled, the slower he ran. As I watched them run in a tight line—Jimmy Mac first, then Marcus then Peter—I got a glimpse of the near future. Neither man would be on anyone else's radar. But existence is existence. Whether they gained entry into the sectional or not, they functioned now like champions.

Jimmy smoked the pace through the mile, and they just kept on charging. With no race stimulus, no medals, and no adrenaline from the crowd, they held it together and raced. In both men you could see the intensity of our quest. You could see the building momentum of our year. Alone on the track their manic drives festered all around, lingering with desire, aching for the thrills of the fall. The wheels came off in the final half mile, but the results were stark. Marcus ran 9:34.0, some 6 seconds away from state qualifying. Peter faded but ran 9:42. Gregorio and Johnson had already run 9:23 and 9:33. Even Meincke, a 3200 meter phobic during track season, had run 9:53. The table was set.

With Marcus and Peter beaten out for their preferred spots, the spotlight turned onto Meincke, Gregorio, and Johnson. All three had dreams of All-State finishes. I was after something larger. Sooner or later any or all three would have to win a big race. The champion's credo says little about moral victories or close losses. I hoped that all three would find their champion's laurels in the late taper of the racing season.

Meincke suffered throughout the outdoor season. After his thrilling breakout race in the MSL Indoor conference meet, he had suffered both a physical setback and a crisis of confidence. Soon after running a fast split on our 4 x 800 meter relay in early April, he came to me with his knee badly swollen. The pain had nagged him even before the race, but the aftermath was uglier. He struggled to bend the joint the next day and was far from functional the week after. Like all good soldiers, he kept training through it, but the crispness drained right out of him.

On top of that he was thrust into a potboiler of intra-team competition. Men get placed into the MSL Conference and IHSA Sectional meets based on the "seed" times they run during outdoor track. Indoor times do not count. Slowly, his teammates started to drop time and plant their seeds. Time after time, we set Monkey up for his big seed race in the 1600 meters, but it never came. He faded badly at both Wheaton and the Palatine Relays. He won a race at the Carlin Nalley Lisle Invite, but couldn't break 4:30.

His frustration moved to a boil. He was not yet mature enough to handle setbacks, and the pressure crumbled the walls of his self-concept. The early-season 4:22 had been magical, yet it spoke blank promises.

After the Wheaton meet, the rest of the team started their uphill climb toward the peak. Monkey stayed on the plateau. Even when his knee returned to full health, his attitude did not. He had the potential to be a state qualifier, had run within one second of the mark in March, but a weak outdoor best would not gain him entry into the fast heat of the sectional 1600 meter run.

So he took the bitter pill and ran his secondary event, the 4 x 800 meter relay. Even a spot in that foursome was no foregone conclusion. We took a calculated risk and held Tim Johnson out of the qualifying race so that he could be at his best in the 1600 meter run. We wouldn't pull that same move in the state prelims the next week if we qualified. It would be too risky. One of the four who ran in the sectional would be pulled. With senior star Ryan McGough waiting on the anchor leg, we lined up Monkey along with seniors Erich Kuerschner and Zach Gates in the sectional qualifier.

As the day built toward the start of the meet, a looming sense of unease crawled into my chest. I fretted all week long about the weather, studying the wind speeds and worrying about the temperatures. Most meets did not carry the absolute need to run fast, but in a sectional qualifier the execution of the various qualifying paces had to be perfect. The wind had to settle at the right time. The sun had to shine. The sectional is an asterisk inside the championship phase. No one cares who wins. It is all about hitting the times. In most of the distance races the coaches will cheer the entire field rather than their own runners. If we can carry the pace with the weight of a group, multitudes of athletes can run standards thought nearly impossible just the week before.

When I handed Monkey the stick on the infield, I looked into his eyes for the clues. He looked nervous, like he wore a brave face to obscure the turmoil. He had not performed at the level we needed in over six weeks. Still, I showed him my confidence. The spot was a big one, fraught not just with the weight of the sectional, but also with the hopes of three senior teammates. Kuerschner had scraped and bled just to make this relay, running frosh-soph and junior varsity for seven seasons before breaking into the lineup. His slower leg speed would be no match for the other leadoff legs. Gates had suffered a stress fracture in his foot mid-season. He and I were holding it all together with bailing wire, glue, and guts. One man didn't have the tools. The other didn't have the fitness. It had to come from Monkey.

The infield was full of relay foursomes and their coaches, nervously wiggling out of their shoes as the slow-paced National Anthem reached its crescendo. More than any other race, this was the one the coaches in our conference loved to dominate. For years I had resisted its siren call. But on this night, with these boys, I stood there and felt its animal attraction. Four boys united as one. The only distance relay in the state. Two of my friends, Prospect's Mike Stokes and Buffalo Grove's Jamie Klotz, had labored for years before winning state titles. My dad's greatest memory had been coaching Tony Taylor, Eric Edmunds, Tauwon Taylor, and Rob Harvey to the 1989 state championship in this race. They ran 7:43.69 to win—the fastest time in the nation that year. It was the only time he would ever touch a state championship.

As I sent Monkey to the starting line with our fate in his hands, I thought also of the larger destiny he controlled. Come next November he would be the one we counted on when the chips were down up the final incline of the state cross country meet. While he had run many fast times in his career, he had rarely come through when it mattered the most. My anxiety was built around the thought that, maybe, he never would. Time after time he had charged with reckless abandon into the abyss before staggering home on empty.

The 800 meters is a graveyard for such spirits. If the pace is too fast too early, the closing meters deliver a sting that can knock a man backward. At 150 meters out the entire top half of your body goes numb. The brain directs all the blood flow to the legs, and the arms, alive and pumping just the lap before, begin an involuntary cease-fire. The lactate demons punish muscles up and down the body, attacking the legs and throwing violent fits in your chest. If you don't play your cards right, the closing meters become a demolition of the soul. All a man can do is relax and maintain a Zen-like composure amid the roiling turmoil. It takes a special breed of champion to close an 800 meter race. After three years, I was still not sure Tim Meincke could do it.

As the starter fingered the pistol and raised his arms, I hoped this would be his moment. For the first six hundred meters, it looked like it would be. He battled hard behind the leadoff legs from Barrington, Lake Zurich, and Deerfield. But that was the issue. He battled. They glided. A man who digs for his speed cannot maintain it for the entire distance. First there has to be ease. Only then can a man dig. Into the final curve, Tim Meincke was all battled out. The top three ran away from him as his muscles started to tie up. Then the rest of the field smelled the blood in the water. By the time he handed off to Gates, we were in seventh place and nowhere near the lead.

Tim Meincke carries the stick early in the 4 x 800 meter relay at the 2011 Palatine Sectional meet.

I immediately felt the sinking in my chest. Meincke's 2:01 split left us far adrift and in need of spectacular racing rather than mundane execution. Behind by half a straightaway, Zach Gates charged straight into the heat of battle. Partially broken foot be damned, he just went for it. He pulled us only back into sixth place, but the gaps had decreased. He passed the baton to Erich Kuerschner, our biggest wild card.

Now three seconds above the state meet pace at halfway, Kuersch had to deliver. All ideas regarding proper pace went out the window. To catch the main running group he ran his personal best four-hundred-meter time in the first half of his race. I knew it was coming. The inevitable tie-up. The implosion. The proverbial "bear on his back." It came, right on cue, with a straightaway to go, but Kuersch fought it with a pride that could only come from a long history of denial. Meincke had been given many chances before in his career and would earn many more. Kuerschner ran with the pride of a man who knew he only had one.

He obliterated himself into the final exchange, passing to Ryan McGough in fifth place. His 2:00.7 split decimated his best and gave us a chance to qualify on time. Immediately he staggered into the infield and fell to his hands and knees. For the next twenty minutes he would vomit, only pausing to look around and watch the race to its conclusion. All distance races involve some species of obliteration. But none can compare to the half mile. The shock of a man going too far, too fast without appropriate oxygen is unfathomable to most. It takes courage both to run the race and to face its aftermath.

With our split at 6:03.4 after three legs, McGough had to run a lifetime best to punch our ticket. He did just that, smashing his way to a fifty-four-second first lap and then hanging on for dear life. He brought us home in third place just under the qualifying standard of 7:58.9. His final split was 1:55.8. Red-faced and heaving under his own burdens, he grinned and patted Kuersch on the back as they both knelt in the infield. Meincke's glum face afterward said it all. The other three had delivered hero runs, poised bits of grace under fire. He could read the writing on the wall. His season was over.

With that race in the bag, the sectional meet acquired its usual momentum. As each event concluded, random celebrations cropped up spontaneously throughout the stadium. A roar from the crowd might indicate another high jumper over 6'5" or another discus throw out beyond 155'0". In the track races the third- and fourth-place finishers held their breath, waiting for their times and their fates. Some saw the numbers and celebrated with glee. For many more the shoulders dropped, and they departed the finish line with drawn faces.

Soon after our relay, the fourteen 3200 meter runners stepped onto the track. All were capable of running the 9:28.8 standard. But fortune is a fickle thing in such long races. A bit of misused oxygen here or a series of strong wind gusts there could derail the whole thing. Running the time had to be both a methodical process and an emotionally charged mission. Those without the proper balance would be left in the wake of those who found it. As Tony and Reuben stepped to the line, their directions were to run seventy-second laps as long as possible.

The race unfolded like a piece of poetry. By the mile mark only six athletes remained on pace, and the assembled crowd willed the field onward. Tony cruised through the race, effortlessly nailing the splits through six laps. Reuben was another story. By lap five his face was a mask of pain. He had earned his laurels in the past year not through any insane speed or talent, but by being willing and able to take the pain. He had trained his mind and body to endure the sting. It allowed him to investigate the edge better than most. As Tony fired away near the front with Lake Zurich's Ryan Moncrieff and Victor de la Torre, Reuben floundered all alone.

Gregorio finished in third, but his near personal best of 9:23 was well under the standard. He ran marvelously. Never one to have much speed at the end of the race, he threw his heart and soul into the pace. Increment by increment, he nailed the race down. With him there were no shortcuts. He couldn't jog through the middle of the race and then push some magic button of speed to bring back the seconds he had given away. He had to earn each hundred meters of speed as it came. If he could battle each increment, then he could climb high.

Anthony Gregorio races near the lead early on in the 3200 meter run at the 2011 Palatine Sectional.

Seeing Tony finish well under the pace, I rushed down the sideline toward the pole vault pits at the north end to get in Reuben's face one more time. He had run magically, way out of his element, transcending everything we thought possible. I screamed *9:05* into his ear and pleaded for him to pump his arms for one last blistering straightaway. Gripped by the pain he got on his toes and found the will one last time. He crossed the tape in 9:26. Both he and Tony had run times in the top fifteen of our school's long history. More important, Reuben would be going downstate with Kuersch. Friends across the years, they had hunted, run, and dreamed together for four long years. Ensconced deep in the junior varsity the year before, both had found the champion's will.

With the relay and the two 3200 meter runners safely qualified, Tim Johnson was the final piece of the puzzle. I regarded his qualification as money in the bank. His inability to run a fast outdoor time left me perplexed, but I chalked it up to bad weather, weak racing tactics, or one of the other excuses I use when things are not going well. Sometimes I miss the reality in the shadow of my denials. Tim had performed gloriously the year before in this exact same race. That effort seemingly assured a spectacular growth curve, a series of breakthrough races culminating in a state title run as a senior. It had worked exactly that way for Mat Smoody and Alec Bollman, two other young men who had earned recent state titles. If it worked for those guys, I thought it would work the same way for the next guy.

The race stank to high heaven right from the gun. The two leads in the race—Barrington's Erik Peterson and Lake Zurich's Pat Juras—were carbon copies of each other. Both were freakishly talented, gifted with speed and competitive fire in equal amounts, yet neither ever showed much inclination to push the pace. Unlike Gregorio, both had "punch the button" speed. If the pace lagged, they could simply use their frenetic speed to get out of tight situations. Right from the opening, the race lagged, dragging limply along through slow splits.

The lagging pace played to all of Johnson's weakest racing inclinations. Everyone else's fears regressed our champion miler back to the "Timid Timmy" of freshman year. Rather than hearing our repeated admonitions to pick it up, Tim dove back into the rail and right into a box. The field enveloped him in front and behind. Outside of his right shoulder, men stacked up two-deep. For some, the lagging pace was a welcome invitation. It allowed weaker men to join the party. The pace ambled so badly into the first straightaway that Fremd's Andy Mack tripped and fell to the track. His fall almost took out Tim and several others. He picked himself off the ground to rally, but catching even a slow pace was tough after such a severe fall.

Rather than stringing out from the gun on fast splits, the field labored to the halfway point. With six hundred meters to go, I looked Timmy J right in the eyes and called for a move. But the box was all. Everywhere around him, men started to drive for home. Yet he was trapped. Finally, nearing one lap to go, he found daylight and moved outside with vigor.

But the twelve-hundred-meter split was a sickening 3:20. To make it now, all of them would need the evil speed. That type of speed isn't portioned out to all men equally at birth. Many guys have powerful speed, gorgeous rhythmic strides that eat up track, but few distance runners can snap it. Just like a rubber band drawn back with tension can be released with full force, so can a distance runner's speed be unleashed if he has a snap kick.

At a lap to go, Peterson and Juras snapped it and broke the race wide open. Johnson worked his way into their wakes, but he had cornered himself in. He could run hard at the end in rhythm with the best of them, but this was no time for powerful rhythms. It was time to take it to the house. He drove on down the backstretch into the tunnel of screams under the bright lights of the stadium, turning for home with all pistons firing. As he ran away into the fully absorbed finality of the race, I stopped and looked at my watch. If he made it, the margin would be thin.

I took off down the center of the football field, chasing the race to the line from behind. Peterson out-leaned Juras at the tape, but both secured automatic spots. Timmy J hit the line third, and I clicked my watch. For a fraction of a second, I held it there, my eyes downcast. Looking would make it final. I finally glimpsed it: 4:22.6. He had missed by one second.

I bent at the knees and took the disappointment square in the chest. I pulled off my "big meet" hat—the weathered Cal hat I had worn to all my state cross country meets and to the birth of both my children. I put my hands through my sweaty hair and tried to figure out what to do next, what to say. The emotions rushed over me. Sixteen weeks of work. All the hard workouts, all the labored discussions and learned lessons, all of it vanished straight into thin air. The regrets lingered and piled. Anger came in at the corners. The racing tactics had been foolish, stupid even. How had he managed to misuse the fitness he had worked so hard to acquire? What had he been thinking? The sympathy came next. Tim would be crushed.

As I stood upright I had to put it all back together. I don't handle disappointment well. Even worse, I can't handle a lack of execution, a thinking mistake that obscures a man's fitness. It's like knowing all the answers to the test, but forgetting your pencil. With Tim the disappointment compounded because of his legacy. He had qualified the year before. Distance running is about progression—of mileage, of tactics, of fitness, and of times. To take a step back is to prompt the deepest manner of soul searching. As I walked to the finish line area to pick up the pieces, I had no idea what to say.

I remember looking over the fence and seeing the concern in Steve Johnson's eyes. He wanted Tim to succeed, but like a good father he wanted to protect him from the pain more. Slump-shouldered, Tim shambled off the track with Coach Sheehan alongside. He had given a great effort, but not a smart one. Inside, the anger smoldered, the resentment at an athlete giving it away. But now was not the time.

We walked off the track in silence and into an uncertain future. Reserved by nature, Tim simply had nothing to say. The disappointment flowed over him as he sat on the ground to remove his spikes. His shoulders slumped forward, and he covered his head with his race jersey. Despite my brief bout of anger, I wanted more to give him a hug and talk away the pain. Tim would run in the state track meet, but it would be as part of a unit rather than for himself. In times past, the team moments—the ones where his friends counted on him the most—had always been his best. That was the angle going forward.

Deeper inside, I worried. Everything that happened this track season was magnified, a piece of foreground in a much larger picture. The preparation for the coming cross country season had dominated everyone's thoughts. Track was the proving ground, and both Timmy J and Monkey had faded when the heat burned hottest. As Tony watched Timmy J put his trainers on and shuffle into a solitary cool-down, he wondered aloud whether his teammate had what it took. From the lofty perch of a recent great race, it was an easy observation, but also a selfish one. All involved knew that Tim Johnson could have the running world at his fingertips. We just had no idea if he would ever grab it.

Twenty minutes later Ryan McGough closed down the anchor leg of the 4 x 400 meter relay in 49.3 seconds and punched our ticket to state in a second relay. Like all sectionals, it was a mixed bag of elation and disappointment. Some seniors slinked off the track for the final time, their careers over. Others would get to run in the premier event in Illinois high school track. For our juniors the growing pains had been palpable. Gregorio performed at a champion's level, but could not close out and win the race. Meincke had floundered and seen the writing on the wall. He would go to state, but only as the alternate. Johnson would take his spot and run the anchor leg. He would do so with an aching disappointment in his center. Whether he used that ache to become a champion going forward or rested on it like the saddest of all unwanted laurels, no one could know.

STATE TRACK

The Saturday morning after that fateful sectional night, both Tim Johnson and I walked into practice with our tails between our legs. We had assumed too much. Hubris, again. In racing, the only thing that matters is the moment that lies before you. Previous history, previous tradition, previous action are just precedents. The races are fought in real time. For both of us, it was a blow.

Still, focusing on the night's one disappointment could not dispel the high spirits of the group. We had qualified two relay teams and two individuals and were headed to the ultimate end point of Illinois high school track. The Big Blue. The hallowed oval of Eastern Illinois University's O'Brien Stadium. I had long attended as a fan of my dad's athletes before coaching my own. Now my career was subject to the same aura of mystery that hung over his career and many others.

Nothing about the state track meet is calm. People look calm on the Thursday before the prelims begin, but for most that is a facade. Too much can go wrong. A false start. A collision in the exchange zone. A hundredth of a second here or there. The meet demanded perfect execution to maintain one's existence. In all the long-distance races, only twelve athletes or relays made it to the finals. Only in the 3200 meter run were the athletes excepted. They qualified straight to the final based on their times in the sectional qualifying races. Everyone else had to fight through the prelims to toe the line for a state title.

Of all the riddles I had worked to solve, performance in the state track meet had been the most difficult. Success in statewide cross country came easy in comparison. Within three years of beginning work with Fred Miller, the boys stood atop the podium to receive a runner-up trophy behind York. But track's individual orientation seemed to drain our athletes' spirit, missing the magical synergies that infused performance when the boys raced as a team.

My early coaching at the state track meet was rife with mistakes. I carried the fear of failure in my heart. So, too, did my athletes. In 2004 I had a 4 x 800 meter relay make the final only to get tenth after James Macatangay ran into a runner in the exchange zone. In 2006 Steve Finley, the state cross country champion, disintegrated in the heat and failed to make the 1600 meter final a week after running 4:11.0. Later that same day, sophomore Mat Smoody found himself boxed and kicked home in thirteenth place, only 0.3 second from the final qualifying position. It may as well have been an hour. The distance between success and failure seemed so acute. I wanted so badly to master this riddle. I conceived of it as a solvable thing, a mystery that others had safely unlocked but remained barred to my understanding.

A year after Smoody floundered in his 800 meter prelim, he and I figured it out. Most of the answer was buried inside his outsized talent and inflammatory speed. The biggest key to surviving state track was to have a freakish talent. Then you could round off the hard edges and fine-tune the details. In the prelims he executed a poised race and won his heat. We had prepared through long discussions and targeted track sessions for all eventualities. Finally the mental frame matched the physical. The next day he blistered the track to the tune of 1:52.57 and won the state title in the 800 meters. The next year he won it again in a Palatine school record time of 1:50.71.

In between he taught me the hardest lesson I would ever learn about the elite track world. It is essentially anti-democratic. The big performances were available only to a few select people who carved up the pie each year with their outsized talent. Sure, a compelling training program and a disciplined athlete could get past more talented individuals from time to time, but I realized from then on that the state track meet was a talented man's paradise.

The two ends of what I did thus fell into a species of sharp juxtaposition. Cross country and track are complementary, yet completely anti-thetical. One is the haven of democracy while the other is the haven of the elite. One rewards teamwork. The other rewards the triumph of the individual. Lesser men could outwork those with more talent over the length of a summer and the space of a three-mile race. The margin for doing so in track was much more limited. When I reconciled myself to these two opposing fates, I found that I was clearheaded enough to find my elites and focus like a laser on bringing them to the top.

Our track season had been built around my visions regarding our three elites: Ryan McGough, Tim Johnson, and Anthony Gregorio. The rest of the team, including my emerging juniors, had made progress as part of the cross country curriculum that underpinned the track season, but only these three possessed what it took to exist in the full-on world of elite track. McGough had been the MSL's 800 meter outdoor champion. Despite his sectional setback, Johnson had been the second-fastest soph-omore in the state the year before. And despite his personal hang-ups and lack of raw speed, Gregorio fancied himself an emerging elite. As we pre-pared for our week of practice, my aim was clear. All three of these young men should end the week with All-State medals hung around their necks.

Johnson and McGough were joining forces in the 4 x 800 meter relay. While both were elite talents on the leadoff and anchor, we still depended on our emergent junior varsity runners to get it done in the middle legs. Kuerschner bounded through the week with newfound confidence while Gates remained confined to limited duty. His aching foot, which we later found out was a stress fracture, gave him fits in the aftermath of the sec-tional. He spent most of the final week biking and convincing me that he should get the stick in the state prelims rather than Meincke. I agreed. Barring further injury, Meincke would be the alternate.

Just as in cross country, Tony had taken a step forward. His time of 9:23 safely secured him a spot in the fast heat of the 3200 meter final. He would put his small frame up against the best the state had to offer. York's Jack Driggs would be the king of the field. Sandburg's Lukas Verzbicas had forgone his senior track season to race in collegiate and international fields. In the month after our state meet, he would break the national record for two miles, running the distance in a previously unheard-of 8:29. A week later, on a rainy day in New York City, he became only the fifth American high school athlete ever to break 4:00 for the full mile.

Verzbicas's shadow loomed over the field as athletes from around the state congregated in the shadows of an empty O'Brien Stadium on Thursday afternoon. A qualifier in both the 1600 and 3200 meter runs, Driggs immediately became the favorite. Standing inside Eastern Illinois's physical education building and scanning the heat sheets, I found our 4 x 800 meter relay seeded near the bottom. That was to be expected since we had qualified without Johnson, but the distance between our 7:58 qualifying time and Minooka's 7:50 that headed the field still sent shivers up my spine. Then I remembered. Seeds did not matter.

Friday's prelim would be a new race with a new set of variables. If we had the confidence and the fearlessness to shape those variables, we would be in that final and running for all the marbles on Saturday afternoon. Even after watching both Mat Smoody and Alec Bollman win individual state titles, I had not unlocked the mystery of the meet. What I had discovered, though, was that only big risks yielded big rewards. Early in my career I feared wasting opportunities the athletes had earned. Now in my mid-career I embraced the opposite. To win you had to love the risk. State track was the gambler's paradise. The only way to win was to bet big.

With that in mind I walked out to the track to talk with my assembled relay. Our heat was an old-fashioned MSL showdown. Barrington and Prospect would also run with us. If we just fought our MSL brethren, then we would be headed to the final. In the shadow of the south goal posts on the hot turf field, I laid out our gambler's risk. Rather than anchoring with our best, we would lead with him. McGough would take the stick first and put us in the lead. I counted on Kuerschner and Gates to up their levels of play in response. Johnson would bring us home. If we ran from behind, we would collapse under the weight of the comeback. If we ran from the lead, we would thrive under its weight. We would embrace the paradox. Welcome to state track.

The next day the sun rose early and bathed the stadium in a welcome breath of warmth. Even into mid-May, temperatures in Palatine stuck in the fifties and sixties. The sticky seventy-five-degree heat was a welcome sensation. As I drove the relay to the track, the old anxiety shivers attacked, but I stayed calm. Running from the outer fringes of the field into the center was straight in the Palatine wheelhouse. We functioned best as underdogs. As we headed into the field house to set up camp, the boys were nervous but focused.

The indoor track just opposite the main stadium was a potboiler of emotion—more staring contest than warm-up area. The athletes stewed in their interior tumult in full view of one another. Before the cross country state meet, we hide across Highway 29 at a closed-down golf course and keep to ourselves. At the track state meet we sit dead in the middle of the tension. We threw our gear down in our usual spot near the emergency doors and sat on a small raised platform to wait for our time. Like hoboes with nowhere else to go, we sat with our backs scrunched up against the wall, making fun of other teams and watching the various bizarre warm-up rituals. Some athletes jogged for what seemed hours on end, aimlessly circling the track and wiling away the time by expending their energy. Others performed endless sprints in their spikes.

It was hard to decipher the serious players from the happy-to-be-here types. The latter crowd would enjoy its two-day sojourn from high school in beautiful Charleston, Illinois. The former crowd had legacies to answer and careers to construct. Even sitting there six months away from the state cross country meet, our aspirations sat in the forefront of my thoughts. I watched Neuqua Valley's dynamic junior Mark Derrick begin warming up for a leg on his team's 4 x 800 meter relay. I saw Alex Riba from O'Fallon begin his strides and prepare for the same race. Both would be serious adversaries in the fall. Sitting there, I wondered what strides Johnson and Gregorio would make this weekend. I wondered how many more rungs they could climb on the ladder to the top.

Fifty minutes from the race, I sent our guys to perform our scripted warm-up routine. I would meet them next in the field opposite "the tent."

Each year, fifteen minutes before a heat goes on the track to race, all of the competitors are called to check in at the tent just outside the track. The officials scan their uniforms and hand out their hip numbers. Then, when it is their time, the athletes finally walk through the tent, past the ivied fences surrounding the stadium, and onto the blue track for the first time. In the prelims, they would be greeted by a couple thousand fans, mostly friends and well-wishers from the various schools. In the finals, they would be greeted with the full crowd, more than five thousand strong. Every seat in the bleachers would be filled, from the handicapped box where my brother sat to the nosebleeds beside the press box.

The space between their check-in and their emergence onto the track was consumed by a demon-filled nervousness that derailed many a great athlete. Although shaded by the sun, the tent boils. The hot metal chairs arrayed inside situate the competitors in neat little rows. The arrangement brings a false order to a deeply disordered set of young people. Unused to such stasis in the moments before a race, they jiggle and shake out the nerves. Some nervously stretch on the fringes of the tent. Those in the front row watch the action outside. Others shakily stand in line for the one porta-potty placed inside the staging area. Friendly rivals share old stories in muted tones, but those genial conversations are simply masks, devices for passing the frightening time. The bodies are there, corporeal and twitching, but the real evil of the tent is the thinking. It is a space for the head alone.

As the officials called for us to enter the tent, I had the guys out in the discus field arranged in a semicircle. McGough stood on the far left with Kuerschner and Gates in the middle. Johnson stood stoically to my right. The sun rained down on us. I noticed that all four, unintentionally, had worn the exact same shirt. Symbolic synergy. I went over the race plan one more time: McGough out in fifty-six seconds through the four hundred and bringing us to the lead, Kuerschner out slower than twenty-eight through the two hundred and then racing, Gates engaging at the three-hundred-meter mark to check out of his rhythm, Johnson finding the aggression to bring it home. Then, through the rush of emotion, I paused.

I looked them all in the eye. The last thing I said was, "When it gets tough out there, remember that you run for Palatine." I poked each guy in the shirt and sent them to the tent.

It doesn't always work out, but those four guys ran their perfect race. We executed every single aspect of the four race plans. McGough came home in 1:55.9. Kuerschner ran one of the most stirring races of my career, and I shed more than a few tears as his 1:58.3 split brought us near the lead. Running on a stress fracture, Gates broke 2:00. Timmy J's 1:56 split secured us a spot in the final. His last desperate lean broke the school record. After watching him weep in disappointment the week before, I swelled with pride at his redemption. His deep care for his team-mates showed in the finishing stretch as he pulled us into third and, even better, into the state final.

The mood afterward inside Lantz Field House was jubilant. Not only had we qualified, but we had the gratification of running our best race. The more I coach, I realize that what I want most is to see my guys run their best, whatever the circumstances. To see men do it under all that pressure is even more gratifying. I gave Kuersch a hug and held it just a bit longer. He had run one of the great relay legs in school history.

Certain guys work so long and hard with so little reward that they just gnaw their way to my center. Erich Kuerschner did this during the 2011 track season. I have a soft spot for kids who succeed against the odds. I was one of those guys myself—small, scrawny, athletically limited, and totally devout. I wanted to be good so bad and worked like a madman to improve. But in the end my championship victories were always vicarious realities. I am a perennial wingman. I live, and always have lived, to see the moment of victory through the eyes of others.

In Kuerschner, I saw myself. Flawed. Too weak. Too slow. Perennially on the margins rather than the center. Competing, but defeated by better talent. The qualities a guy like Kuersch had going for him were perseverance, dedication, and their on will. As a junior he missed the entire outdoor season due to an injury. To make matters worse his father, Vaughn, had a heart attack. He survived, but the trauma was not easy on

Erich and his family. His best eight-hundred-meter mark before his senior season was 2:08.

During indoor track, he ran like a changed man, setting PRs left and right at all distances. Still, I doubted him. What use could a man with a fifty-six-second four-hundred-meter best be on the state level? His answer: Get faster. His races in the MSL Conference and the sectional both ended with him on hands and knees, vomiting furiously and then staggering away to put on his sweats. With a week to go, he looked me straight in the eye and said, "Coach I don't know how many more good 800s I have in me."

As we walked to the tent for the final, I looked Kuersch in the eye and answered his question: "Do you know how many more good 800s you have in you? One." Erich would not run in college. The state final was his last race. To watch him kneel on the medal stand and end his career as an All-State runner would be worth any of the small sacrifices I went through to help him along. It certainly would be worth all the big sacrifices he went through. Running doesn't always pay off in such an outsized way, and I've learned to love the many small favors it offers. The hard finish. The taste of fresh air. The mingling of sun, sweat, and salt in the summer. But all of those pale in comparison with the thrill of a well-earned victory.

The night before we sat together in our hotel and discussed the next step. Johnson's lean had already broken the school record. Our time of 7:51.50 was far above what we had expected. So we decided that we would put the entire load on McGough's shoulders and try to win the whole damn thing. It wasn't feasible, sitting there with Gates's foot in a bucket of ice and Kuerschner already near his limits. But if we could get a 1:53 to 1:54 leg from McGough on leadoff, then we would have the lead and the momentum. Anything could happen from there. We decided to have him run the opening leg like it was the 800 meter final. He would hit the six-hundred-meter mark at full go and try to hang on.

That is exactly what he did. With 150 meters to go in the lead leg, we were winning. Then McGough tied up. Bad. Epically bad. The more conservative leadoff runners streamed around him in the final straightaway, rocking the baton into the exchange zone with full heads of steam. It was no matter, though. McGough got Kuerschner the stick in a tie for fifth, and we were in it from then on. Kuersch dropped another 1:58 while Gates faltered in the closing meters but kept us in eighth. He gave way to Johnson with Hersey clear in our sights.

This was Johnson's moment, a chance at redemption. Through all the frustration he and I had experienced over the years together, I still believed one basic precept. Timmy J always brought the heat when it mattered most. This faith had taken a blow the week before. Watching him scorch the backstretch and run right up onto Hersey's heels for seventh place offered a hint of revelation. Maybe Timmy J didn't have the inner desire, the necessary selfishness to go out and punish people for his own good. But he could pull away from his kind nature to punish people for others. He could do it in the service of the team.

The glimmering fire in his eyes shone in his bodily action. He ran tall and rhythmically. He didn't possess snappy speed. He didn't have that gift. But in the space of those eight hundred meters, in the 1:56 seconds of action he needed to hold on to eighth place and secure All-State honors for his teammates, he showed his team speed. The passivity of the sectional final was replaced by an urgency that he rarely summoned. It could only be the speed of great service.

Watching Ryan McGough, Erich Kuerschner, Zach Gates, and Tim Johnson earn All-State honors was one of the highlights of my coaching career. I've seen three of my athletes win state titles, yet I took just as much joy out of watching these young men get eighth in the state. We were well out of the championship, running 7:52 to finish nine seconds in arrears of Minooka, who won behind a great 1:51 leg from their senior star Joe McCasey. In the end we ran our best and nothing could be better.

When they presented the All-State medals to my relay, I had already left the stands to find Tony in the field house. I heard them announcing the medalists over the loudspeaker, and I paused at the fence that rings O'Brien Field and found a small hole in the ivy. All four of the young men had great stories. Ryan McGough had moved to Palatine as a sophomore and found his ultimate potential as a leadoff man. Zach Gates persevered through a stress fracture to run in the state track finals. Tim Johnson erased the disappointment of a week earlier through his service to his teammates. But hearing Kuersch's name over that speaker was the one that did it for me. All I could do was grip the fence and weep with joy.

The medal ceremony over, I jogged quickly into Lantz Field House to find Gregorio and take him to the tent. As we walked, I went back over the race plan. Commit to the pace. Find the All-State group and hang on. Play to your strength rather than depending on finishing speed. When the race broke just past the sixteen-hundred-meter mark, be ready to shift. Commit. Commit. Commit. Usually such an intonation was unnecessary, but I sensed his growing fear as we stood outside the tent and waited for the official to call the fast heat into the cauldron. As the rest gathered, I saw the same odds he felt. He looked like a miniature next to the tall and lean men he was about to race. Hinsdale Central's Billy Fayette towered over him, as did York's sleek Driggs and Oak Park–River Forest's powerfully built Malachy Schrobilgen. He looked like a boy among men.

As we parted, I remember thinking he had never looked so scared or out of his element. Even the big chip on his shoulder, the attitude he used to attack those whose talent he envied, couldn't hide the fear. I left him with words of confidence, but sensed his doubt. Despite all the miles and the fast times, he still didn't believe.

As I took my seat near the top of the straightaway and watched the Class AAA fast heat jog out onto the track, I knew that his mind was blown. The crowd. The size of the field. The résumés of the competitors. The pressurized atmosphere. It all conspired against him and any others who had no logical signpost on which to hang their belief. Rhetoric could only give a man the brave face. To wear it he would have to earn it. Tony had earned his laurels in cross country, but this was no grassy field among the late-fall elements and the comfort of the extra mile.

Tony's race the week before had been expected and consistent, and nothing that happened in the early going should have dissuaded him from contending. Edwardsville's Garrett Sweatt hammered the early pace, but not hard enough that it fazed anyone. The pack worked methodically through the early laps, jockeying for position and struggling to relax as the tension wound its way through the field. After three laps, men began to leak out the back, first in singles then in a steadily drawn-out stream. They looked like the wagging tail of a dog. Sooner or later the move would go down and the field would explode.

Each lap I implored Tony to relax and stay home. He had been swallowed by the pack in the first lap and tentatively rode the metal rail that kept the competitors from stepping onto the infield. I could hardly see his small shape, hidden as he was by the bigger men, but I hoped that he was taking it easy and biding his time. As the field strode down the front stretch toward the halfway mark, I gripped the rail on the bottom row of the stadium and leaned in: "It's gonna shoot! It's gonna shoot! Here it comes!" Long-distance races have the potential to transfer steady kinetic energy to explosion in the blink of an eye. It just takes one man to light the tender and set the race ablaze.

The move was predictable. Schrobilgen began his bid for the win by taking the lead on the third lap, but he turned it up heading through the sixteen-hundred-meter mark. Immediately, the contenders scrambled. Maine South's David Eckhart and Neuqua Valley's Mark Derrick deftly covered in rhythm. As Tony scrambled, he nipped the rail with his left foot at the top of the backstretch and stumbled ever so briefly. That was all it took. With the pace turned up, he suddenly found himself off the back.

I saw it in his body language immediately. He panicked. His formerly steady chin swung from side to side punctuated every few strides with a dip down toward his chest. He was reaching. In calm rhythm he could run with the field. But the second the thought entered his head that he didn't have the speed to cover that move, his brain attacked his muscles. The desperation took over, and he began the slow fade of a man thrown out the back of the race. I watched him run the last three laps and gamely pretend to stay in it, but there was no obscuring the obvious. One second of inattention had smashed his hopes to pieces.

As I sat down to watch him finish out the string, I thought of all the work we would have to do over the summer to bridge the gap between the champions and the pretenders. It wasn't just physical. In fact, most of the land to be conquered lay squarely between the ears. Like most in the race, Tony possessed qualities of a champion. But only Jack Driggs had what it took to be a champion. After years of seeking, he seized the lead at the bell and held it all the way to the line for his first state title. He tacked on the 1600 meter run later that day. Watching Driggs, another link in the mythic York machine, I once again came face-to-face with the tall task before us. He ran for a program that knew how to fill in the championship gaps. For us, this would be a journey of first discoveries.

The mood in the van on the ride home to Palatine was a mixture of exaltation and quiet contemplation. Every individual athlete's season is a narrative. All of the young men I coach have a story to tell and—like a movie or a great novel—their running is the medium through which they tell it. Our three seniors had written a beautiful final chapter. Johnson had written one about redemption. Gregorio had scribbled a tome about defeat amid his notes for the future.

As the sun faded from the horizon and the boys drifted off to sleep, I retreated into my head and began composing the next chapter. Driving north up Interstate 57, I gripped the wheel and lost myself in a flurry of aspirations and machinations. Our cross country dream had dominated the track season, always in the background of every practice and race. We had all paid outward fidelity to the track season, but our common mission had ridden unspoken underneath everything we did. For the last eighteen months, we had been shaping this coming team, sculpting it bit by bit and mile by mile toward a future vision. At least now we would start living that vision out in the open. The summer was upon us. It was time to jog out to the cliffside and dangle our toes over the edge.

SUMMER

On the Tuesday after the state track meet, we held our annual sign-up meeting for cross country. The message was clear. No breaks. Returnees who made it to the state track meet would take seven to ten days off before resuming training, but the rest had been on hiatus already. On June 1 the summer training would begin. It wouldn't be organized—not yet—but the buildup would commence. On that date I would hand out the mileage charts with the suggested miles for each week of the summer and turn them loose. While I recuperated and graded all the AP English papers I'd let accumulate over the last three weeks of the track season, the machine began to roll.

The summer is meant to be transformative. For much of the year we run moderate, consistent mileage. It probably totals more than most programs do around the state and nation, but the miles per week skirt the upper edge of sanity. During the summer, we charge straight into insanity. By August most of the varsity will reach eighty to a hundred miles a week. Even the old guys, myself included, get after it. For the last ten years, barring a couple periods of injury, I have averaged more than eight hundred miles during the ninety-two days of summer training.

In the team meeting we unveiled the butcher paper upon which we first sketched our dream back in January. As we looked back over the past track season, the boys could see how things had developed. Five returnees had logged 3200 meter times of 9:53 or better. Our developmental guys, juniors-to-be Zambrano, Smith, and Stella, all ran better than 10:15. Noah Brown, a convert from soccer, had also slipped under that mark. Our rivals had made similar progress, but the feeling in the room was one of control. No more would we chase from behind and hope it all turned out. For once we would not have to supplant some immovable force. The shaping of a title would be in our control.

I introduced the meeting with a quote from legendary Arkansas track and cross country coach John McDonnell. He had this to say about winning: "I thought I was one of those guys that was snake bit—that couldn't win the big one. I have an old saying, 'Once we kicked the door down in '84, it seemed like it was open to us all the time.' We learned how to win. It's very hard to learn how to win, and after we got that habit, we won meets we shouldn't have. The highlight of my career was winning that first national championship. That's all I ever wished for—to win one. I never thought it would mushroom the way it did— not in my wildest dreams." From 1984 onward, the Razorbacks won forty-two national titles in cross country, indoor track, and outdoor track. Their habit of excellence started with a single accomplishment. We hoped to start a similar habit.

When I looked around the room, the assembled men filled all the desks, even leaking onto the floor and spilling into the foreground. All of them were here for a reason. For some, it was to get in shape and be part of something big. For others, it was a quest to find their full potential. I had wanted to win ever since I was a little boy sitting in the stands at Peoria High School watching York win state titles year after year.

Since those early days, I had become a connoisseur of championship celebrations. I remember weeping at the television screen as Michael Jordan hugged that first NBA trophy. I lay on my college dorm room bed and watched Steve Young of the San Francisco 49ers hug the Lombardi Trophy and cry those tears of joy. Just once, I wanted to feel that ecstasy. I wanted to love that tangible object just for a second as an expression of all the intangible forces that led to it. I also knew, in the back of my head, that the first would be the sweetest. It would change everything else. It would liberate us, set us free, testify that the grand things worth doing in life were doable. As I looked at Marcus, Tony, Peter, Timmy J, Monkey, and the rest, I felt it was our time.

As the meeting drew to a close, I looked at the seventy kids in Room

216 and asked for everything they had to give. The ruling construct had been set long before: The five guys make the team, the team makes the five. I told them each year that it would take every guy finding his limits to make the whole operation go. This year I meant it more than ever. Our aims were ambitious, challenging, and partially psychotic. As a varsity team and a coaching staff we had agreed on one principle. If we were going to beat York in the Illinois state meet for the first time, then we were going to have to out-train them.

I remember the first time I ever read Joe Newton's summer workouts for the York varsity. My dad took me to one of Newton's speeches at a local shoe store in the Quad Cities in the summer before my senior year. My dad had known Coach Newton for a long time. He had coached his entire career and beaten a Newton-coached team only once. It was the only time that a team from Moline ever beat York in a varsity cross country race. Such statistics resound throughout the state of Illinois. For my dad, coming from the western part of the state, York was simply untouchable. You could say you wanted to win. You could put your heart and soul into the training. The only problem was that their training existed outside of the rational mind.

My dad bought me Joe Newton's book *Running to the Top of the Mountain* that day, and I still have it in my library with his signature on the cover page. Little did I know that one day I would try to coach a team past a legend. Even a couple years north of eighty years old, Joe Newton is still the edifice of Illinois cross country. He's the base, the walls, the height, and the grandeur. To become anything as a coach or athlete, you have to go through him and his boys first. It's not impossible. Many teams have found a way to beat the Dukes for a year, maybe two. But they have never been supplanted.

I remember opening that book for the first time and looking at the summer training schedules for his 1987 team. I got the book in late July, so the summer training for our senior season was well under way. My friends and I had grand plans of a state championship and were running near seventy miles per week. We returned five of our seven men and York was squarely in our sights. I guess they were until I read those training logs.

In their first week of training, May 25–31, 1987, they ran eighty miles. That was the easiest week of the summer. The numbers escalated into the triple digits and stayed there, week after week. To my young eyes, it had to be a myth. It just was not possible. But all the evidence was there. The twenty-seven state titles could not lie.

From August 9 to August 18 of that year, Newton conducted "Camp Olympia" in Elmhurst. The total running load for the ten days was 216 miles. That's more than twenty miles a day. How could high school boys, youngsters like me, ever run that much? It had to be a lie. No one could run that schedule and survive much less have a life, play in the school band, watch television, get good grades, or have a girlfriend. The same tune played throughout the season: 122 miles, 114 miles, 117 miles, 100 miles, 99 miles, 118 miles, 96 miles, 95 miles, 93 miles, and then 67 miles the week of the state meet.

I am sure that some of those training schedules are hyperbole. Maybe a few guys ran that much, but certainly not everyone. Maybe it was all a lie, a fantasy. The real irony is that he published the training schedule of a team that only placed fourth in the state meet. If this work hadn't even yielded a state trophy, then what did the state champion teams do?

In running, just as in most things, there are many ways to fry an egg. Mimicking Newton and York wouldn't do for us. We had built up to running sadistic amounts of mileage over the years, and we had done it our way and in our good time. The week before our sign-up meeting I talked with Marcus, Tony, and Peter—our mileage leaders—and we agreed that this was the summer when we would take what Palatine did and send it over the edge into irrationality. We agreed that when our Early Bird program began in mid-June, we would already be at seventy miles a week. From there it would accelerate throughout the summer until we were all hitting hundred-mile weeks by early August. Previously we had found single men who could live on this edge for an entire summer—James Macatangay, Sagar Patel, Adam Bethke, Colin Morlock—but the ambition had shifted. This time around we were going to do it with twenty guys all at once.

The beauty of summer running is that it goes beyond team training and is shared with many members of the Palatine community. Started in 1989 by former girls coach Pat Gleason, the Early Bird Running Program grew from its humble beginnings to a machine that runs 150 people strong. The high school boys and girls were the bulk of that participation, but the numbers were also padded with youth runners, adults, and even a few senior citizens. Throughout June and July we all meet at 6 AM each day of the camp in front of Palatine High School for some real community running. Most of the time, the high school students train together as a group, but it is important for their training to be informed by the efforts of others. Many of our athletes started running as youngsters when their mom or dad started bringing them to Early Bird. Of course, many also returned the favor and introduced their parents to running. While most high school group members develop an insular bond with one another through school camps, we train alongside Boston Marathon aspirants, fitness joggers, mothers and fathers, and returning alums. The camp is more familial than the alternatives.

Our adult running group is now anchored by Paul Herzog, Diane and Scott Starcevich, and Kristen Jordan. Paul had been a friend of both the boys and girls programs for years after his kids ran for Palatine. Diane and Scott caught the running bug in a bad way as their son Jacob ran for the boys program in the mid-2000s. A veteran of four state champion girls teams, Kristen Jordan comes each day and runs with the same intensity she used to place All-State three times. Even after three kids, she finds solace in the run. One of the best age-group athletes in the area, she is a constant reminder that the Palatine tradition is for life.

I am sure that our high school students provide some manner of inspiration and freshness to our adults as well. A day at Early Bird can have that effect. The entire exercise brims with its own brand of lunacy. We all wake up at an ungodly hour throughout the summer to push the limits together during the hottest time of the year. Like all good teams, every part is necessary to create the whole. Early Bird is about perspective, community pride, and connection to the larger exercise that runs behind our athletic aspirations. Running cannot be contained inside a season. It is a lifestyle.

Some in our school and community would find *cultish* a better descriptor, but we are used to it by now. Something in the aspirational closeness of Early Bird frightens people. At its core is always the question *Why?* I remember asking that question when I first met the Early Bird crew. When Fred Miller told me that we would be meeting at 6 AM, I was stupefied. In the summer? Every day of the program? As an outsider, I couldn't believe that high school kids would get up at that hour, much less train. But they did.

Soon I grew to love the early mornings, the camaraderie, and the outsized glee I felt when I saw the group assembled each day. It was as if our group captured something essential about the community in which we lived. Every day just half a mile from the school, the Palatine bike path fills with fitness joggers, cyclists, and families out for a stroll. Even in the winter, we have compatriots, fellow strivers who feel the need to hit the whitewashed pavement no matter the temperature. Early Bird captures that spirit in its largest relief—young and old, men and women, fathers and daughters, coaches and athletes. The boys and girls who run for Palatine are simply products of a larger wellspring of community energy.

As the guys ran throughout June, ramping up their miles for the big training weeks that would commence with the start of Early Bird, our thoughts turned also to Colorado. With Coach Sheehan getting married in early August and my wife due with our third child just after, we rescheduled the varsity trip for the last week of June. For ten years we had planned our varsity trip for the last week of July, the week that precedes the "no contact" period in Illinois. Usually, the group built across the summer. We got to see who was in with both feet over the line and who still straddled the fence. The varsity trip then united the group. This journey was going to be different.

We selected fourteen boys back in March and decided that we would light the fuse earlier than normal. The group included a careful mix of young and old, experienced veterans and naive newbies. A number of our boys from the previous year's trip returned, with the Fab Five at the forefront, but we also mixed in the up-and-coming sophomores with the already established varsity. Each year this transition engendered a combination of sadness and freshness. The bonds from the previous year would inevitably start to break. While the Fab Five got up each day to pursue their common dreams, senior graduates Reuben Frey, A. J. Laskowske, Ryan McGough, Zach Gates, and Erich Kuerschner would be safely in bed. Most of them would "play" at coming to Early Bird, but the sanctity of their commitment dissolved on graduation day. Their futures lay elsewhere, and their absence would be palpable throughout the early parts of the summer.

Bonds once formed in the bedrock and turmoil of common difficulty shattered overnight. They were all still friends, but the seniors could no longer share in the journey. Through the sadness and already increasing nostalgia, a new group would form. Each team has its own identity, and it is my job each year to find it. Bemoaning the greatness of past teams is not a passage into a pleasant future. At the start of each varsity trip, I tell the team that who we are as a group will emerge somewhere along the way. I never see much use in looking for it or inaugurating some series of tired guidance-counselor games to find it. Somewhere along the line, given the right circumstances and a deliberate openness, our new identity reveals itself. The concept lingers around us in the ether before suddenly crystallizing into a solid and viewable shape.

Along with the coaches, Peter, Tony, Marcus, Timmy J, and Monkey had found the "pearl of great price" somewhere on the trek up Blue Ridge Road the previous summer in Winter Park. At the top of that devilish climb, the tears had mixed with heartache and exhaustion. When we jogged back down from that peak, we were a unit. The bonds with the just-graduated seniors vanished. When we hit the cabins and packed our things to go home, the team was set.

This year's crew would enact the same process but in a different place. We would still fly into Denver and stay in Boulder for two days, but the back end of the trip was wholly new. We had booked our rooms at the YMCA of the Rockies in Estes Park. Just outside our back door would be the lofty peaks of Rocky Mountain National Park. None of us had ever been there before.

Outside of the top five returnees and fellow senior Noah Brown, our group was buoyed by the addition of six talented but inexperienced juniors, one incoming freshman, and one senior aspirant plucked from our junior varsity squad. We determined early on that these nine held the greatest potential to help us. Brian Smith had been the token sophomore the year before, and he paid back that bid with a phenomenal year of training. The track season brought a new 3200 meter best and a burgeoning confidence. Tall with bright orange hair, he joined fellow "ginger" Andrew Clingerman. Oft-injured, the intense Clingerman had been a star in the making since freshman year. Sporting a brand-new tattoo on his back, Clinger brought some muscle and badness to the bunch. More half-miler than distance runner, he trained with ferocity each day. Men with a slightly loose screw are a definite asset, and Clinger certainly was a consumer of life out on the edge. Since freshman year, he had performed diamond push-ups to remind us just how strong he really was.

Christian Zambrano fit more closely with Smith. Quiet and methodical, he endured nearly two years of pain due to Osgood-Schlatter disease in his knees. Each day he ran, he answered to that pain. Never once had he intimated that he would quit or back down. We adjusted the workouts, and he just kept dealing with it, day after day. Somewhere in the middle of the track season, he had broken the disease's spell. Finally he had stopped growing and now neared six feet in height. With the pain gone, he turned the volume up to full. His reward had been a MSL conference title in the frosh-soph 1600 meter run.

Two fellow juniors, Tyler Squeo and Joey Mars, were not quite as sure as their more experienced friend. Both still carried an air of fear when we discussed varsity workouts and the intensity of the training. Tyler had all the moxie of a great one, but not the speed or the health. Competitively he reminded me of an annoying little dog that constantly yipped at your heels. He raced like a pest. Too often, he had pushed too far too fast in training and ended up injured. A stress fracture in his shin had been the price he paid the previous cross country season. Mars struggled with both motivation and confidence. Gifted with raw speed and a competitive edge, the task with Joe was getting him to the line in one piece. At various times both his mind and body had fallen apart. Even as we prepared to leave for Colorado, I wasn't sure we could keep him put together through the entire summer. He had nearly quit the previous spring.

The sole remaining junior, Zach Stella, was one of the biggest enigmas of my career. A tall and awkward character, Zach provided numerous challenges on his journey to the varsity. Loyal to a fault and deeply aspirational, he had failed to win many friends on the team. During his freshman year he had twice stopped running within sight of the school and refused to finish. One time I spent thirty minutes convincing him to stand up and walk the final block. These outbursts frustrated both his coaches and teammates, but I sensed that Zach was someone who needed a good mentor. He and I became close, bonding over our common love of reading and writing. He grew slowly, two steps forward and one step back, but the momentum had been forward. In his first varsity workout the previous fall he fell off the pace and threw a temper tantrum. When he took off his racing flat and spiked it into the ground, I kicked him out of practice. Crying and distraught, he came back later and apologized. Still, I stuck with him. He had talent. He also had an incalculable ability I couldn't overlook. No matter how big a mess he was in training, he nearly always raced well. I guessed that was better than having the opposite problem.

Our senior aspirant was Devin Hein. Just the year before I had plucked "Devo" off the scrap heap of the football team. He took to running immediately and labored to get in shape for his junior cross country season. Devo lost forty pounds and became an inspiration. Still, his hard work brought him nowhere near the varsity level. His 19:00 three-mile personal best was just barely faster than the recovery pace of our varsity. But he kept working, earning the respect of the frosh-soph and becoming a vital leader. By his junior track season I saw his fuller potential. He was captain material. The Fab Five had lived throughout their careers in the rarefied air of the varsity. Devo lived in the material world of the broader team. He had the ability to connect and unite the two halves of the team. So I pushed him. He ran a 5:19 mile during track season. His road run paces got quicker. I put the bug in his ear about coming on the Colorado trip, and he blasted straight through his end-of-season break, building up his mileage and his hopes. We weren't sure he could keep up, but I invited him anyway. Devo was the heart and soul of the team. If we were to find our identity, he would have to be there.

The last member of our travel group was a curious choice. I had followed Graham Brown's junior high career with great interest. In fact I had followed him every summer since he was in fifth grade. With his sister, Courtney, on the girls varsity, Graham's mom Sharon decided that the entire family should start coming to summer running. Graham was not pleased. Each day as I went out to monitor the Early Bird runners, I would find him walking or lagging behind. He grew from those humble beginnings to become one of the best prospects of my career. In seventh grade he ran 5:07 for the full mile, a time unheard of in our junior high feeder schools. Watching him dominate eighth-grade competition with a beautiful high back kick and an obvious nasty streak, I salivated at his potential. I knew I was witnessing an emerging All-Time Great. The big dilemma heading into freshman year was whether he would play football or not. That actually made him more attractive. Cross country programs rarely get athletes. Graham had the same genetics that helped his sister run to fourth place in the state, but matched those natural abilities with the smash-mouth mentality of a football halfback. No freshman had made the Palatine varsity since 2002. Quietly, I believed that he could find a way into the top seven.

As I prepared for the season by upping my own mileage, I knew that everyone would have to be all-in. Peter had made that declaration the previous December, and it had resounded ever since. In the preceding two years, I had treated my own running like a coward. Dealing with the first injuries of my thirties and the growth of my family, I sank into an athletic somnalescence. I convinced myself that I would never run faster than I had in my youth. I imposed limits: no marathon under 2:50, no more 5:00 miles, no more Boston Marathons, no more big PRs in the half-marathon, no more sub-17:00 5Ks. Somewhere in the middle of June, in the midst of a fifty-mile week, I decided that I should stop worrying and just go for it. If I believed in limits, then so would they. During a solo fifteen-mile long run around Busse Woods Forest Preserve in Schaumburg, I secretly resolved to push the envelope in the coming months. If I was asking them for a thousand miles, then I would follow suit.

The next day we flew to Colorado and began the process of seeking our shared dream. The trip was grandiose in both ambition and canvas. We were going to run the full fourteen-mile out-and-back on Magnolia Road just outside of Boulder. We were going to push through the thin air above eight thousand feet straight to our breaking points. We would do it willingly. Somewhere out there, we would drain ourselves to exhaustion. Then we would stagger to the bottom of some formidable peak and will ourselves to the top. I hoped that the majestic canvas of the Rocky Mountains would be the site of our cleanest revelations. Somewhere up among the thin air and the peaks, we would find out just who we were.

BOULDER

The varsity team and coaches pose as a group of western outlaws in Estes Park, Colorado. Note Tim Meincke dressed as a woman in the center.

Late in June I found myself checking into the Silver Saddle Motel in Boulder for the second year in a row. A dingy multi-unit motel near the intersection of Arapahoe and Canyon Boulevard, the Silver Saddle is as far removed from suburban standards of comfort as you can get. It's basically a dive. Most of our kids are not used to such bleak accommodations, but the spartan environment of "the Saddle" dovetailed with our aspirations. Cross country running is about being good rather than look-ing good. It's about functionality rather than impression. A roof over our heads and hot water would do just fine.

As Coach Sheehan and I checked into our room behind the main office, I sent the majority of our guys up to the motel's dingiest building, known simply as "the bungalow." For three days, eight of them, includ-ing Jimmy Mac, would inhabit these close confines as only a band of dirty athletes could do. The bungalow supposedly had air-conditioning and ventilation, but by late afternoon each day it reeked of sweaty shoes. As we walked in their eyes certainly did not light up. The television was a sad relic, equipped with rabbit ears rather than basic cable, and the fur-niture showed the nicks and bruises common to any low-rent institution. Savvy as always, Tyler Squeo quickly grabbed some couch cushions and made a nest by the window. The rest grabbed spots according to the team's internal pecking order. The next day, when we would run Magnolia Road, I went to wake them, only to find most sprawled pell-mell all over the floor. The older guys got beds while the incoming juniors and Graham tried to find comfort in their sleeping bags.

The rest of us, including the seven seniors and the coaches, grabbed more normal rooms with double beds on the first floor of the main build-ing. The year before, Marcus had been fixated on the hotness of one of the maids. This year he would have to make do with several long-term res-idents, men between addresses, who spent most of their time sitting on a bench outside our rooms and smoking cigarettes. Their hidden stories and haunted pasts fit within the broader tableau. Each year the boys were excited by the basketball court at the end of the property, but its bent rims, absent nets, and gravelly playing surface cooled that enthusiasm. The only quaint touch that all enjoyed was the bottled-Pepsi machine by the lobby door and the view of the mountains from the front porch.

At least the view did not fall prey to our silly expectations. Each morn-ing when the sun beamed through the drapes, I could open them up and see the Rocky Mountain foothills. Unlike the big mountains of Rocky Mountain National Park, these were the starter set, big enough to impress flatlanders like us but still within reason and conquerable on foot. At these relatively low elevations, the pine trees still covered the slopes, interspersed with large boulders and dusty foot trails.

For most of our guys, running is an enjoyable activity, but their perceptions remain skewed by the blighted reality of the suburban environment. We do have access to two wonderful forest preserves in Palatine at Deer Grove East and West, but those places are just that—preserves. They are keyhole glimpses into nature amid a landscape of tract houses and sameness. For most, runs in Deer Grove are subject to the same repetitive dullness we feel when we look at our neighborhoods and see the same house over and over and over again. In the mountains we return to our primal state, explorers and survivors, curiosity experts with a nose for adventure. Running up in the thin air away from the fresh comforts of our safe lives reminds us of the beast lurking within. It is in our nature to run. That's why the bungalow's broken television, dented coffee tables, and outdated wall paintings need not matter. We weren't there to be at home. We were looking for something different.

Aside from the mangy hippies and the homeless, the bike trail down Canyon Creek just outside the Silver Saddle felt like home. It had different aesthetics and a few more good-looking women, but the trail still resounded with the trappings of normal life—families on bikes and in-line skates, joggers with their headphones, crazy college kids rope-swinging into the freezing water. But somewhere in this landscape there existed a place beyond our reality. It was up to us. We had to follow our noses and keep seeking. At some point, with maximal effort, we would enter alien space. Only then could we truly learn what the land had to teach.

We began our trip with an "easy" introductory run. Although not nearly as high as places we would run later, Boulder is still situated at fifty-three hundred feet and offers a stark contrast for any Illinois athlete. Even as we headed down the Canyon Creek bike trail toward the campus of the University of Colorado, I could feel the guys breathing heavily. As we turned off the trail and headed uphill toward the football stadium, the altitude immediately punched all of us in the chest. Hearts pounded more quickly than normal. The lungs struggled to get a full glimpse. As we ran, I tried to joke it away, but I could sense our new-comers' fright. By the time we circled the campus and headed downtown, most were breathing a little easier. But when we hit the Pearl Street pedestrian mall near its western end, we took a hard left and threw down the pace.

The year before, our first run just outside Boulder had been with American Olympian Jorge Torres. Tim Johnson's father, Steve, knew Jorge from their common junior high coach, Greg Fedyski, and he had arranged for the boys and I to visit Fight Club—the property made famous when the Torres brothers and Dathan Ritzenhein starred at Colorado. Before showing us his house, Jorge took us on a run up the Betasso Link Trail. We parked just off Canyon Boulevard before it went through a tunnel. The trailhead didn't look auspicious, but it immediately went vertical up the mountain. We started running at Jorge's easy pace, pretending we were fit enough to keep up. Several minutes into the run I thought my heart was going to explode. I looked down at my watch, which read three minutes and fifteen seconds. The switchbacks were relentless, and I was overwhelmed by the need to walk. We finally reached the top of the trail and leveled out onto a trail system that overlooked Boulder, but the point was taken. This was Jorge's playground. The rest of us had a lot of work to do.

The veterans wanted to deliver a similar shock. I could feel it in Marcus Garcia's body language. We hit the Red Rocks Trail near the end of Pearl Street and headed straight uphill. I paused for a second to take attendance and noticed that Graham Brown and Steve Johnson were nowhere to be found. As the team filed by, I fell in to take up the rear. The beginning slopes were gentle, even encouraging for the affrighted members of our crew, but the trail quickly gave way to punishing uphill. Enter heartbeat. Enter lung trauma. Welcome to the thin air. We climbed gently and gradually, not wanting to give it all with the next day's long run on the horizon, but the message was clear. This would not be normal training. At the front Marcus and Tony drove the pace with a punishing fury, trying to break their teammates. They also frolicked uphill, happy to be at play and running free.

After pausing to look down over Boulder and across the way at the Flatirons, we began the dangerous descent. You can read a lot about a man's nature watching him descend. I stayed near the back with Peter and Timmy J, carefully choosing my footsteps and methodically working down the trail. Up ahead, Marcus, Tony, Clingerman, and Squeo charged down the mountain, vaulting off the rocks at high speed. It would take both hard-chargers and methodical men to make the team go. I was glad to see that we had both.

After collecting the group we jogged a brief cool-down and then headed back across Canyon Creek to the Silver Saddle parking lot. There we found Steve J and Graham waiting for us. Graham's eyes were downcast while Steve wore a whimsical grin. At lunch Graham had eaten his own hamburger and then helped two or three of the guys finish off their meals. It had been the wrong proving ground. Somewhere just before we began the ascent, Graham peeled off from the group and gifted his lunch into the front yard of some lucky Boulder resident. A parent for years but a runner to the end, Steve consoled the young man only after remembering to take video on his iPhone. Devo had christened the talented freshman "Prodigy," and everyone had a blast welcoming him to the realities of distance running. Graham took the good-natured ribbing in stride. I assured him that he would look back on these first moments fondly someday. Perhaps a future state championship would make us forget such a humble beginning.

As we headed down to Pearl Street to grab dinner, I could feel the team inventing itself. The first run, the dingy motel, Graham's front-yard episode, the creekside high jinks—all conspired to begin the fusion. Watching the streetside buskers and going through the eccentric shops gave everyone a set of memories to hold on to. But those memories alone couldn't create a bond. A team that goes to see something interesting is together, but not fused. The fusion can only come through difficulty. As we enjoyed the beauty of a late-June sunset, we knew that everything would change in the morning. A first jaunt up a small mountain was one thing. The next day we were going to run fifteen miles on Magnolia Road.

Chris Lear first popularized "Mags" in his book *Running with the Buffaloes*. Lear followed the Colorado men's and women's teams throughout the summer and fall of 1998, and his chronicle yielded one of the finest tomes ever written about the process of forging a championship cross country team. Through the injuries and the heartbreak of that season, from Jon Severy's untimely death to Adam Goucher's national title, Lear gave us an inside look at the dynamics of a major college team. Central to that story had been Mark Wetmore's mileage-based training, a nose-to-the-grindstone ethos that took champion runners and made them elite while molding walk-ons into stars. At the center of the book was the long run.

Magnolia Road begins as a winding offshoot that runs due south from Canyon Boulevard. The drive up the canyon to the junction is gorgeous. Boulder Creek, formed from the meltwater of the mountain snows, rushes down toward Boulder while the mountains steadily grow all around. The turnoff to Mags is a small sign, and if you didn't regard it as something iconic you would miss it entirely. The ascent is devilish, unsafe at any speed, especially when you have Steve Johnson driving and talking into his cell phone. The road twists and turns through a series of steep switchbacks and residences before leveling out just above eight thousand feet. The year before we had simply followed Lear's instructions. The run started when the paved section of the road ended.

The holdovers from the previous year had done their best to frighten the newcomers, but even they did not know what lay in store. The year before we had chugged through the high pastures and ranchland adjoining the road in the bright sunshine and heat of late July. We ran Mags for seven miles to its terminus at the Peak to Peak Highway before heading back and reaching the cars at the ten-mile mark. Back then, that distance had been enough. It wasn't anymore. The pact today was deeper. It was the full fourteen for everyone, or at least for the major players. Devo, Prodigy, and Mars might have had the ten-miler in their heads, but the rest were full go.

As we parked off the side of the road and prepared, the guys scrambled into the woods to take a final piss or just to enjoy the panorama. Nothing about Illinois is panoramic. It has a copious flatness that lets you see for miles, but none of the relief. Just farms and silos and a view that runs straight to the horizon. Colorado has snowcapped mountains and high-altitude wildflowers and a stark clarity of view sharpened by the thinness of the atmosphere. Despite the overcast nature of the day, we could still look to the north and see Longs Peak. The only "fourteener" in Rocky Mountain National Park, it dominated the landscape, even this far to the south.

I lingered a bit longer pre-run than usual, sitting on a boulder and looking north while fixing my socks. The pause was a gathering. My foot had been killing me for the better part of a week. I had no idea if I could even run, much less go the full fourteen. Like the boys, I had to face the daily realities. The numbers on the chart were always there whether the body cooperated or not. Before we left, I had sliced up some RockTape and applied it to my foot. The intersection of the two pieces of tape rubbed the ball of my foot, and I worried about blisters. But I couldn't let them see my fear. This was a man's run, and I was going to pass the test, same as them.

Mags has a three-hundred-foot elevation increase over the course of its seven-mile run out to the highway, but you wouldn't know it from the start. We started downhill, joking and laughing, drinking in the peaks that towered all around. We had agreed to keep the group tight and the pace easy through halfway. Then we would put the hammers down for the second half and test our collective form. Despite the genial beginning, I knew what was coming. Just over a half mile in, the road kicks uphill for a good six hundred meters and the real running begins. Just like the year before, the incline knocked my face off. I immediately dropped back and went to the shuffle, a respectful degradation of pace reserved for survival. The thoroughbreds just took it in stride. The strong men—Marcus, Tony, and Peter—were quickly joined by Timmy J at the front. The year before Tim had climbed into our support vehicle at the base of this first climb. Later that night, a visit to the emergency room confirmed that he had mono. Now he ran easily, glad to be back in the fold and comfortable with his boys around him.

As the run went on, the hills failed to shock as much, and the group's rhythm increased. The dreary weather and intermittent sprinkles proved a welcome relief compared with the scorching weather of the year before. Again, I could feel the closeness. I ran alongside Jimmy Mac, my trusted alum, and fell into easy talk and happy associations. We had performed similar rituals together when I was a young coach and he was an emerging star. The elapsed time had done nothing to decrease the bond. Amid the mountain peaks and the difficulty, our center remained as strong as ever. Watching the current boys, I wished they knew how deep it could all get later, the meaning our intertwined lives could still bring when the runs were all played out and the seasons' stories were all spun.

As we kicked down a long incline near the five-mile mark, I looked up the road and saw the Fab Five locked in tight formation. In the high meadow the views extended miles in every direction, christened at intermittent spots by snowcapped peaks. Up ahead, I saw Meincke split off to the side laughing—either the prankster or the pranked—and Tony gave him a playful shove. Such interplay had been the framing experience of my youth. The six men I ran with in high school remain the six closest friends in my life. On those long ago runs with Johnny B, Awesome A, Verstraete, Funk, Pankey, and Roehr, I had done the same. With them I still had the instant rapport and comfort of assumed friendship. We could be apart for years, see each other for an instant, and immediately step back into a groove. The difficulty of it all—the training, the heartbreak of our bad races, the edification of our best, the yearning—had made the bonds timeless. If they only knew . . .

Jogging with Jimmy Mac, so many years after we had bonded on the run, I realized I would never have to tell them. At the end of this whole journey, somewhere past the state meet and the concrete doing of it all, the bonds would persist, informed by memory. Their play and turmoil on this road was all. It was as big and real as the tangible mountains, dwarfing the simplicity and vacuity of the task we supposed we were really about. In their youth, winning a race would appear to be their end. Later, wisdom would reveal the means as the end, the goal incarnate, with no need of tangibility. Even in their powerful youth, striding along at eight thousand feet I bet they could sense it, too, like a wisp of intuition floating in the breeze.

Bad foot and all, I finished our jaunt out to the Peak to Peak Highway mid-pack and feeling strong. The foot ached as usual, but my spirits rose to match the elevation. We jogged across the road to look at the continuing trails that sprouted on the other side. We briefly contemplated a run into foreign country, but decided getting lost while exhausted and without water wouldn't be a smart proposition. While we looked at the map, American marathon and 10,000 meter ace Fernando Cabada reached the end of Mags, briefly nodded his head at us, and then took a right down the highway. Such casual encounters were common in Boulder. The year before we had shared runs with Jorge Torres and Pat Rizzo, a Schaumburg alumnus who later finished thirteenth at the 2012 American marathon trials. If we wanted to be in shape and elite, we clearly had come to the right place.

As the rest of the team straggled in, we gathered our exhausted selves and prepared for the real test. Magnolia Road actually loses elevation from its end to its beginning, but after a net elevation gain on the way out, the return would still be devilish. I could see in the eyes of a few newcomers— Prodigy, Mars, Devo, and Squeo—that there was no way they were making fourteen. We agreed to have Steve Johnson pick them up at the ten-mile mark and bid adieu.

Immediately on the return, the Fab Five got down to business. Even Meincke, usually a long-run hater, attacked with vigor. The easy memories and collegial groupings of the early run evaporated. The return would be defined by the traumatic bonds of heaving struggle. The way out had yielded casual memories that could only be fused by the shared torment of the return. Quickly I lost sight of the group as they hammered the first uphill, a devilish eight-hundred-meter ascent, and vanished around the curve.

Jimmy Mac and I settled in for the long haul. By ten miles my foot ached palpably. Jimmy dragged beside me as we kept the shuffle in motion. When the limp started in the last two miles, I shrugged it off as best I could. There would be no more physiological gains. Making it would be all. I had never seen Jimmy so bereft. After moving to Chicago from Palatine, his running had suffered, and he had arrived at this training camp well off form. His usual bouncy stride flattened into a shambles as we strode along silently.

As we emerged from the heights one last time, we finally caught sight of the Fab Five. The decline we had enjoyed at the run's outset proved to be a forgotten challenge. Across the mile of ground between us, I spied Marcus and Tony hammering up the last incline with Monkey, Peter, and Timmy J just behind. They ran in a single-file line, suffering in unison. In six months the same five would have to attack a similar psychic incline in the finish of the Illinois state meet. My whole body shivered at the connection. The hairs on my arms rose, and I attacked the final rise with as much vigor as I could muster, limping badly but driven by the image to dig a little deeper. With a quarter mile to go I could see all five of them stopped now and cheering wildly for us to finish. After fourteen miles of exertion and the pain of a mangled foot, my speed was gone, but my spirits soared.

The next day we packed up our things and left the Silver Saddle and Boulder behind. The drive up to Estes Park was a charming one, full of manic cyclists hammering out on the highway and magnificent views of the emerging Rockies. Our journeys into Rocky Mountain National Park would take us even farther toward what we needed to find, but the first inklings of discovery had been revealed out on Magnolia Road.

I had flown halfway across the United States, leaving my pregnant wife and two young children at home, because I was looking for something. As I struggled to that finish line, slapped those high fives, and stood atop a boulder to cheer on the rest, I couldn't tell you what I wanted, but it was on the tip of my lips. The indefinable piece of mystery we had all come to find reared its nebulous head and floated around us out on Magnolia Road. In the coming days, I wanted more. I wanted to touch it, master it, and bend it to our will. If we played it right, the spirit would serve us well in the tight moments. I wanted no more mountain mysteries. Somewhere up in the highlands, there would be clarity.

CUB LAKE

The "Fab Five" pose at over eleven thousand feet in Rocky Mountain National Park. From the left, Peter Tomkiewicz, Tim Johnson, Marcus Garcia, Tim Meincke, and Anthony Gregorio.

Sometimes silence is the center of all things. It's a powerful mistress, a brazen declaration, a whim. The descent of the trail that day was rocky and dangerous. The sun shone brightly, but spiky boulders rendered the path uneven. The group strung out badly. Up ahead Tony and Marcus ran with urgency, and the tail of the group could barely see the head. The descending path wound quickly through the curving bend, lending a first glance of the lake, covered in lily pads and bedazzled in late-afternoon sunlight. Unlike the other "sights" we had seen that day, there was no rushing water, no epic force, no smallness of man next to nature. Oezel

Falls had been all brutal discharge, a rushing torrent blasting from the side of a mountain. Cub Lake quivered slightly, but offered little else.

Ahead of me I focused on Timmy J's feet as I looked squarely at the trail. Stealing a glance meant almost certain doom in such a rocky descent. All I heard was the slight crunch of rhythm, the metronomic pattern of feet, rubber on the trail, element to element. Reaching the bottom, the trail smoothed and the dense boulders became more sparse and were replaced by soft pine needles. The soft crunch became a padding. The men ran with merely a shiver. Up front Tony and Marcus disappeared, drawn into a rush. My anger spiked. In their haste, they had run right by the lake. I figured it was marked on the map for a reason.

Then I realized why. I heard the cavernous silence. It drew me with a force I had not felt in some time. I had to stop. I needed the silence. I called a halt and drew the leaders back to the group. The front trio padded dutifully back, a bit upset at the interruption in rhythm after such a long and tricky descent. I called the guys into a circle.

I told them, "I'm going to give you guys a big treat. Just humor me. Let's spend ten minutes here along the lake in silence. Everybody spread out." A bit shocked, but willing to play along, they dutifully scoped out spots amid the shaded pines.

As they fanned out, I jogged backward up the trail. I had picked out my rock the second I thought of the exercise. I left the group and proceeded quietly off the pine-needled trail to a large boulder that jutted out into the sun-splayed lake. I scrambled up carefully and drew my knees up toward my chest. I took off my watch and threw it on the ground along with my map.

If only I could describe to you the angle of the sun, the brilliant reflection of the lake, the swinging of the lily pads in the faint breeze. If only I could show you the snowcaps, framed by the V-shaped descents of the lesser peaks. If only I could describe their lordly display in earnest, with more urgency in my voice and a flame in my eyes. If only I could tell you how much I admired the trees on the far bank, especially the young ones, the light green firs emerging into beauty alongside their more weathered brethren. If I could tell you, you would be there.

But being there never has to do with seeing it. The images—the mountains and the sun, the glimmer and the ghosts, the heartbreak and the runaway—are pictures we think we know. But only experience could do justice to that perfect cavern of silence. Words cannot express true negation. They exist as tangible digits waiting to form rational sense. They can't fully describe the power of nothing at all.

Trust me. I submitted to the little lake and its silent charms. It spoke to me as only a colossal silence truly can. Ever since the summer started I had been adrift in a sea of wrong directions. My wife and I bemoaned our lack of an adult life. We complained about how the pregnancy was keeping us from enjoying our older kids and traveling. We wished that Madeline and Christopher were older so that we could do more interesting activities and see the "real" world. While sitting on that rock, I heard myself wishing for a future life, one I could fast-forward to rather than live toward. If we won the state title, I'd be happy. If we had more money and freedom this summer, we'd be happy. If we could just be somewhere other than where we were, life would be better. I had been living in a sea of contingencies with no idea that I was swimming upstream against a rushing torrent of shaded realities.

After about ten minutes, I asked the big questions: *Why am I here? Why am I sitting on this rock, at eight thousand feet, half a continent away from home? What am I looking for?* It was only at that exact moment that I knew what I wanted out of this cross country season, out of my life, out of my wife, out of my kids, out of my career, out of my coaching. I wanted to enjoy my time with these people—my family and the guys—realizing suddenly just how ephemeral that time was. The need to win, to work harder, to do more just drifted away within the space of a lazy ripple. I ran because I loved these guys. I wanted to see our efforts as the exponential fury of our passionate drift. To run with such ardor and connection would be freedom itself.

I will never quite forget the silence that saved my summer. The sun's arc kept tracing downward toward the snowy peaks, and I knew that my time was short. In that moment I realized time had ceased inside the pocket of that gracious silence. I had been there forever and a moment. The brilliant sun and the glimmering ripples. The forest and the rock. The mountain and the trail. They had been there much longer than I and carried the weight of that wisdom. The entire scene was a call to being. A humble portrait of eternity. All of it was just sitting there on Cub Lake waiting for fourteen restless pairs of eyes to give a moment's consideration.

I stood up and brushed myself off. I jumped into the nearby bush and retrieved my watch and the map. Then I turned around to see it one last time. Standing there enveloped in the caress of the silent lake, I knew that I had received what I had come to find. With that in hand I walked slowly back up the trail. I found the guys seated near the less brilliant end of the lake and hoped that they hadn't just spent the time chatting. After watching them giggle, I guessed that Monkey had screwed off the whole time, like a student forced to study, but I hoped that hadn't been the case. I pulled everyone in and tried to tell them what I had been thinking. It came out all wrong. I just couldn't pull the trigger. We continued down the trail.

But I just could not let it go. Marcus, Steve Johnson, and I had spent some time earlier that morning sitting in a creek near the Wild Basin Trailhead. The rest of the guys had gone to the car, but we lingered. The creek water froze our feet almost instantly with its newly thawed power, but we played at it, sitting on boulders in the middle of the creek and dipping our feet in with momentary splashes before cringing and retrieving them back into the sun. Marcus and I sat there lazily before Steve ran up with the fire in his eyes. He wore this look only when he got really pumped up. He plopped down on a log that had fallen astride the creek and spent a minute absorbing the silence. Finally he looked at both of us and declared, "Guys, I don't know who I would be without running."

He then told us a story I will always remember. He had recently traveled abroad for Hollister to Copenhagen, Denmark. At first I was excited when he began to talk because I had yearned to be abroad and away from my mundane life. But his story was not about that. While traveling alone and far from home, he had seen many supposedly interesting sites, but each one left him feeling more spiritually dead. The entire experience had been like walking around inside an inch-thick glass cage. He could see it all, yet felt nothing. Yet here, out on the trail to Oezel Falls, he found a spark. You could see it riding in his eyes. While we cavorted high up on the mountain throwing snowballs and sliding down the immense drifts, he had stayed near the trailhead and run intervals. All alone and in love.

His story ran repeatedly through my head as I joined the group in the rocky descent from Cub Lake. Both his experience and mine sat at the same center. For both of us, joy and purpose intersected in the act of running. The physical and the spiritual coalesced. Sharing it with other people only intensified the connection. After considering his story, I knew what I was doing out here with these high school guys. I knew why Jimmy was out here so many years later. I stopped the group again near another small pond and arranged them on a boulder outcropping.

Only twelve of the guys and two of the coaches made it out to that rock and heard my talk. Coach Sheehan and Devo had to walk that afternoon because of injured feet. Prodigy was too young to come that far on a second run. I knew that this was the moment of our trip, and it had to happen far out here on the ragged edge of this basin, next to a quiet pond amid the fading rays of a brilliant sun.

After a carefully orchestrated pause, I let it out. There had been too much complaining on the trip thus far, too much moaning and petty fighting. It had to stop. I told them how I had used my time at the lake to think about our purpose. No one joined the cross country team or came on a trip like this because it was easy. Everyone was searching. None of them would go through all of this suffering because what they were looking for was easy to find.

I then related to them Mr. J's story about Copenhagen. For good measure I added the coda. That morning while we were up throwing snowballs near Oezel Falls, he stayed down near the trail's bottom and ran intervals by himself. I could understand that. We all could. When I go out and ride a bike, I can't embrace the pain. I quit before it hurts. But when I run, I lust for the pain. I want it to render me so full of hurt that I know that I am alive. And I want to feel that hurt with others around me. I paused for a second, seeing that I had their rapt attention. Here it was, the simple moral. Guys, we get to do this together. What is winning a race next to the incredible power we all feel when we are together? Everyone here is looking for something, and I know now what that is for me. I want to be with you.

I had a lot more to tell them out there on that rock, but I left the rest of the story to the look in my eyes. I loved these guys, I loved their fore-bears, and I would love the ones I hadn't even met. I did not feel ashamed to tell them that I loved them. The declaration crossed all the lines of professionalism and broke all codes into a shambles. So what. Love is real. The only bigger disservice to them would be sheltering it and scorn-ing it in the face of "rules and regulations."

In the end I hoped that it was love that got us to the line in the state meet, not a better set of intervals or a smarter race plan. If we loved one another and the run hard enough, someday the biggest win of all would come to us. For now, winning was the enemy. It haunted our purpose and diminished our acts. To spend all of my time thinking of winning was to miss what I truly loved. The guys. The doing of it together, each day, day after day. The guys and the pursuit were continuous. If we did it this way, then the season could never end. Somewhere out on the lake I had tapped into the mysticism of the task.

Sitting on that outcropping far from home, more than a few of them cried, too. They felt it. Why else would they have flown to Colorado to endure two hours of running each day, with most of it at eight thousand feet? Who else would put their bodies on the line in the hill intervals I was going to surprise them with the next morning? Why else would they tape together the broken parts and pour their patchwork selves into the run? The exercise made us whole. They were the purity of the run.

We ran out the trail and found Prodigy, Devo, and Coach Sheehan standing in the freezing shallows near the Cub Lake Trailhead. Steve J filmed us as we chugged up the final ascent, and Tony and I crushed the pace as the run came to an end. I felt joyous and free and Tony laughed and said, "Chris Quick taking it to the house!" I pointed my finger skyward and ran the trail out through its final bridge.

As we crashed to a halt, I made it a point to shake hands and look each guy in the eye. For the emerging juniors, this had been a first dose of heavy varsity emotion. I hoped they understood now why the team meant so much to the departing seniors each year. For Marcus, I looked him straight in the eye and gave him a half hug. This trip had brought us closer. Time had deepened our loyalties, and I was glad for it. My talk had sealed what we had both been feeling. Same with Timmy J, Tony, Peter, and Monkey. Our sense of mission was powerful, but I also knew that our bonds were deepening. If being together was the payoff, today had been a good day.

The handshake that mattered the most came from Jimmy Mac. In typical James fashion, he just said, "Thanks, Quick." James had always sought solace in the run, and there was little that could mean more to me than sharing those powerful moments with him. I had loved him with veracity for years and knew that our connection had only deepened. The fact that he was still out here with me, running and laughing, betrayed a devout commitment that only the best Palatine guys demonstrated.

I stopped for one last handshake as I caught Joey Mars staring upstream. More than any of the others, he found something important up on Cub Lake. Joey had been through a lot in his family life lately, and he intimated near the end of the track season how hard the spring had been and how much he was suffering inside. He just looked me in the eye and said, "I don't ever want to leave this place."

I had no idea what went through each guy's head while we sat next to Cub Lake. Some found depth. Some found boredom. Others felt at peace. Whatever happened, those thoughts are theirs. I certainly found my center. For some reason I had always known that love is what really kept the whole thing going, but I had rarely put it into words or shown it so nakedly. It felt good. It felt true and honest and simple, like all good things. The silence out on that lake prompted me to speak what I had been dying to say. These people were what I was looking for, and I was happy to have found all of them just when I needed them most.

OLD FALL RIVER ROAD

The varsity team poses before heading up Old Fall River Road for the annual challenge run.

Two days after that revelation, we prepared for the final ritual of the trip. The morning of the varsity challenge run I lay awake in bed long before the alarm went off. I peeked out my window just waiting for the first glimpse of light to crest the Rocky Mountain foothills to the east. It was still dark, but my eyes felt intense and awake. The motor in my head ran with anticipation and fear. Even I was not sure that I could do the task I had set for the boys. There in bed I began the bargaining of the long-distance runner. How hard would I push? I was not training for anything. It would be perfectly acceptable for me to take it a little easier, to minimize the pain.

I put my feet on the floor and went over to the dresser to check the time: 5:07 AM. Wake-up call for the boys was in twenty minutes, and I crept out so Coach Sheehan could finish whatever sleep there was left. I slipped on the last of my clothes, the ones I had saved for this specific run: mesh racing socks, my short racing shorts, and my sweated-out Palatine XC long-sleeve. The back simply read, CHAMPIONSHIP STANDARDS = CHAMPIONSHIP RESULTS. I hoped I could live that motto on the way up the mountain. I crept through the early stillness in our cabin (named Golden Eagle because it was much sweeter than the Bald Eagle Cabin across the drive). Our porch faced to the south and the east, and I sat down to freeze and shiver in my favorite spot.

The first glimpses of daylight were coming over Estes Park to our east, but no one at the YMCA of the Rockies would directly see the sun's rays for another hour. The rays huddled behind the smaller mountains to the east of the Estes Park Reservoir, and I pulled my knees up close to shelter myself from the cold. I turned to contemplation. The trip had succeeded beyond my wildest dreams. The trails and hikes around Rocky Mountain National Park had been stunning, full of beautiful sights and animal life. I knew the boys had cherished their time together, and I hoped our final run would be the lasting memory of the trip.

I looked across the valley to the southeast and wondered what would have happened if we had pulled off our first choice for the challenge run. Just across from our cabin a lonely residential road snaked up the next mountain over, leading the residents ever upward through fifteen to twenty devastating switchbacks en route to their mountain homes. I had wanted to run it ever since I saw it, but the road was closed to the public, and we had to look elsewhere. The problem was complex. Even in late June most of the roads and trails above ten thousand feet were penned in by snow. We needed to find some real uphill distance. Until a stroke of luck, our search for the perfect challenge had been stymied.

Two days prior to the final run, Coach Sheehan, Steve J, and I spread out our topographic map of Rocky Mountain National Park on the broad kitchen table and tried to find the perfect run. We had driven up to twelve thousand feet on Trail Ridge Road, but it was absolutely frightening to drive, much less run. There were no shoulders, and the road dropped off precipitously at certain points. Coach Sheehan had exited his van in a cold sweat after driving through one portion where a single swerve would have taken our rental van down a cliff on either side of the road. Running the main highway was not an option.

Running on any of the myriad trail systems also proved unsafe. We would not be able to offer the athletes water or medical assistance if anyone suffered dehydration or an injury. After thirty minutes of scanning the map, my eyes alit on Old Fall River Road. The terminus of the road was down around 7,800 feet, but it appeared to rise all the way to the ranger station at 11,700 feet. Further investigation revealed that this had once been the main road for vehicular traffic through the park. Upon the building of Trail Ridge Road, it had been largely decommissioned for cars, but still existed as a gravel trail for hikers. We were in business.

I drove to the visitors center at the Beaver Creek entrance, hoping against hope that the trail would be clear of snow and available for some real uphill running. The nice young woman at the desk quickly dashed our hopes. Her trail log indicated that no one had hiked it beyond a mile due to snowbanks and impassable terrain. My heart sank. Every year the challenge run was the culminating experience of the varsity trip, but now we had nothing.

We decided to persevere and check out the trail for ourselves. We fooled the guys into thinking that we were going for an easy trail run, but instead sprang a series of hill repeats on them. We told them at the beginning of the trip that we would do one thing that they would not expect and one thing that would be near impossible. The hill repeats were the former. We parked in the adjoining parking lot, which butted up against Fall River, and the guys calmly (some grimly) prepared for the arduous workout. We gave them a simple bargain that doubled as a means of escape. The hill repeats would be a workout without coaches. They could decide how many they wanted to do while we went off and jogged on our own. They took the change in stride, and we left them alone to run savage repeats on the opening incline of Old Fall River Road.

The trailhead was a simple gate at the bottom of a gravel path. One directional sign marked the trail. It was a speed limit sign setting the speed at fifteen miles per hour. Beneath it was an arrow, pointing heavenward, that declared NEXT 9 MILES. ONE WAY. UPHILL ONLY. The boys thought we were just here to run hills. Really, I hoped and prayed that we could run this trail all the way to the top, right up to the heavens and the Alpine Visitors Center at 11,700 feet. As the boys started the workout, Jimmy Mac and I set off at a jog up the road. The lack of oxygen slammed both of us, and we immediately gasped even at a light jog. We reached the point where the boys would finish each hill repeat and gazed across the gorgeous valley to the south. The early-morning sun bathed the valley, and I thanked my lucky stars for the opportunity to be in this place. Jimmy and I turned uphill and ran.

About ten minutes in, we jogged luckily into our first piece of hope. Two rangers were up the trail in their truck, and we stopped to inquire how far the trail was open. They had not been up the trail in nearly a week, but they had just made it two miles before they hit snow. Since Old Fall River Road ran on the north side of the valley, its surface was exposed to the sun. It was melting quicker than other areas of the park. We continued jogging uphill, going steady for two minutes and then walking for one. We felt ashamed at the concession, but the going was brutal.

Past the first pair of switchbacks, we spied a fit woman jogging above us and recognized immediately the shape of a real runner. I drive around Palatine all the time evaluating people's running forms, and I knew right then that she would know how far the trail went. She looked like one of those trail runners you see in *Running Times*. She told us, "The trail is open to at least five miles if you are willing to scramble over some snowdrifts." She had just run the whole thing and looked none the worse for wear.

We knew then that the challenge run tradition would continue and that we had conceived the granddaddy of them all. The year before up Blue Ridge Road had been phenomenally difficult—beautiful, poetic, and grotesque all at once. I had collected some of the most enduring memories of my life on that run. Running that mountain with Reuben, A. J., Kuersch, and McGough created a lasting bond. I remembered men pulling off to throw up and then continuing. I remembered the soft slipperiness of the muddy road and the intermittent boulders. I remembered the exact moment that I emerged above the fog and saw that wonderful blanket of low-hanging clouds quilting the valley below. The sun, the snow-white soup of clouds, the pain all wove together to frame a group in full drive. Finishing that run with those boys created a bond I would never relinquish. I hoped this would have the same effect.

Reflection aside, I looked at my watch and noted that it was go time: 5:31 AM. The wake-up call provoked a grim response. Halfway groggy and halfway scared, the boys pulled on their gear and climbed slowly up the stairs from the basement. Right away I saw that Marcus Garcia wore the intensity on his face. A year ago, he and I had climbed the last impossible mile of the Blue Ridge together. He stopped to dry-heave just past the last rocky switchback, but he never quit. When we hit the false flat at the top, both of us threw it into one last gear and smashed it to the finish. This trip had only intensified our bond as we swapped iPods and told filthy jokes. I knew he would kill it up the mountain.

Slowly the guys grabbed their Gatorades and walked out into the early-morning dark. The chill in the air knocked more than a few off stride, and most came jogging back in to grab a long-sleeved shirt or a stocking hat. For our final drive of the trip we chose Nine Inch Nails' series of Ghost records—a perfect soundtrack for the brooding concentration that took over the van. The quiet dominated as each guy locked in to fear and apprehension. None of them knew where we were heading. Most had built a legend in their head of what this run would be, and they were all left to face the ghosts of their own creation.

On the way in to Estes Park we passed by the snazzy German restaurant that sat creekside and watched the torrid rush of the mountain streams for one last time. The furious snowmelt of early June had turned the local waterways into raging cascades of nearly frozen water. Absorbed in the music and the beauty of the creek, I nearly missed the obvious. A gigantic elk, with a massive rack of antlers and a newborn following it, stood on the shoulder of the road. I slowed to a crawl, hoping it wouldn't attack the van or bolt. Instead it stood its ground, anesthetized to the dangers of humanity so near the luscious sanctuary of the park. We crept up to it in our van so close that Marcus could have touched it out his passenger-side window. Its gigantic glassy eye scanned the window before the great beast dropped its snout and casually went about eating its breakfast. We drove quietly past before bursting into laughter.

We continued into the park, taking a new way to an old place. As soon as I took the left-hand turn, the thinking men on the team knew what was up. We drove west down the same road we had traveled on Thursday, through the alluvial fan caused by the 1982 flood and right back to the base of the hill. The flashbacks began. The painful memories of Thursday's workout had not subsided, but little did they know that the same hill continued for nine miles at the same grade. This time, there would be no rest. This time we were going uphill until we could go no more.

Coach Johnson had volunteered to mule some Gatorade up the mountain, so we were surprised to run into him at the base of the climb. As they huddled in a semicircle near the gate and the speed limit sign, I let them in on the metaphor: "Each year the challenge run is a symbol of what we hope our season can be. The challenge is tough just like winning a state title is tough. This run is going to be a lot like the season. You will have mental ups and downs. You will face pain and hardship. You will have setbacks and then regain momentum. The most important part of the journey is to keep going. Nobody quits. Everyone is going to the top except Graham. Graham, you try to make it through the three-mile mark at least.

"According to the trail runner we met, it is over five miles until you hit the snowpack. When we can't go anymore, the run is over. There are some small drifts that we can scramble over, but our runner friend told us that we would know the end when we saw it. That point is somewhere up this road at an altitude of eleven thousand feet. Last year, we climbed fourteen hundred feet in just under five miles. This year we're doing the same distance, but doubling the climb. No one runs alone. Find a partner and stick. You can walk if you need to, but the challenge is to stay moving the entire time."

After listening patiently, the guys got into battle mode. A few shed their sweatshirts or ditched their sweats. The emerging juniors—Mars, Squeo, Stella, Clingerman—had a slight tinge of fear in their eyes. Tony Gregorio was pissed. Like usual, he had to go #2 but couldn't get it done. The rest of us had to live each day with Tony's overactive colon so we delighted in his grumpiness. With all the talking aside, we headed straight up with no end in sight.

I will remember certain aspects of this run for the rest of my life. My first memory was a near flashback. A year before I had started in last with Brian Smith, then a sophomore, and we'd proceeded to pick off the early burners due to our measured pace. Here we were, a year later and stronger, starting out in the back again. At that moment all anyone could hear was the delicate crunch of footsteps and the labored respiration. On our right side the foreboding cliffs of the mountain towered above us, threatening to rain down boulders. To our left we could see across the valley. A raging creek split the two mountains, and its throttling chorus accompanied our every move. Two days previous I had run up high enough to see the origins of the creek, to the exact moment where you could see the snow melting on the mountainside and cascading in an elegant waterfall from high above. I hoped the boys would savor that sight as much as I had.

Past the top of the first rise, the terrain became virgin territory for everyone but the coaches. Timmy J and Marcus quickly started killing it off the front while my other two senior leaders—Monkey and Peter—passed me with the hammer down about ten minutes in. Tony was nowhere to be seen. Finally at the first bridge he came tearing past, screaming something about "goddamn pooping in the woods, my stomach is killing me, yadda yadda yadda . . ." His anger fueled my drive for a moment or two, but I quickly settled back in.

The pain and the climb were relentless. A more poetic writer once referred to this pain as the "loneliness of the long distance runner." I assured the boys that it was okay to walk and recover if necessary. None of them would. In fact most of them probably hated that I'd even mentioned the option. None of them was going to walk, not when this was the ultimate test. Any man who truly runs long distance knows that he can make the pain stop at any moment in time. The real truth was that we all had a wicked love affair with the pain, with the pulsing reminiscence of a calm breath, with the gasping drive for more air, with the ultimate sadistic burn. Distance guys want the pain.

The first set of switchbacks blew my legs to pieces. Our struggle was writ large all over the mountain. Even the strongest among us labored grievously. I saw the boys arrayed above me as the trail switched savagely up. The normally large group dissolved into dribs and drabs, pairs of souls clinging to one another for life and motive. My body turned to trash, a staggering mass of confusion. The thin air played the role of torturer. The lungs heaved at the same rate, but drank in far less oxygen than normal. All I could do was concentrate. One foot. The other. One foot. The other. One foot. The other. One foot. The other. Solace laid only within the single step.

Past the mile mark I linked up with Tyler Squeo. Tyler is affectionately known within the team as "Squeef," a mixture of old-time juvenile humor and hardwired truth. Squeo is a feisty little booger, a bit annoying at his best, and he had earned his filthy nickname early on and for good reason. What Squeo lacked in talent, he certainly made up for in will and spirit. I was glad to find him because the suffering extended deeper than I could imagine. The uphill surged relentlessly, leveling out a bit before kicking again and again. Each corner yielded more desolation, more gravel to crunch, more climb and less oxygen.

In normal circumstances the scenery would be sublime, a mixture of awe and wonder. To see it while running was to enjoy something more aesthetically grotesque. The south face of the valley shone starkly in the now rising sunlight, snowcaps glistening above the tree line. Around the two-mile mark the boys saw one of the origin points of the raging river that thrummed quickly below, some five hundred feet down the cliff. Water first trickled, then poured into a cascading fall that bathed the mountains in mist and spray, seeking its way to the bottom. No matter how beautiful or how pleasing, it all came through the same human filters, all overtaken by the pain.

I gasped at Tyler as often as I could, beckoning him to look around and take it in, but his concentration was intense. Slowly and steadily we climbed by most of the team—first Mars and Clinger, then Coach Sheehan and Jimmy Mac, then Smitty and Noah. We did not run fast, but we clung to each other. I knew that if we split up I would crack.

After nearly twenty-five minutes of running, a little over two miles, I witnessed the most depressing scene I could imagine. The leaders were stopped in front of an impenetrable mass of snow. Disappointment overtook me. How could it be done when we had so much left to give? Marcus had been leading, and he stood there flabbergasted with a wry grin. This was no small snowbank. The avalanche of snow had apparently washed away the road, taking with it trees and massive boulders. Gigantic pines stuck out from the middle of the mass, and the road terminated in a litter of broken branches and discarded boulders. I stood atop the drift and looked for the road, but it was gone, vanished under a cold blanket of semi-melted snow and dead trees. No way. This could not be the end.

For a couple of moments we cheered as guys dribbled in alone or in pairs. Marcus was disappointed. We scanned up the cliffside and saw a ledge. Maybe that was the road above us. We decided to climb the drift and see. Ascending the slippery snow in the early-morning chill was neither fun nor safe. But it was crazy, and crazy was what we sought. We set off up the avalanche pile, picking carefully through overrun branches for footholds and wondering what that ultra-trail-running lady had meant when she said that the road was open to five miles. We cursed her openly.

Later, we discovered that peeking over one downed tree would have revealed a switchback to our right. At the time we knew that we could climb the avalanche, but no one had any idea how we would get back down. When we got to the top, we took off running and the decision was final: We were going to ride this run to the limits. The impetus was to keep climbing.

Squeo and I quickly found each other again and fell in line behind the Fab Five. I'd like to say that we happily continued, that the rest of the way was a breeze, but all I remember is the devastation of my muscles and lungs. The searing pit of fire in my lungs scalded each breath. I was not going to walk. No way. Past three miles and ten thousand feet Tyler slowed for a couple of seconds and contemplated stopping. I shot him a glance and gave him a quick word. No way. No walking now, not this far up. I wanted to walk more than anything in the world. I would have sold my soul for a full and easy breath, but the impulse to finish was too strong. He came back.

Nothing I had ever attempted in my life was quite as relentless as that mountain. As we crept toward the tree line, the cold became overpowering. At lower elevations the sun threatened with its warmth, but not here. Here, the sun had failed to melt the winter's snow. The only reminder of a warm thought was the trickle of ice water in the gutter of the road. After stopping once to urinate, I scooped some of the fresh meltwater into my mouth and onto my hat to slap me back toward normality. I still noticed the beauty and the rushing sound of the water and the thinning of the trees, but mostly I just climbed. One foot. The other. One foot. The other. One foot. The other. To quit this mantra would be to quit the challenge. I couldn't believe that the boys were actually doing this with me. A year before Squeo had been one of the most recalcitrant of runners, a man whom I had to push and prod to do even basic work. Here he was a year later suffering with me. Riding the line with him up that mountain is something neither of us will ever forget. We wish the best relationships would be born out of love, but most often they are forged in the heat of pain.

Just past the four-mile marker we saw the first of the snowdrifts. We saw the fresh footsteps of the varsity seniors ahead and scrambled over. Now the way was obscured more and more, first periodically and then constantly, with snow scrambles and drifts. You could tell that the patches of road up this high were newly exposed to the sun. Branches and assorted sticks littered the road. The encumbrances just made the pain worse as we churned through slippery, ankle-deep snowdrifts and jumped stray wooden barriers before resuming whatever rhythm we could manage.

At this elevation the peaks we had gazed at from the trailhead now appeared within our grasp. All around us we could see the fields of snow encasing their crests. The trail ran straight toward them into a gigantic bowl before turning abruptly to the right and heading off to the north, straight uphill at a monster grade. It was right at that turn that we first heard screaming. It snapped me out of a painful trance, and my initial reaction was that someone had been grievously injured. We picked it up and ran toward the source before realizing that the screams were celebratory. Marcus stood atop a gigantic snowdrift screaming his lungs out as he saw his teammates approaching. The run left all of us in a desolate physical condition, but the mood was anything but. We had done it.

There was much hugging and high-fiving and even a few tears as every last one of our guys trickled in to the end. Joe Mars and Christian Zambrano started the run nursing injuries, but persevered all the way to the top. Even Devin Hein, nursing a sprained ankle, sucked it up and ran all the way. We covered more than five and a half miles in just under an hour. A later examination of our finishing spot on the map showed that we reached just over eleven thousand feet before the snow blockaded further running.

With most of the team up, we sought out the sun. Just off the road a gorgeous and semi-swampy clearing opened in the middle of the mountain crescent. All around on three sides, the snowcapped peaks lorded over us, but between them we found an elevated clearing that was bathed in radiant morning sunlight. Arrayed around this circular clearing were a series of stones, and we sat, mostly in quiet, to take it all in. We had won this moment together through dire effort. After a few minutes of muted conversation, we heard a voice through the trees, someone still trapped up on the road. It was then that we saw Prodigy, a week ago just a naive freshman, stumble down the embankment and into the clearing. After depositing his lunch into someone's front yard in Boulder, our incoming freshman star had acquitted himself well. Rumors of his talent and drive had superseded him, but that moment when he burst out of the trees at the top of that mountain sealed the deal. There would be no friction if Graham challenged for a varsity spot. He was one of us.

Graham's arrival brought a wave of cheers and sparked everyone back into revelry. The entire exercise was designed to demolish barriers. Everything we had just done was novel—a new meaning of pain, a new threshold of possibility, a new aesthetic vision regarding the landscapes that surrounded us. More important, we had discovered an animating spirit. If we wanted to see who was in and who was out, we had our answer. Everyone was in. No man would do that run without putting all his chips into the middle of the table and betting big.

We savored our time. We lingered. We watched a delightfully playful bird hop across our circle. We felt the cleanliness of the thin mountain air. We marveled at the sights we had seen and wondered whether we could have made the entire nine miles to the top. We laughed at our craziness. We just sat and soaked it all in. After all, the waiting was worth it. Five and one-half miles back down that road we would find our car, and from there we would find our cabins and then be gone to the airport and home. It would be back to dreariness and diligence from then on, running in the sculpted suburban landscape of places we had already been and runs we had already done.

Before starting the long trek to the bottom, I called the guys into a circle. We would stand in such a circle many times in the season ahead, but this was the first one. I talked to them about the relentless nature of the bond we had just created. Our training in Palatine, although more boring and normal, would be just as relentless. Each man would have to bring effort each day. We talked about holding one another accountable.

More than anything the moment allowed the depth of our task to sink in. Every man had run up a mountain for the cause. We had moved past "trying to win" long before this day, but the run up Old Fall River Road cemented the motive. It was an embrace of common zealotry. We had run with the fervor of revolutionaries. For better or worse, winning the Illinois state championship had just moved from a race we wanted to win to an epic quest.

In that circle I looked each man in the eye. Fused into a motivated whole, the vows we said were the silent kind, the implied kind, ones that spoke far beyond what words could say anyway. The way down was full of impish play, damaged quads, and exhaustion. We stopped and marveled as the river blasted through a tunnel of ice. We enjoyed the feel of the warming sun on our salted skin. Mostly, we enjoyed one another. When we left, the summer and the season would continue on apace, but some piece of this had to be eternal. It was too good to end. The all-consuming quest might be the animating force, but I had an inkling that the potentials of November would also carry a touch of sadness. We were sprinting toward a defined finish line, but no one wanted it to end. It would have to, as all great times do, but jogging down that mountain we all wanted to hold the picture a little longer and savor it all with glee.

THE RAIN RUN

When we returned from Colorado in late June, the summer still had two months of grind to go. Even as the weather intensified and the humidity clung, the mileage demands increased. Through the humdrum days of seventy-mile weeks, through the fifteen-mile days, through recovery days that totaled two hours of running, we persisted. By July the seniors had organized daily second runs at the school without coaches. I'd stop by on our available contact days and fill my chart, too, jogging into the dusk with my boys.

Noah Brown quickly became the face of our summer. A convert from soccer during his junior year, Noah showed a penchant for incredible levels of work. During track he started shadowing the varsity, and no one had dropped him ever since. Something in his inner workings, in his circuitry, made him well adapted for big mileage. Not gifted with a ton of foot speed or the lean musculature of Meincke and Johnson, Noah just kept plugging. By mid-July he crossed the ninety-mile-per-week threshold with no intent of stopping. He would run over that threshold each week until the end of August.

No one knew whether Noah would make the varsity seven, but he drove the training. Few could match his intensity. Marcus missed days here and there, still running, but framing the whole exercise on his own terms. Monkey and Johnson did their work dutifully, learning from long experience that complaining about the volume and the pace led nowhere. They buttoned up into a stoic quietness and did the best they could.

Only Tony and Peter could match Noah. After attending a double run with only a smattering of frosh-soph and JV guys and no varsity, Tony stepped up his leadership. He made the phone calls. He took over the group and threw it on his back, corralling Marcus and inspiring the rest. He wanted all of them to burn with the fire he felt inside, knowing it couldn't be replicated but striving for it nonetheless.

Quietly and off to the side, Peter matched him, stride for stride and mile for mile. Previous divisions were forgotten amid the work. Of all the guys, Peter was the one doing the most mileage "off the books." All of my great made men had done it. They would run with the team on the assigned Early Bird contact days, but then some compulsion would drive them back out the door later on.

More than a few times, I heard a knock at my door around nine o'clock at night and knew that it was Peter. I'd put down my book, grab my running shoes, and hit the pavement with him into the darkness of the summer. Those meandering runs through town were the pleasure of my summer. Even after a ten- or twelve-mile morning, we'd just start talking and moving our legs. We'd haunt the hill over at Riemer Reservoir or the late-night pickup basketball games at Birchwood Park. No matter where we went, the runs took us deeper. Peter no longer needed me to salve the bonds with his teammates, but in each other we found the comfort of a fellow striver. I understood the driving compulsion of a man on the make.

By the end of July I knew that we had driven out to the edge and survived. Meincke showed up with an inflamed iliotibial band, but outside of that we had built the physiology with the poetry and precision of great art. Even at twelve to fifteen miles per day, they thrived. As I left them on their own to observe the required two weeks of "non-contact" in Illinois, I hoped that the ownership was strong enough. It was their team anyway.

While they labored through the one-hundred-mile weeks of early August, I stayed at home with my kids and recharged my batteries. Meredith and I were due to welcome our third child on August 24, and that took some girding. We'd decided to leave the sex of the baby a secret so I busied myself setting up a "neutral" room for the baby while struggling to keep my miles up all alone. With practices for the full team slated to begin on Wednesday, August 9, I laid the plans and concocted the first big test. On the first Saturday, I would bring them in at 9 PM. It was a devilish move.

As I rode my bike to school for that night practice, there was no indication of rain. Instead, the fading summer sun shone in pink and purple gashes as it receded over the houses near the school. Heading through the east gate, my stomach churned with pale nervousness. Tonight's workout was not for the weak, and even I did not know how I would acquit myself. The boys knew nothing about what would be required. The call to practice at night had been unexpected, and this mini drama suffused the morning session with a combination of surefire dread and electric anticipation. They knew it was going to be hard. Running eighteen miles in a day is a tough task for the best-trained runners, much less going to the well way past the time when most people are in for the night watching baseball or sipping lemonade on the back porch.

To preserve the drama I rode by the varsity as they gathered in the parking lot, staying coy, lazily shading by as I drifted out to unlock the track. Coach Sheehan pulled up moments later and fielded their questions regarding the workout. He, too, relished the drama and left the big reveal for me. The workout harked back to an article I read the week before in *Running Times*. The piece profiled Midwest rival Columbus North, Indiana, a unit that placed third in the nation the year before and was the 2011 pre-season national number one. Their coach had proudly shared their toughest workout, and tonight we were going to try it.

We had run quite a few extended tempo sessions before, but this one was different. We would start with a five-mile road run where the last three miles came home at an accelerating pace. From there we would move on to track segments of two miles, one and a half miles, and one mile. Each interval break lasted only five minutes of slow jogging. The rest would be needed because the pace increased as the distance decreased. After eight miles in the morning, these ten miles would say much about the team's character.

The workout was more transitional moment than physical test. The buildup to every season involved work. But this was a different workout for a different time. This night was about engagement rather than commitment. I anticipated a level of emotion that had been missing in our summer work. Engagement requires sacrifice, and asking a group of fourteen teenagers to give up their final Saturday night of the summer surely fit the bill.

I walked my bike back from the track through the lengthening shadows of a Midwest late-summer night. The fading sunlight refracted off the building clouds, blending the creeping indigo blue with passion pinks and purples, the dying embers of the day. From then on we would be creatures of the night. As I walked up to the burgeoning group, I felt their anticipation. Peter had on his NXN race jersey while the other seniors—Garcia, Gregorio, Johnson, and Meincke—had all donned similar regalia. The jerseys showed that they meant business, and my own internal mercury rose in accordance. They were far from bothered by the lateness of the hour and the sacrifice of the moment. Even our varsity newcomers—Zambrano and Smith, Mars and Squeo, Stella and Clingerman—appeared moved by the challenge. They had been through the trials of miles over the past ten weeks, but this run was something else entirely. This peak week for mileage had been virgin territory for most involved. Ten miles of hard running to cap an eighteen-mile day on the back end of a ninety-mile week must have boggled their minds.

The seniors had come to expect this kind of challenge, but even they had to doubt whether they could run the assigned times. For Peter, Marcus, and Tony this night capped a 105-mile week. The past three weeks had all been run on the edge of the envelope, on the thin ribbon that separates greatness from breakdown. Thursday's session of thousand-meter repeats at the course had been expected, but ten miles of long intervals? Tony's steely eyes betrayed that simple mix of resolve, scorn, and slight anger I had come to know and love. I never knew if he loved me or hated me in these moments, but I knew one thing for certain. This was Tony's "fight face." He wore it when he understood the pain of a nearing effort.

The faces of the milers betrayed no such resolve. Johnson stitched on the veneer of confidence that he wore in such moments while Zambrano simply looked bemused and frightened. They would do the workout, but without the sick love of dull pain evinced by the true distance men. The world of the middle-distance runner is more manic electricity than muted current, and both this workout and the preceding weeks lacked in the quick-firing simplicity that the milers loved. For them tonight prescribed more of the same—difficult emotional acceptance mixed with bodily distress on a cellular level. They had to suffer in the company of three true distance runners, all of whom had embarked on a singular quest to be the team's alpha male.

Arriving just a moment late on his road bike, Tim Meincke showed none of his trademark congeniality and good humor. His past two weeks of training had been derailed by iliotibial band syndrome, and we had pulled him from running for a weekend in the hope of averting disaster. He continued to work through it, but his health and our season hung in the balance. Push it too far and it could mean six weeks of inaction. Leave it too late and he would miss fitness he could never regain. Already the leaders of the team knew that our hopes of winning the state title would probably come down to Tim Meincke's performance in the last mile of the state meet. For years he had been a fader. He simply lacked the requisite patience and fitness so necessary over the three-mile distance. It had been our mission to equip him with the tools, but his injury impeded all progress. We stood now at the turning point of his season. Like me, he would be riding the bike for the first five miles before joining the team for the track portion. Sometimes an injured athlete needs to roll the dice and see if injury time is over. I hoped that we would roll big in this workout. Otherwise our season might be over.

After I announced the workout amid the small cluster of cars in the deserted parking lot, everyone dispersed to pursue the last rites of men readying themselves for large doses of self-inflicted pain. Marcus knelt down to retie his shoes and secure the right tightness across the bridge of his foot. Tony stood and cracked his neck. The others stashed their warm-up shirts in one another's cars. Much of the effort this night would be far from maximal, but that changed nothing. The workout would build toward a symphony of self-destruction.

As we took off down the first blocks of the Morning Loop, the difference in tone was pronounced. Usually our warm-up and recovery runs resounded with chattiness and the sound of young men joking away the coming effort. As we drifted through the last shreds of light into the dark tunnel of the sidewalk, the pace slowed to a veritable dawdle. Only the dull silence of concerted foot strikes interrupted the concentration. I rode silently in the street, watching the sparse neighborhood traffic as Coach Sheehan drove his Ford Escape in support.

At the turn onto Hicks Road, the boys snaked around the electric box and the pace quickened. This slightly downhill section of the Loop had seen many accelerations over the years, and this time was no different. The tempo would not start until the two-mile mark outside Popeye's Chicken on Northwest Highway, but on Hicks the run acquired the tone of young men moved to industrious action. Garcia and Tomkiewicz led through the mile mark in a pedestrian 7:45 mile pace. Back in the pack the juniors nipped at the heels of their older teammates, afraid of the coming pace but looking for early action.

Gregorio took over from Garcia just past the bike path and kept the pace at an even keel. Marcus's need to lead usually edged our runs into the red zone far earlier than anticipated. Every team has a pace-pusher. Marcus was ours. He treated tempo runs like he was a cascading torrent of water rushing down a series of rapids. Each step trended toward acceleration; each slight surge by a teammate provoked a subtle rush of more pace, more pace. Before long the group would hurtle along at the behest of his efficient ferocity. When the rapids hit their peak, the water would hurl from the mountainside, and the run would rip until it plummeted back to earth. Running with Marcus involved a marked appreciation of his fluid intensity, but also a fine knowledge of the warning signals of an impending rush. Like Tony, I recognized Marcus's too-early pace impulse. This night held no room for too fast too soon.

As we approached the takeoff point, the fear from the back end became apparent. Although they had been assigned paces varying from 6:00 to 6:20 per mile for their first segment, they knew that holding back also betrayed weakness. Each man competing for the fifth, sixth, and seventh spots knew a sad truth: Controlled and consistent training was the most logical road to the varsity seven, but only guts and panache could convince the coaches and team captains. At the assigned mark, the pace jumped abruptly like a driver edging up on the gas pedal of a high-performance automobile. Peter, Marcus, and Tony revved their newly acquired engines and happily took them out for a ride. They cared about the team, but each man could only gain the champion's edge by showing his dominance.

The early pace down Northwest Highway destroyed the back end. At the turn onto Rohlwing Road, the front four remained together with the rest of the varsity safely ensconced in their assigned groups. Now running fully in the dark down the uneven sidewalks, they simply glided away. The Morning Loop has its own rhythm, and they carefully acted out the script—shooting the downhill past the split-rail fence, carefully blasting through traffic at Palatine Road, then crossing over to the east side of the street for the last mile. Their faces betrayed no effort. Eyes straight ahead. Jaws relaxed. Maximum efficiency.

After tailing the back end through the four-mile mark, I headed toward the front at full steam. I raced through the murky yellow shadows cast by the streetlights and rode hard with knees driving, reveling in the infectious energy of a team going full-bore. When I reached the creek bridge, I felt the first drop of rain. Oblivious to weather reports in my late-summer haze, I'd had no inkling that rain was in the forecast. For a moment I feared lightning and cancellation. That fate did not transpire. This felt like a cleansing rain, the kind that washes the sweat away and provides a respite from the salty sun. The raindrops sprinkled on the road under the streetlights, first in isolated spots, then in patterns, then in clusters, then in droves. As the leaders hit a half mile to go, they flew through the newly drizzled night with their spirits soaring and the pace on cruise control. I rode up alongside and gave them the instructions. First to the school, then five minutes of jogging, then right onto the track for two miles at 5:20 pace. The rain amplified their already elevated spirits.

As we rounded the circle into the Palatine parking lot, the rain hit full volume. The boys streaked toward the light pole in front of the athletic doors, rattling the pole with their open palms as they declared the first interval done. Coach Sheehan parked at the finish, and we all took off our extra clothing and gave ourselves over to our rainy fates. Past a certain level of discomfort, all runners move into kinship with their surroundings. Like Henry David Thoreau said, if the world proved to be mean then we would "get the whole and genuine meanness of it, and publish its meanness to the world." I threw off my now soaked windbreaker and prepared to test my mettle.

We jogged slowly around the front driveway of the school as we cheered the rest of the team to the finish. Graham Brown splashed through the growing puddles en route to completing his first varsity workout. In junior high they canceled runs on rainy days. In high school he had no such luck. With the rest of the group safely in, we jogged lightly toward the track. Meincke joined the top group of four now, and the six of us prepared for the increased pace. Rain cascaded in torrents across the lights in the stadium parking lot. Sheets of warm rain soaked us to the bone in an instant, overwhelming the drains on the track. By the time we reached the starting line, lane one had flooded by the concession stand and the entire backstretch was underwater. When we hit the line, the watches clicked for the two-mile, and the group exploded straight into pace.

Down the backstretch it was clear that Tony and Peter were going to run away from the group. Johnson, Meincke, Garcia, and I ran rhythmically, our Nike Lunar racing flats dancing on pillows of warm water. After the first lap we saw that Timmy J's dad, Steve, had made his way over from their house just up the street to film the workout and shout encouragement. Steve stood at the fifty-yard line reveling joyously in the spirit of the workout. He had left the house without a jacket and stood fully doused, a wild man in touch with his inner child. His reckless joy inspired all of us, and we picked up the pace once again. In Colorado, Steve J started a ritual of chanting "Palatine XC" when something got really good. Seeing him, I told the guys to prepare on three for a power chant. I counted off one, two, three . . . and then we let rip with a blistering "Palatine XC" chant that cut through the cables of rain shaking the track. The chant would remain with us throughout the season, a mantra to invoke when the run or the race got to its best, a wording for feelings that went beyond words.

Tony and Peter were now well clear, and we set about maintaining our rhythm. By lap five I felt the common pain of the lesser runner. My form started to break down, and all three chided me to stay on pace. I decided then to do the counterintuitive move I had taught them: When you start to see it slip away, pick it up. I took the lead. Somewhere in the middle of the interval Zach Gates, All-State the previous spring, showed up and joined us. He and I did our best to cut a path through the storming surface of the track, moving past tempo to our race-level efforts. The trio behind us kept their glide. And the rain kept coming and coming, sheet by sheet. From the backstretch we saw only the silhouettes of the rest as the light from the parking lot strained to find its way over the bleachers and into the stadium. I had hoped this run would be conducted under the ambience of the moon and stars. Instead, we ran as phantoms through the rain.

Straining through the last couple of laps, I tucked back in and relaxed my way to a 10:57 clocking for thirty-two hundred meters. The top duo ran 10:41 and set about running their rest interval in the opposite direction. They cheered us to the finish both as encouragement and as testament to their prowess.

The rain lessened a bit, but now came the time for hard truths. The novelty had worn off. The accrued mileage had run off the last of the day's adrenaline. From then on we would resort to something else entirely for inspiration. We jogged slowly back to the starting line, sloshing through the middle of the north curve and marveling at the scene.

I knew before it started that I probably could not hang with the pace in the next interval. With Tony and Peter already gone, Gates and I did what was required. We couldn't keep the pace, but we could lead it out for the rest. I scorched the first four hundred meters, and that got Marcus's dander up. Heading into lap two he put his head down and charged ahead through the rain alone. On the other side of the track we could see the top two faintly outlined through the din and patter of the storm. Marcus set his target and got moving. Johnson and Meincke valiantly followed him out, but couldn't hold with his sudden fire. They fed off each other, gamely knocking out 5:10 pace deep into the night. I rigged quickly from exhaustion but found rhythm enough to hang with the second group. It was clear from the myriad shouts and manic pace making that everyone was nailing it.

Somewhere near the end of that rep I saw Marcus narrowing in on the top duo, staring them down with laser eyes. Gates and I were running just over 5:20 pace, and he was threatening to lap us. Jogging backward in preparation for their last rep, Tony and Peter joyfully showed me their split: 7:41. Catching them from behind throughout the rep, Marcus finished just in arrears. The rest finished either faster than or right on their times.

I held back and grabbed some extra rest and attached myself to the Stella, Zambrano, Brown, and Smith group. The spirits in this group remained high, but I could sense their doubts about the last rep. Most of these guys had broken 4:50 for the 1600 meter run the previous spring, but trying to break 5:00 on the final rep still did not fit their inner compasses. Even I had no idea what remained in the tank.

We took a running start into the final rep, and it quickly became clear that we all had the magic. The eighty-second laps felt effortless. Zach Stella and I matched strides as we cut a swath through the fading rain. Fully locked in, we increased the pace and started to drive for home.

I could see the powerful legs of the varsity five as they hammered down the homestretch. Their bodies shone only from the waist down. The light leaked in through the chain-link fence and illuminated the piston drive of their legs, the quickened cadence of their arms, and the bounces of each foot strike. With four hundred meters to go, I shifted gears and let out one final burst for the line.

In its best moments the act of running separates from its actual doing. It is as if consciousness itself can no longer process such a strong combination of movement and joy. In such moments the runner's spirit dances outside and around the body, enveloping the physical being inside a cocoon of possibility. To be on a great rep, a great run, or a great workout is to feel divine inspiration. On most days we are all conscious of the slog. The ennui of the committed runner overpowers the spirit more often than not. But in his finest hour the runner gets to momentarily touch his true force. It's the moment that keeps us all coming back.

As I drove for home in what we all hoped would be the greatest of all Palatine seasons, I wondered at the inspiration these boys provided. I had left my own running career for dead, but here I was hammering paces I had never run in my life. I finished the final rep in 5:13. Three weeks later, I would run a half-marathon in 1:16.43, an average of 5:49 per mile. I had ceased to be a passive actor in my own career. Like mine, their results on the final rep were stunning. Marcus finished the final sixteen hundred in 4:45 while Tony and Peter both broke 4:50. The top five all finished sub-5:00 for the last mile. Meincke shrugged off the lingering pain and doubts from his injury to finish the final rep in 4:57. He bubbled with confidence at the finish and manically slapped high fives with his teammates. Monkey was back.

To win the Illinois state meet, we knew we would have to finish off tough efforts. As runner after runner completed the workout, we all knew that greatness was in our grasp. I still had one surprise, though. The workout they knew about had come to a close. The workout we had withheld still had to be run. I decided one day while daydreaming in the shower that we should make six-hundred-meter repetitions at the end of hard workouts a special emphasis. The distance from the deep corner at Detweiller Park to the finish line is roughly six hundred meters, and the zigzag before the final straight is exactly three hundred meters to glory. We huddled them up and gave one final challenge. Tony's shoulders slumped when he heard the news, but they adjusted quickly. They knew that the extra rep would test their poise and mental toughness. They begrudgingly trotted off across the turf football field to the starting line.

Feeling his track legs, Andrew Clingerman bolted to the lead. Often injured but powerful, the curly-haired redhead relished track work and the raw speed generated by his powerful pack of leg muscle. He had gamely survived eighteen miles on the day and made his bid for workout supremacy. At the halfway point the varsity dutifully shifted into one last gear, and Tim Johnson came to the fore. He had endured a summer of drubbings in long runs and tempo intervals, but the track was his turf. He exploded down the backstretch, arms driving and legs flying. At 150 meters to go, he looked back over his shoulder to assess the damage. He had dropped all the usual suspects. Only Peter remained.

Down the homestretch Johnson held gamely to his form, but Peter was not to be denied. Ever since track season he had been a different man, a zealot of the first order. Fifty meters out he flattened Johnson with one last surge and barreled to the line with his tall frame in full gear. The stopwatch clicked at 1:35. He had been a man on fire for some time now, and once again he stamped his authority on the team.

As the rest streamed in, it became clear that the summer had done its job. Strong as bulls and sleeked out from the heat, they now possessed the wiry frames and strong hearts of the distance running elite. As we gathered in the north high jump pad to enjoy some post-workout Gatorades, we marveled at how the power of the group and the power of the weather had pushed us beyond our preconceived limits. As the grounds guys circulated in their cart and prepared to lock the track, we ambled off content with the night's effort and enjoying the happy chatter of men in recovery. There would be more workouts to share and possible victories to celebrate. Right then none of it mattered. The spirits of the running gods had been in the house. Everyone had felt the magic. We hoped there was more in store as we piled into our cars or rode our bikes homeward for a late supper and some well-earned rest.

HINSDALE

The next week school began and our relations shifted out of the summery dreamscape back into reality. In the summer, running had been all. Now there were normal life functions to balance. Homework. Studying. Teaching. We tried to shove the season and our practices back into a manageable corner, but we felt their omnipresence in everything we did. For better or ill, the rest of it would be a charade. The goal had consumed us long ago, and we did our best each day to hide just how much it meant.

As I welcomed my newest batch of Advanced Placement English-language students, I tried to shove aside my anticipation of practice. I tried to stop running target times through my head. I tried to sit patiently and grade papers. But I couldn't focus. It all faded next to the deeply emotional bonds we had developed. I spent most of my time yearning for 3:30 PM and the final bell that would set me free. Call it monomaniacal, but nothing could compare to the incredible experience we had wrapped ourselves within, no other bonds could supplant these, no one could know the fervency we shared as we performed the mundane acts of our days. I would see Marcus in the hallway and trade a fleeting glimpse that spoke legions.

The one place where I didn't feel the pull of distraction was at home. In the late afternoon on Monday, August 24, Meredith and I welcomed Joshua Jeffrey Quick into our lives. Back in January, when the five guys and I outlined our plan for the year, I knew that our pregnancy would be running in a parallel stream. To be privy to two emotionally full experiences was more than I could bear. As I rushed over to the warmer to hold his hand for the first time and look into those baby-blue eyes, I considered myself blessed. Family at home. Family in the team. Never had I felt such a sense of ease.

The following days were trying. Meredith and I struggled with little sleep, breast-feeding schedules, making time for the two big kids, and trying to keep our lives from disintegrating. We had done it twice before, but this one was different. We had become used to the ease and fun of two kids who could walk, talk, and entertain themselves. Going all the way back to babyhood was like rounding the board in Monopoly but not getting $200 for starting over. This time was more work than pleasure.

It didn't help that the team flitted incessantly around my edges. Meredith had grown used to my divided attention during cross country season, but I still struggled to be present and accounted for at home and at work. Furthermore, the burden of formally running the team each day descended with its full force. No longer were our practices casual and athlete-driven as in the summer. Now I was expected to be in full command each day, sometimes twice a day, orchestrating the individual training of sixty-five different boys. It had always been our compact to train every man. Each day thus necessitated a script that considered all variables at once for every guy—age, ability, summer training, injury history, competition schedule, appropriate weekly volume, appropriate intensity, and on and on and on. We had made the pact long before. The five would make the team. The team would make the five.

Unlike most other sports, cross country and track do not recognize levels. I coach every man from the slowest freshman, to the sophomore upstarts, to the returning All-Staters. This divided agenda creates some difficulty because it requires a split focus. The team of the present has to be front and center, but your thoughts can never deviate too far from the team of the future. Focus on the former too much, and you'll find the program lagging in two years. Focus on the latter too much, and you'll disappoint the now. Each year is a delicate balancing act between two equally important poles.

The year before I had wrapped myself into the wrong mission for half the season. In our first time trial, held on grass in mid-August, we found only two freshmen capable of breaking 6:00 for a mile. Eddie Graham and Dean Kolar ran 5:55 and 5:57 while none of the others was remotely close. Argeni Bailon struggled through the first mile in his clunky cross trainers while Emil Kozakiewicz bobbed his head and threw his arms wildly across his body, trying to grind out more speed. Marco Chilelli looked more like a pushcart being pulled by a donkey than a high-speed Ferrari. Gabe Flores trailed badly behind everyone, managing twelve-inch strides out of a six-foot frame. Rushi Patel dragged his seventy-six-pound body around like he had yet to be introduced to his first muscle. He and Will Padilla brought up the rear, struggling to jog the one mile out to Hamilton Reservoir without walking.

To maintain our program, we need five guys capable of getting it done by senior year. Nothing about those freshmen told me that any of them would ever make a top seven at Palatine, much less run inside the top 50 at the state meet. Watching guys struggle through an eight-minute timed mile (ten minutes for some) was enough to shake my faith. I started to panic. I questioned whether our program could pull these guys up from the doldrums. I questioned whether I was a good enough coach for them. I doubted my faith and cursed the running gods for always making this so tough. Where was my hermetically sealed distance ace—one with the winged feet of Hermes, the racing wits of Apollo, the steely toughness of Ares? Where was my Grecian metaphor for greatness?

After a week spent bemoaning the fate of our program, I shaped up and got to work. There was no time to complain. I had to believe that these men possessed the will and the skill. So we went old-school. Every Monday, we ran a 1600 for time followed by 8 x 400 with a ninety-second rest. We started in early September, and I made it my personal quest to turn these young men into runners. My thinking became absurd. For a while, I forgot about that year's varsity, the ones trying to win a state title. They were a finished product, at 90 percent of completion. If we didn't intervene, then where would we be in three years? By mid-September I realized that no varsity was ever a finished product and divided my attention more rationally, but for a bit the freshman challenge consumed me.

This same struggle happens every year at the beginning of cross country. The program has built to a point where there is no letdown. The expectations are sky-high every year, not just to win big meets and place well at state, but also to guarantee the same vibrant and incredible experience for each group. For many around the state, the cross country season lasts three months. In the good programs, it lasts four years and begins the day that the incoming freshmen first show up. Then, the clock starts ticking to that November day in senior year when the chain of greatness will have to continue. To ignore the clock is to risk the legacy.

So you can see how a year later, even amid the expectations of a state championship team, a pre-season number one Illinois ranking in all the major newspapers, and a number twelve pre-season national ranking from Marc Bloom's Super 25, I was just as obsessed with leading my sophomores out of the wilderness. By their freshman track season we had improved enough to arrive at our most ambitious goal. We were going to win the frosh-soph MSL conference meet. I told them then, with total seriousness, that I thought winning that race would be even more challenging than the varsity winning the state title. A bit hyperbolic, but they believed it. Through the summer months, the five-man group of Eddie Graham, Emil Kozakiewicz, Dean Kolar, Adam Brauer, and Argeni Bailon trained alongside our varsity. They ran beyond their abilities and then some, training with a faith and diligence that I had rarely seen, even in our most dedicated classes. These men were not fast, but they had the fused spirit.

Our first major test of the season, the Hinsdale Hornet–Red Devil Invite, was thus a test of far more than our varsity seven. It was a referendum on the state of the program. A year removed from an utter blowout, I hoped our sophomores could acquit themselves well, maybe even earn a top-five finish. Winning would be tough since we faced both Neuqua Valley and New Trier, two powerhouse programs with more than 150 runners each. The year before in the freshman race, New Trier had triumphed over us by a score of 27–220.

Neuqua Valley would also challenge at every level of competition. Throughout Illinois cross country history, York had always dominated, but in the four preceding years Paul Vandersteen and his Neuqua Valley boys had threatened to tear York's choke hold asunder. In 2007, they had seized their first state title behind Chris Derrick, one of the best runners in state history. Two years later, they won again behind an incredible display of teamwork. The year before, they had edged us for a third-place state trophy by a scant 9 points. Our battle had been ongoing for years, and this meet was our only battleground before the state final. Each year it was a referendum on two dueling programs both attempting to usurp York.

The complicated history of the previous year also imbued this first race with more significance than normal. The snafu over the scoring at the 2010 NXN Midwest meet had boiled the blood on both sides. I remained close and cordial with Coach Vandersteen, but the boys on each side let their competitiveness simmer underneath the veneer of such politeness. Our boys, including all five of our now returning seniors, believed we had beaten them fair and square on that dreary day in Terre Haute and had deserved a berth in the Nike Cross National meet. Their boys believed that they had been vindicated by the rules. In an odd way, both were right. The fact that Neuqua Valley had been invited to the national meet and placed twelfth still stung. In the days leading to the meet I could feel our boys' animosity, slightly tinged with jealousy, approaching a boil.

To make matters worse, the weather mirrored the sentiment. As I walked out to get my morning newspaper, I was enveloped by insidious humidity. Cross country racing is fraught with variables that impact performance. Heat is first and foremost. It's the great equalizer. We had all trained through the heat of the summer, but for most athletes this would be their first race since track season. Cross country in Illinois always moves through a similar cycle of heat, beauty, and then cold throughout its three months. As I stepped inside to read the Friday-night football scores at my kitchen table, I had absolutely no idea what impact the heat would have.

I walked to school with my normal race-day excitement, but felt a nervous trepidation. It wasn't just the heat that gave me pause. The past two weeks had been full of distractions. Having a baby is no small event. I had missed school and more than a few practices to be with my family. To make matters worse, our team had attracted more than its usual share of pre-season notoriety. Reporters from the *Chicago Tribune*, *Chicago Sun-Times*, and *Daily Herald* had been out to take pictures and conduct interviews with Tony and the other top returnees. My phone had been ringing off the hook with feedback and—get this—congratulations from alums and well-wishers. One conversation with an overzealous alum ended with us being crowned state champions before we had even run a race. I should've sensed the foreboding whispers of impending meltdown.

The adolescent mind jumps easily from notoriety to reality. Cross country runners fall prey to this delusion all the time. Many of them, including the coaches, are incessant "results hounds." We pick apart the returnees from the previous year and start to write the next season's scripts the moment the results roll off the press. We take the times from the previous track season and extrapolate the returnees into their three-mile futures. The deeper the investigation, the deeper the potential delusion. Add onto that the false acclaim of a few state and national rankings, and you can understand how a young athlete could confuse the magical universe of imagined place with the hard realities of an actual race.

So we swaggered off the bus at Hinsdale Hornet–Red Devil into the boiling heat of a humid September morning and headed straight into a trap of our own making. Neuqua Valley, New Trier, and the other perennial contenders at this meet never rolled over. Now they also had the incentive of a number one state-ranked target to shoot for. Sitting in the parking lot waiting for the boys to unload the tents and the water jugs, I looked Coach Mark Hajik in the eye and declared, "It would probably be the best thing in the world if we lost today."

I meant it. I love to win. I would have loved to win every meet for the entire season, but I could smell the hubris as I tailed our guys into Katherine Legge Park. They were right to be confident in their work. The summer had been physically and emotionally transformative. But I had not liked our day-to-day rhythms in the week that I had been back from paternity leave. Tyler Squeo contracted strep throat. Tony and Timmy J got sick, grew fevers, and missed school. Joe Mars had to be coaxed back onto the team after a bad week of training. Zach Stella fell apart under the pressure of his newly rigorous course load. The distractions went on and on. The group that had labored so long and hard all summer, so diligently and collectively, had fallen apart. By the end of the long two weeks that began the school year, the only thing we could cling to was our headlines.

The grounds of Katherine Legge Park are physically gorgeous. Started as a recreation and welfare center for women, the park is peppered with aged oak trees. On afternoons when it isn't invaded by legions of adolescent runners and screaming coaches, I assume the park takes on a beautiful serenity. The copious shade and venerable trees create a gorgeous tableau each season for our first meet. The beauty also belies the course's difficulty. The three-mile course at Legge is physically demanding on a nice day, but even more brutal when the temperature ratchets out of control. It begins with a concerted three-hundred-meter downhill that leads to a narrow opening between the property's fence line and a grove of trees. Get out too fast and you might pay for the rest of the race. Get out too slow and good luck working your way up. For the past two years Marcus had taken it upon himself to set land-speed records to the first turn. I now hoped for more control.

From there the course jogs out to the perimeter and the loops begin. The athletes trace the perimeter of the park three times. On each loop just past the mile and two-mile marks the field heads uphill and the real racing begins. Near County Line Road they turn right and head downhill for the creek jump. For years the jump over the creek was a highlight moment, replete with some nasty spills, some graceless athleticism that only cross country runners could manage, and big moves. Lately, the creek had been filled in to create a small path, but the small alteration in the terrain still broke the race's rhythm to pieces.

The varsity race also offered a view into the contrasting racing styles of Neuqua Valley and Palatine. For years Paul Vandersteen had constructed his program around smart, methodical training and pacing. His athletes knew pace like a metronome. They would lay back in the first mile, and then begin moving up gently and in rhythm through the second mile. Then it was all release. Aerobic and composed, they would charge through the last mile, mowing down places and hammering to the line. Through whatever manner of voodoo he possessed, this race plan had been ingrained down into the cellular level of his athletes.

At Palatine our style was built long before I arrived. From Joe Johnson down through Steve Currins and Fred Miller, it had always been a charge-hard philosophy. Get to the front. Establish position. Hang on. Depend on your guts and desire to get you to the line. Currins had won five state titles in girls cross country doing exactly that. When the girls ran 2.1 miles in Illinois, his teams treated it like a one-mile time trial. Each year, you'd see four or five Palatine girls up front hammering inside the top ten. Then they'd fade like crazy and hang on. That tactic had brought home state titles year after year.

Later, the distance moved to 2.5 miles and then 3 miles for the girls, and that thinking had to shift. Dominance on the girls' side shifted to Naperville North amid their strength orientation and their methodical pacing. Throughout my career, I had questioned the virtue of this charge-hard philosophy. It had been ingrained in my DNA, too. Literally. My father knew no other way to coach. *Get in the thick of the battle and fight* had been the mantra of my youth. Even when we started winning state trophies—runners-up in 2003, 2004, and 2005—I wondered whether we would ever win the state title with this philosophy. Not only had Paul and his boys started to beat us in the intervening years, but they had thrown us from our game. I had written internal memos and done chalk-talk sessions with our boys, preaching the value of moderation and medium rhythm. Every time we tried it, though, the result was a failure. It was like acting as something you were not on a date.

The state final the year before was the ultimate clash of the two philosophies. The scores at the mile mark of the 2010 state final: Palatine 57, Neuqua Valley 452. At the mile-and-a-half mark: Palatine 115,

Neuqua 378. At the two-mile: Palatine 157, Neuqua 273. At the finish: Neuqua 180, Palatine 189. Even reciting the scores a year later, I can hear their footsteps coming from behind. The contrast in styles as well as a mutual respect had turned our rivalry into one of the great ones in our sport. For the past four years, they had owned us.

Watching our guys warm up in the quickly escalating heat gave few clues of an impending meltdown. I should've sensed the faux confidence from miles away. We looked nervous, especially for a group of guys who had competed at levels far above this one. A coach can see the tightness. Tony looked scared rather than wound up, hesitantly doing his strides, worrying about beating Peter and his other teammates rather than the opposition. Try as I might to squelch it, the battle to establish an internal pecking order had been fierce. Peter's emergence threatened to alter a number of self-concepts. He alone looked confident. He had trained with the hunger of a starving man, and this was his first real opportunity to feast. Marcus glowed with his usual strut. Timmy J and Meincke looked less than sure about themselves in the pre-race warm-ups. I had chided Timmy J over the summer to take it up a notch, but his training had been nothing more than diligent. I still harbored a belief that he could be the top man. Meincke's iliotibial band syndrome had largely healed, but the reduction in training had led to a predictable reduction in confidence. Try as I might, the ongoing battle against his mind raged. I hoped he could overcome his doubts and the oppressive sun.

As the athletes lined up for the start, they glistened with perspiration and the excitement of hard training come due. I headed down past the grove of trees and over the creek to take a quick lounge in the grass. Reclining at ease, I chatted with my coaching buddies and tried to quell the early-season nerves. After a summer of waiting, it was finally time to enjoy the scene. The call of men moved to action. The sun and trees and wind. The gorgeous contrast of the school colors on the starting line. For my entire life this scene had been the animating force, a regular call that the quest resumed again with the fall. I hoped this one would end as my father and I had so long wished.

With the whip-crack of the starter's pistol, I punched the timer on my wristwatch and sprang up ready for action. Some coaches find a cozy spot and watch a race. To the chagrin of some, I get after it. Watching a cross country race can be a uniquely participatory event. No one goes to a basketball or football game and plays along in the stands, but at a meet I can throw on my running shoes and get from point to point around the course at will. I hope that my energy and spirit are an aid in troubled times.

Through the first grove of trees, our top guys showed small hints of composure, but they still found themselves on the lead by the half mile. Marcus hit the far turn up by the road in full groove. His eager one-stepping prompted his teammates, and Tony, Peter, and Timmy J smoothly glided up to challenge at the front. Winning the individual battle would be no easy task. New Trier's Leland Later had run 4:14 for 1600 meters the past spring and was swollen with confidence. The pre-season chatter indicated an even more impressive growth in his form. Neuqua Valley's duo of Mark Derrick and Taylor Soltys also stepped in and started to play. Old rivals by now, they would be a match for our seniors throughout the season.

By the mile mark we looked dominant. Timmy J had fallen slightly off the front, but our top trio looked composed and in rhythm. I searched vainly for Meincke and found him well back, but looking good. With the front four gunning it, we could withstand a solid but unspectacular race in his first big effort back from injury. Behind him, I found a void. The early pace, the heat, and the pressures of their first varsity race cooked my juniors. Christian Zambrano tried gamely to get into it, but the rest had the big eyes and labored breathing of first-timers. I could smell the choke in their body language. These races were for learning, but their fear left us with no room for error. As the race chugged up the first hill, I thought we could hold off the Neuqua charge.

I was wrong. Far wrong. By the two-mile mark, the fade began in earnest. Marcus's early confidence masked deeper issues. He melted badly in the heat. The sweat dripped from his slick black eyebrows, and his red

Photo by Cindi Johnson

Tim Johnson, Anthony Gregorio, and Peter Tomkiewicz surround eventual state champion Leland Later early on at the Hinsdale Hornet–Red Devil Invite.

jersey clung to his back. With eyes downcast, he tucked himself away into survival mode. Timmy J wasn't doing much better. His powerful quads produced less and less lift with each stride. Soaked with perspiration, he resembled a pogo stick running out of energy, bouncing less and less with each foot strike. Johnson managed to hold his position relatively well, but competitors streamed by Marcus on each side.

Just past two miles, Neuqua Valley's back end found its groove and went to work. Running in tandem, Alekh Meka and Nick Buschelle motored up through the field, on the balls of their feet and charging with the force of men who had played their cards right. Marcus had no response. Tony and Peter were still battling inside the top five, but it took more than two to win. I hoped against hope that Meincke could come

201

from behind with all of the answers.

It quickly became apparent that was not going to happen. Never a good finisher, Monkey looked stuck in neutral throughout the last mile. He grinded slowly up the far incline while his fading body unleashed precious little force on the downhill that preceded the finish. The weeks off had robbed him of some fitness and most of his confidence, but my mind immediately returned to the background fear. I wasn't sure if we could ever win with him as our fifth. No one race is conclusive, but there are trends. This one was a big one. As he staggered home in twenty-seventh, I looked up the finishing incline and realized how soundly we had been beaten. A couple of guys had run well, but the team had melted under the insidious heat.

As I walked up the hill to our team camp, I mulled my options. Make excuses and blame it on the heat. Get angry and call them out for their weak practice habits. Use it as a teaching tool and remind them that early-season races are test tracks and nothing more. Shame them into trying harder. Blame myself. At certain points in that confused walk, all options seemed true.

In the end I chose poise. No screaming. No fearful displays or projecting too much from one heat-addled race. I would frame it as a learning experience and a motive for returning to the basics. The performances from our juniors betrayed the normal jitters of young men in their first varsity races. A couple of our guys suffered in the sun. A few more suffered from weak tactical choices. Some, like Peter and Tony, turned in superlative races. The end result found us second by 17 points to a talented Neuqua Valley team that was obviously more ready to race. We beat them marginally through three runners, but they devastated our back end with the strength of their tight pack.

I was surprised by how calm I felt during and after the race. Through long practice I had trained myself not to get emotional about early-season races. Early in my career, they meant everything. Now they were simply places to experiment. Much would change from beginning to end. In the aftermath I found our guys contemplative rather than sullen, reflective rather than angry. We talked about what we had learned and moved on. Disappointed, but unshaken, Marcus doused himself with water and promised to do better next time. Even Meincke took his race in stride, happy to be back racing if not satisfied with his time or place. If our goal was to engage in fulfilling process, then we had to include broken races. Only one race was an end point. The rest were all points in evolution.

Photo by Cindi Johnson

Tim Meincke returns from injury to score as the fifth man at the Hinsdale Hornet–Red Devil Invite.

Blaming the elements is always a fool's game, especially in a loss, but the debilitating heat affected many. It skewed the day's realities. Marcus Garcia had run 15:40 the year before. Was he now a guy who could only pump out a 15:52? I thought not. Was Tim Meincke really slower than the year before and less capable of serving as fifth man because he ran 16:03? I thought not.

We needed to look no farther than our sophomores to find the value of team cohesion. Close friends and diligent training partners throughout the summer, Dean, Eddie, Emil, Adam, and Argeni had become a force. A picture of them taken just before the mile mark shows them trailing a front pack of ten to fifteen guys, but they ran in tight formation. The picture embodied "the power of the fist." Cross country racing can work in two ways: All five guys can run alone and exist as solitary fingers of the hand, or they can group together and possess the power of the fist. A slap only stings. A punch has real power. Running alone and fading alone, our varsity had tried to throw Neuqua Valley aside with a slap. The sophomores delivered a punch. The five grouped so tightly that each man could reach out and touch any of the four others.

In the ideal world the five-man fist never disintegrates, and they finish together. This rarely happens because ability and fitness can never be distributed that evenly. But the deeper that grouping lasts, the more incentive each man has to bleed for the cause. Slowly but surely, they peeled off, but the attractiveness of the group did not fade. They stayed close to that power. In the middle mile Emil Kozakiewicz took charge and pushed the pace. As guy after guy dropped back from the lead group, they were picked up by a successive line of our eager sophomores. Just past two miles our guys were in ninth, tenth, eleventh, sixteenth, and twentieth. They faded in the finish up the hill, but their performance was one of the most stunning reversals of my coaching career. The year before we had placed seventh in the freshman race and were handily beaten by New Trier. Neuqua Valley had placed seven runners in front of our best guy. A year later, our sophomores were third. They not only beat Neuqua Valley but also reversed their previous deficits versus Wheaton Warrenville South and New Trier to a manageable handful of points. The scoring: Wheaton 53, New Trier 58, Palatine 96. I once thought that this group of sophomores would be our downfall, the end of the line for all that we had built. Now they looked like saviors.

As I gathered our varsity to break down the race, I needed look no farther than their race to find the moral. Rankings did not make a team.

Ambition and love had to be fused together. Our varsity would need to run together or die alone. Marcus and Monkey knew that their isolation had led to ruin. Even Tony, who had placed fourth and run well, knew the score. Worrying about Peter and fighting for his spot on the team was a distraction. From then on, the pecking order could not matter. The team result had to be all. I saw the frustration in Tony's eyes. He had hoped to win the race. In reality, Peter had given it to him, chugging through the heat despite his massive frame and battling with Leland Later deep into the final kick. His second-place finish, in a staggering personal best of 15:14, was the grand transformation writ large. A year ago, we hoped he would be a manageable number five man. Now he was the top dog. The rest would have to learn not just to embrace it, but to love him for it.

PEORIA

Photo by MaryAnn Graham

The entire Palatine boys cross country team poses after winning all three levels at the Peoria Notre Dame Invite.

In the wake of a blowout loss to open the season, I chided the varsity to remember our mantra. The five make the team. The team makes the five. Our sophomores had reminded us of what we had so easily forgotten in our preoccupation with rankings and team pecking orders. Working as a group was our most valuable commodity.

So on Monday, Labor Day for those inclined to irony, I created one of the hardest workouts of the year. We jogged out to Deer Grove East to run our varsity course three times. After each three-mile repetition, the pace would increase. That was nine miles of hard running with much of it faster than our young men had run in the previous Saturday's race. I knew we couldn't hit the assigned times. What I wanted was for each guy to believe that he could do it if he ran with the team. Noah Brown and our juniors would do only the first two reps plus the first mile of the last one. The Fab Five would do all three.

I met the guys shortly before we ran and went through the group guy by guy to point out all of the distractions. The last one to get a piece of the blame was me. My family life had been upended, and I wanted them to know my own culpability. Over the summer I made a compact with them that I would run every day, and I did it to the tune of nine hundred miles. But as soon as the summer was over and the baby was born, I let the streak die. I could have run. I just made excuses. Apparently we had all been thinking alike, stuck on ourselves and in a funk of complacency. So on Labor Day, I brought my running shoes and prepared to attack the workout with them.

We took off on the first rep, trying to cruise along at 6:00 mile pace. We hit the quarter mile way fast and promptly had to back off. Other than Stella, Squeo, and freshman Graham Brown, the group hummed along like a well-tuned machine. I dropped back and let Stella have it throughout the rep. Zach is a massively talented young man whose head too often gets in the way of his physical gifts. Upon completing an 18:30 clocking in the first loop, he said the wrong thing: "I just don't have it today." I kicked him out of practice. Now everyone was awake. The season had officially started.

For the second one I knew that 17:00 would challenge the group, especially our eight juniors who had run between 16:30 and 18:00 in their first race. I was not sure I could run the time, but I gamely slipped on my Nike Lunar Racers and told myself that anything was possible. Before starting I reiterated the point of the workout. I knew that many of them would not be able to run the time, but if they were standing on the starting line they better believe they could.

We launched off the line straight into a torrid pace. We settled in to a 5:32 first mile. I looked around, and most of the guys were still there. By the two-mile, I was running with the six seniors and a lone junior,

Emanuel Rosales. He was the last leaf to fall off the tree. I was dying, too, but the power of the fist was in full effect. There was no way I was quitting. When I glanced back our juniors were off the pace, but working. We motored home to finish in 16:57 with the six seniors and I together. Joe Mars, Emanuel Rosales, and Christian Zambrano came in sub-17:20. Mars and Rosales ran both reps faster than their race paces from Hinsdale.

The last rep was a sterling piece of brutality. Asking them to run 5:20 mile pace after six miles of hard running was a dictator's bargain. I was counting on their bond with one another to bring them home. They responded at first with bravado, as Peter and Tony led the group through a scorching 5:08 first mile. From then on it was a death march. They did not just slow down. They retreated into a collective agony that only the best cross country teams can access. The workout went past the point of physicality. They survived on spirit. Just past halfway, Tony powered away while the other four struggled to keep their proximity. The grippy pain shone on their faces, but the times were stellar: 16:09, 16:20, 16:30, 16:45, 16:51. They also did not matter. The soul of the workout was committing to the effort and believing the group could will it into being.

After that workout, the worm turned. Our annual overnight jaunt to Peoria for the Notre Dame Invite was on the horizon, and I knew that we would come out breathing fire. Each cross country season our varsity uses the Peoria Notre Dame Invite as a simulation of our state-meet trip. We leave on Friday, drive down over the exact same roads, order the exact same meals from the exact same places, go through our exact warm-up procedure, and hope to run exactly as we would in the state finals. The early-season loss also guaranteed something more vital. We would finally run with the emotional connection we had built during that long suffering run up the mountain.

Each year we are allowed to take one van full of guys, so that meant only seven athletes would earn spots. The competition to get in that van animated the first portion of our season. At Hinsdale, the Fab Five and Zambrano had all earned their spots. The wild card choice ended up being Zach Stella. After his early exit from the Labor Day workout, the rest didn't trust him, but I believed in second chances. He had observed the same trial of miles they had over the summer. His race performances reflected his manic work ethic. Chemistry-wise, Noah Brown was the popular choice, but performance won out and Stella seized his first chance to run varsity.

Excepting the year our van broke down at Exit 75 on Interstate 80 just outside Lasalle-Peru, the drive was the same. We dialed up some stand-up comedy and got down to relaxing and enjoying our time together. Tony was a veteran of such trips. He had been there two years prior, pushing the van, when we strained up that exit ramp and down into the Shell station that became our home for the next four hours. He had been there through the disappointment of a sixth-place state meet choke and the exhilaration of our fourth-place near miss. He had been there the year before when the ride home was the quietest anyone could remember.

There is a picnic table somewhere near the Detweiller Park exit. The previous September, it had been the scene of one of my most brutal speeches as a coach. Unlike the mature contemplation occasioned by our loss at Hinsdale, this one provoked nothing but sincere outrage. After finishing eighth in the Peoria Notre Dame Invite, our season felt lost. I exiled the varsity squad to an hour-long run up among the hills that framed Detweiller Park. Whether they came down with any answers or not, I had no idea. In the interim my anger boiled. I sent them away so I could calm down and get rational. Instead, I found more anger.

I rarely yell at young people. After a while the volume drowns out whatever message you might have. But I could not help this one. Anger as inferno. Anger as evisceration. Anger in my bones. While often disappointing, performances rarely made me angry, but our thunderous flop set off something within me. Any honest person knows the truth about yelling at others. Sometimes you only do it because you are angry at yourself.

When they returned from their run of shame, I stood on the picnic table and looked down at the ten sullen faces below and let them have it.

I called out each guy in turn, railing on weak practice habits, the lack of intensity, poor racing tactics, or whatever other charges I could trump up on the spot to fan the flames. When I had screamed my fill, we shambled silently to our District 211 van and rode home in quiet. As Marcus reminded me, there were only three words spoken during the entire drive back to Palatine: "Gimme my chips." Marcus broke records finding my potato chips from the back of the van.

It was within this context that we returned one year later to the scene of the crime. Four of the guys in my van had been part of that crushing loss. Now we looked back on it in detached bemusement. It was as if the coaches and athletes who suffered that loss were simply former versions of ourselves. We looked at them as quaint relics, precursors to the newly minted unit we had become. As we slowly rolled up the long asphalt drive that runs beside Detweiller Park's main field, that loss lingered more as a humorous aside. We were serious as salt about winning on Saturday, but proceeded about our business with amusement. We made fun of the Hersey freshmen, who ran all of their strides from the box at maximum effort. We changed our clothes, bumped along to the Chemical Brothers, and marveled at the disgusting smell of Marcus's shoes. He seemed to think that socks were optional. The rest of us dealt with the aftermath.

It would have been natural to proceed quietly and gravely through our practice and into our meet the next day. After Neuqua Valley's stumble at the Peoria Woodruff Invitational the week prior, the pollsters had once again voted us the number one team in the state. But the tone had changed. No one thought anymore about the rankings. We simply went about our business, and it was comforting to relax and enjoy our time together. We ran through the mile mark at 7:15 pace and worried if we had lost all our fitness on the ride down. We wondered why more people didn't run into the electrical boxes on the course. We discussed how Peter had become a giant, towering over shrimps like Tony and I with hovering impunity. A year ago I had stressed out about all elements of our preparation. This time, we worked through the finer points of racing the Detweiller course with ease. The guys knew the right tangents to run.

They knew how to correct the errors from both of last year's races. The whole exercise felt like filling in answers to a test made easy through long bouts of preparation. We ran our simulation of the first eight hundred meters, and the top five smoked through the half-mile mark in 2:16. We were ready.

Dawn broke crisply the next day, and we all felt fall in the air for the first time. As we stepped outside the Spring Hill Suites into the parking lot, it smelled like cross country season. The slight chill. The changing of the leaves. Per ritual the guys performed our ten-minute morning jog, trying hard to run for exactly ten minutes. Timmy J tried to nail it on his watch but came up just short—9:59.88. Unlike two weeks before, the good-natured ribbing disguised no inner nervousness. At Hinsdale we had run to protect a ranking and a reputation. Now we acted ourselves.

As the boys ate breakfast in the hotel lobby, I sat alone and watched them. All the trips and long runs had created a sense of ease. Most cross country teams are close, but this one eclipsed the other great ones I had been around. Glancing around the edges of my morning paper, watching their easy joking and casual repartee, I realized what it was. They carried the easy manner of family. The stories were assumed. The memories ran deep. The jokes and conversations flowed back and forth like they did among a troupe of actors after long practice. Actors worked long and hard to capture such rhythm, but for the boys it just flowed, an assumed comfort that had taken years to build.

Marcus slumped in one of the big cushioned lounge chairs with his feet up on a coffee table and his fingers tapping out texts on his phone. With one earbud in, he zoomed in and out of conversations, pausing every now and then to punctuate one of Gregorio's jokes with his laugh or a tagged-on finish. A joker to the last, Meincke sat eating his bagel and banana with that mischievous glimmer in his eye. He looked like a sly devil, a conspirator about to pull off a big heist. Across from him, Timmy J methodically ate his oatmeal. Quiet by nature, he rarely stood out. Over time I had learned the value of his sly wit. He played the straight man to Meincke's raging comic. Peter sat with them, but his thoughts at eating time never tended toward conversation. Everyone knew not to get in the way of Peter's appetite. Eating was serious business, and his large body demanded calories. The night before he had eaten an entire large pizza before finishing off some pasta and buttered bread.

Slowly by dribs and drabs they retired to their rooms and prepared for the race. I busied myself gathering the water and food into the van, hoping that the rest of the team was faring well on its 5:30 AM bus ride to Peoria. As the assistant, Coach Sheehan had drawn the responsibility of bringing the rest of the crew from Palatine. Despite the earliness of the wake-up call, the experience of running on the state course was too important to pass up.

On the way to the course we argued about what this year's theme song should be. It was a silly topic, but Zach Stella was adamant that we needed one. It seemed natural to have a "go-to" song for the van ride from the hotel to Detweiller Park, but the entire exercise felt forced. In 2008 we adopted "Under Pressure" by Queen. The two preceding years had been dominated by some horrendous techno song that Mat Smoody selected. All I remember is that it rattled the cheap factory speakers and that the drop centered around some guy saying "Sex and Drugs and House." Not our finest hour. Stella thought an AC/DC song might fit, but the rest disagreed. Like all theme songs, it would have to be revealed rather than chosen.

Entering Detweiller Park is always a magical moment, whether it be for a regular-season invite or the state final. We wound slowly through the neighborhoods on top of the hill, glancing at the opulent houses that dot the top of the bluff, before descending through the hills to the park. Even now, after thirty years, I still feel the rush when I turn right from the stop sign and head up the long drive that skirts the course's perimeter. The girls races were already under way, so we got a quick taste of what lay in store. The buses and team vans lined both sides of the drive, and frantic high schoolers jogged back and forth across the road. There was no option but to proceed at a creep. The slow drive only accentuated the moment's good flavor. The nerves churned and tumbled around in everyone's bellies. Instantly the weekend shifted from a fun trip to a competitive reality.

We reached our team camp near the back corner of the park and found the rest of our crew already moved in and warming up. Our freshman-sophomore team would be up first, with the varsity and junior varsity to follow. Already, our girls team had taken the course and finished second behind four great performances from our established stars. Despite this, their search for a fifth runner would continue. No matter the level or the gender, five is always the magic number.

Our frosh-soph team promptly stepped onto the course and proved it. Immediately Graham Brown shot into the lead group and refused to quit the pace. It was the first glimpse of Prodigy's outsized talent. He kept mowing down guys into the last mile before finishing third overall in 15:45. The time was staggering. In my eleven-year career, no freshman—even the ones who ended up All-State or as state champions—had ever broken 16:00 on the state course in September.

Graham's heroics moved his sophomore teammates to furious action. Running behind a lead dog for once, the pack ran with unfiltered confidence. Just as the week before, Eddie, Deaner, Emil, Argeni, and Adam ran like a shape-shifting amoeba, clinging to each other, fighting the unified fight, punching throughout. Fifth man at the two-mile, Emil lit up a fabulous late-race move and powered through the field into the top twenty. He finished in 16:17 with the rest behind him in close order. Door closed.

Even during the race, watching it happen, I couldn't control my emotions. I frantically scrambled back and forth, punching the air, letting them know that we were on the lead. As they hit the final straightaway, and I saw Emil coming from behind, I paused long enough to take it all in. Here were my ultimate projects—an entire class of them—blowing the doors off a major invite. In my entire career we had never come close to winning this frosh-soph race. Now, with the worst group of freshmen I had ever coached, we found a way. When the scores were tallied, we found ourselves on top by a solitary point over York—101 to 102.

If this was a preview of what winning the state meet might feel like, then I was all in. The mood in our camp was ecstatic. The coaches and varsity had shared deeply in the transformation of our sophomores, and watching them win a major invite title—the first one in school history at this race—told everyone that the magic was in the air, inside the wings of this season, just waiting to take flight. Their race had been a beautiful synergy, a perfect melding of up-front talent and striving will. When we heard the score, a massive cheer erupted from our camp. It was an uncharacteristic bout of joviality for a regular-season meet, but no matter. The entire crew had bought into the larger team goal. The five make the team. The team makes the five.

Our frantic cheer coincided with the finish of the varsity race. After watching our sophomores pull off the surprise, our varsity took no prisoners. They stormed the field en route to an 80-point victory. It was a statement win. The inclusion of York in the field for the first time only made it sweeter. Regular-season meet or not, this was only the second time in school history that our varsity had defeated theirs. Our team average of 14:55 was the fastest in school history, even including our program's great races in the state meet. There was no need to glorify individual results or lionize one man's great race. The team result was all. Our varsity charged fearlessly to the front of the race and defied the field to come and get them. The past November such a tactic had been a precursor to a late-race fade. This time, they belonged. Even better, they knew it.

Soon after, our junior varsity threw down six runners in the top fifteen and a perfect afternoon was complete. The meet organizers kept no score in the open race, but we would have won handily. The emphasis from the start had been on what the broader team could give to the varsity and what the varsity could give to the broader team. Our team meeting in May, the moment I had asked each of them for everything they had to give, seemed so long ago. Now here we were, together and firing on all cylinders, a precision machine from top to bottom. For one afternoon, we reached perfection.

As we pulled out of the park, I grinned and thought about the instability of success. Any team could be a loser in September and end up being the biggest winner in November. We had proven as much the year before. Now the shoe was on the other foot, and we would have to be wary of the volatility. No team is any better than its last race. No lead is immutable. Winning in the moment was not a curse, but I could easily see how it could become one. As I turned our van homeward up Illinois Highway 29, I knew that the coming weeks would provide trials we had not imagined. But for one afternoon at least, we had run like kings. Whether we would be crowned at the end was another matter entirely.

THE PALATINE INVITE

The boys varsity poses after winning our program's second-ever title at the Palatine Invite. From left, Christian Zambrano, Peter Tomkiewicz, Anthony Gregorio, Zach Stella, Tim Meincke, Tim Johnson, and Marcus Garcia.

After Peoria, the challenges kept coming quick and fast. It felt like moving up levels in a video game. First, a mid-week conference meet versus Barrington. Then the Palatine Invite. I had arranged the most brutally competitive individual and team fields in the history of our meet. A week removed from the fastest race in school history, we had to turn right around and get up for an even bigger test. The Palatine Invite had moved beyond just another race long ago. For the other schools it was just a tough invitational. For us it was a spiritual capstone to the regular season, a time to gather with parents, alumni, and friends. For most of the season we run in wide-open spaces in faraway places. The Palatine Invite is a party in our own backyard.

We began our day together with a meeting in the team room—a rather small rectangle just off the main gym in the foyer of the boys locker room. Designed for basketball teams and equipped with twenty school desks, the room was not built to hold an entire cross country team. That is part of its charm. Regardless of the team's size, the Palatine Invite speech and all subsequent team talks are given in this room. The veterans run in to seize a desk near the front. The floor ends up littered with freshmen, and the standing-room crowd promotes a clear intimacy. With the men of 2011 packed on top of one another, I began my annual talk.

Sometimes I bring fire, sometimes I bring anger, and sometimes I choose to bring them some soul. Our preparation thus far had focused on becoming a truly great team, not just a group of people that rode on the backs of five talented individuals. In this endeavor we had stressed that every man had to count. So I talked about my heroes. The year before I had told them about my father and my brother and what they meant to me. This time I let them know what they all meant to me.

So I told them that Emanuel Rosales was one of my heroes. The year before his brother had been shot in a gang-related incident. Emanuel had chosen an opposite path and sacrificed his time and energy for the team. Ever since freshman year, he led recovery runs even though the pace was insane and he had no prayer of staying with the group. But each run he made it farther and farther. Eventually he became a runner to be reckoned with, and I let him know what an honor it would be to watch him run.

I also told them about Argeni Bailon. In his first time trial as a freshman, Argeni shambled through a 7:53 mile in his cross trainers. I told them how I initially looked at him and saw nothing—no potential, no way forward, no way that he would ever run fast. I had been wrong. I told them that I could not measure Argeni the person just by looking at him. He worked. He demonstrated character, drive, sacrifice, and dozens of other admirable qualities. And here he was, fresh off a series of incredible races, staring straight at a top-ten finish in the Palatine Invite sophomore race.

Lastly, I told them about Peter. I told them how he had come to me the previous December and told me that he was going to give this team everything. He had done just that. The previous weekend he had run 14:43 for three miles and finished top ten at Peoria. Today he was attempting to go out and win the toughest Palatine Invite in our meet's storied history. All three were my heroes, but I could have said the same about so many other men in the room—Will Padilla, Jon Young, Devin Hein, the Much twins. Most would never place in a race or win a medal. They worked without guarantee of recognition. It was easy to be good and stay driven. Heroes needed no such guarantees, and we had built the team on such men.

The vibe reflected an assumed electricity. The time of the season for yelling and screaming had not yet arrived. The implicit message was not lost. Every man sitting in the room knew that he was capable of extraordinary feats if he stayed true to the team. Building such faith across the years had not been an easy task. It involved collecting extraordinary people first and then hoping they could perform extraordinary athletic feats later. That was no guarantee, but men like Emanuel, Argeni, and Peter showed that humble work and diligent drive could be the precursors to actualization.

With the tone set we shuffled quietly out of the room and onto the bus. Our goals were twofold and ambitious: Every man was going to run a course PR, and we were going to win all four levels of team competition. Both tasks were daunting. We had built the field into the greatest collection of talent ever seen at the Palatine Invite. Elmhurst York, with the collective weight of twenty-seven state titles, would have their entire program—some two hundred boys—contesting races on all four levels. Their varsity was ranked third in the state and rankled after we had defeated them handily the week before. They aimed to take back the number one ranking. Emergent powerhouses such as New Trier, Barrington, and Lake Zurich would be out in full force. To top it all off, I had invited two of Missouri's finest—St. Louis University High and Rock Bridge. The Rock Bridge squad arrived the day before having ridden two yellow school buses all the way from Columbia, Missouri. They were ranked number one in their state and spoiling to make a mark on the regional scene.

Individually, we had arranged the deepest field in our meet's history. New Trier's Leland Later was quickly establishing himself as the favorite for the Illinois state title. Rock Bridge's Caleb Wilfong had won the Missouri state title at 1600 meters the previous spring. Barrington's Erik Peterson was a local nemesis, the MSL Conference champion and the second returnee in the state. For the first time ever, St. Ignatius was entered, and their star junior Jack Keelan, the fastest man in his grade, would be there. Grant Nykaza of Beecher, the favorite for the Class A state title, had been specially invited. The list went on and on. Men who had run 9:20 for 3200 meters the previous spring had to wonder when they boarded their buses whether they could make the top ten.

Photo by MaryAnn Graham

A year after running in the junior varsity race, Peter Tomkiewicz challenges the national-class runners at the head of the Palatine Invite varsity field. From left, Barrington's Erik Peterson, Rock Bridge's Caleb Wilfong, York's Billy Clink, New Trier's Leland Later, Beecher's Grant Nykaza, and Loyola's Todd Ford.

For the second straight year the Invite would be contested on our remodeled course. For the previous nine years, the races had been run on a pattern of trail loops through the Deer Grove East brush. We had cut and maintained the paths for years, but a Cook County Forest Preserve decision to turn parts of the park into wetlands had destroyed our course. While the changes ruined some of the aesthetics of the race, the unintended effect had been to intensify the large crowd's interactions with the races. In the last quarter mile, the runners would descend into a tunnel of screams as fans lined the ten-foot running lane on both sides. Most invites in the Chicago suburbs have a solid base of fans, alums, and parents. The Palatine Invite is an event.

Each year my favorite moment occurs when the team pulls into Deer Grove East on the bus. Usually the quick jaunt over from school is quiet and nervous. As the team rounds the bend past the water pump and the bike trail, I stand up to give my final instructions. What I love is the look they get in their eyes when they see the course—our course—all dressed up in its finery. The turn marking the exit from the gravel path will be dressed up in new pennants. The yellow caution tape will be stretched from tree to tree. Later in the day it will cordon the runners off from the fans as they descend into the scream tunnel. If it is a nice day the sun will illuminate the fresh dew on the early-morning grass and bathe an old place in a new light. The tents of the early-arriving teams will be set up in the far west field, a kaleidoscopic array of colors and logos. Thickets of runners will be walking the course, learning afresh patterns we already know through deep communion. The Palatine parents will be working diligently, some in the concession stand, some as course marshals, others as traffic control cops. In this moment you can see a simple realization. All of this is for them. This scene is our special treat.

As we got off the bus I got the same old Palatine Invite feeling. It's that "game on" feeling you sense in your bones, one that can only shiver its way into your interior when you truly know that the best are in the house. The Palatine Invite has a gravity that is part of its greatness. Even though it is a mid-season meet, it has the weight of the post-season infused into its nooks and crannies. The small parking lot at Deer Grove East fills up an hour before the first race, and you can see the people streaming in from the surrounding neighborhoods, as if magnetically drawn. It has the feeling of a sold-out arena, or a concert where the promoter has over-booked the venue. In the end we put on a show for the best of the best to do what they do. We call it the Meet of Champions for a reason.

As at the state meet, the excitement builds through the morning to the two races everyone comes to see—boys and girls varsity. The races started promptly at 9 AM with the freshman boys. For Palatine and York, it started with a bang. Right from the gun fans were treated to a devel-oping rivalry that will play out across the next four years. Lauded in the pre-season as a potential heir to multiple state champion Donald Sage, York's Matt Plowman put together a sterling junior high résumé and positioned himself to be their next great champion. The week before, Graham Brown had scored a narrow victory in their first meeting. It was clear that Plowman wanted payback, and the two engaged in a heated dual. They sprinted the entire last quarter mile side by side, sparring neck and neck, neither man giving in. Ten meters out Graham threw down a burst that provoked a dive from Plowman at the line. Prodigy took the victory by less than a half second and the course record by a sin-gle tenth. The race got the crowd buzzing, and you could feel the day's intensity start to gather.

As our varsity girls prepared to race, I checked in with my varsity. They stretched silently and intently just behind the main pavilion. I sensed a slight nervousness but also calm. The week before at Peoria we had run shockingly well. Our front four all set personal bests on the state meet course. The task now was to manage expectations. As they stretched I quietly gave each man a touch, reminding him of his race plan. We wanted to stretch the race out in the middle. From the one-mile mark to the two-mile mark we wanted to deliver a knockout punch. As we stayed glued in our packs of two, we hoped that the increase in pace would decimate our rivals. From the turnaround point at a mile and a half, the race would proceed for a half mile straight away from the finish. Psychologically, the athletes could not see home. Every man knew the finish would come, but the brain would have its doubts. To move when the race heads away from the finish and the safety of the crowd is to make a champion's move.

Despite my confident rhetoric, I sensed something missing. Being used to fields of this quality, I did not suspect fear. Instead, I felt a numb complacency, a general lack of engagement. Ever since the beginning of the summer, I had spent countless hours around these athletes. At times our language moved past words to a deeper and slightly less detectable vocabulary. Looking at their lackadaisical stretching, I sensed that we were about to get beat. Arrayed in their stretching circle they appeared like men who had ridden the tallest of all waves the week before only to just now be coming up for air after the crash. I wasn't sure they were ready to ride another wave. They would do it, but I knew after watching them that this victory—if it were to occur—would be workmanlike. Even Marcus, usually coldly focused and intense, lacked spark. Had this been the state meet, I would have worried. Instead I reminded myself that this was all part of the process. Every meet can't be a peak.

After watching our girls varsity fumble around in their continued search for a fifth runner, we got ourselves together into one final huddle. We went over the cold logic of our race plan for the final time, but even our cheer felt mechanical and formulaic. Noah Brown still rang out his illogically loud "Pack on three! One, two, three, PACK!" in our huddle's center, but I walked away hoping that my senses were off. After all, this was the Palatine Invite. If we couldn't get emotionally engaged for this, then what would it take to get us fired up? I fretted. I paced and talked to my assistants, awash in doubt. We had won the Palatine Invite only once in its storied history—a single-point win by our 2007 team. Even worse than disengaged, the boys seemed bored. I tried to shake it off as I focused on the starter's pistol.

As the field charged up the opening incline, I knew that my feelings were right. A week after being disassembled by a couple of teams, the young men from York fired out of the box with unified purpose. The contrast between our boys and theirs was immediately evident. By the quarter mile, all seven York runners were near the front, racing with an urgency they had clearly lacked the week before. We looked shocked, but poised. Perhaps we were good enough to physically dissociate ourselves from our mental lapse. A well-conditioned runner does not always need grand emotion or massive jolts of adrenaline to get it done. In running, poise is physiological. The mind may disengage, but a big heart can save you. As I saw Tony and Peter, Marcus and Timmy J, and Monkey and Z group into their assigned pairs, I hoped that we could be clinical. Now was the time for cold-blooded execution.

By the mile mark, we had moved up beautifully, matching York's early exuberance with discipline. Rock Bridge's front trio tagged into the lead group, but so did our top four. Under strict orders to lay off the early pace, Monkey began to move up through the field with Zambrano in tow. Into the scream tunnel they raced through the hundreds of assembled spectators, wrapping themselves in the energy of the blanketing cheers. Just as the group moved toward the turnaround, Later, Keelan, Nykaza, and Loyola's Todd Ford shot to the lead and strung out the pace. It was clear that all four aimed for Jack Driggs's course record of 14:34.

At halfway Tony stuck tight to the lead group, but the rest splintered apart. A week removed from his finest hour, Peter slid helplessly backward. As they entered the trail to the back corner of the course, Johnson also dropped off badly. Despite his fitness and enormous talent, his mid-race fades would cause increasing consternation throughout this race and the rest of the season. Once the string tying him to his teammates snapped, he would fade into oblivion. The week prior, we blamed his collapse in the last mile on an overzealous race plan. He had opened at 4:44 and faded badly. Now, after a more sensible opening, he still could not cling to Marcus. Was the training wrong? Was he hurt? Was he sick? Was he not tough enough to stick? Was there a better race plan? Timmy J's race provoked nothing but questions.

By the time I hustled out to the two-mile mark, we were running individually well and collectively terrible. I could see each man battling, but their incentives diminished as they became more and more isolated. One look into Tim Meincke's eyes and I could tell we were in trouble. I knelt on the ground at a mile to go and reached for the jockey's whip. No manner of urgency, cheering, or angry oral jolts was going to get him moving though. His mid-race move bankrupted him. His quads barely pushed his legs onward, and I felt anger when I saw the blankness in his face. He looked like he wanted to give up. Desperate now, I counted all seven York runners ahead of him and all five from Rock Bridge. My worst fears were realized. Tim Meincke was going to lose us the meet.

Leaving the back corner, I booked it across the field to get one last look. Tony battled with all his might near the front of the race, but it became clear that he would be fried by the kickers. He settled for eighth place and a new course best of 14:49. Behind him, the boys straggled in like the remains of a beaten army. Peter gamely tried to hold his rhythm, but he slid backward and was enveloped by the entire front trio from Rock Bridge. Even worse, York's junior star, Scott Milling, caught him in the kick and pulled a 2-point swing. Peter slid into a no-man's-land where he could do nothing but hold his spot. Luckily, Marcus powered home the last part of the race and nearly caught him. They finished within two places of one another in fifteenth and seventeenth.

In the sprint to the finish Johnson suffered madly. Harnessed to great half-mile speed, he was supposed to be our closer in tight places. Now adrift from Marcus he fought in vain just to hold his spot. As an entire thicket of runners passed him, I screamed for a response, but it never came. He floated to the line, the victim of the mid-season haze and possibly a few too many miles. He hung on for twenty-fifth.

Now our fate came down to our fifth. Cross country coaches are used to this phenomenon. We all know our teams can only be as good as our fifth-best athlete. In most sports the best of the best decide the outcome. In cross country a man who is far from your best always carries the load. Up in the top ten, fading ten seconds might cost 3 or 4 points. Back by the fifth men, points change hands in swaths. Five seconds could be 15 points, three men per second, fates changed in mad rushes right at the line. A championship team needs a closer in the fifth-man spot. Watching Tim Meincke stagger into the final four hundred meters, I saw both our day and our season meet their match. No manner of prodding could summon more power. His legs completely flattened out. Even his eyes sank, first into his skull, and then downward where he bored two finely lasered holes into the ground. His chin showed defeat.

As I chased the race to the line, I suddenly saw Zambrano pull alongside his beleaguered teammate. For a brief second Monkey recognized the challenge and gave a burst. The anger welled up inside my chest. He couldn't sprint for the team, but he could sprint for his spot on the team? I put it all aside. Zambrano had found the gear. He went to his arms and put the accelerator through the floor. A miler by trade, he gloried in his speed. As the five-deep crowd screamed at full throttle, he got to the outside of the running lane and took us home. It was a magic-carpet performance.

The totals would later say that we won the race, but it never felt that way. Zambrano's magic finish obscured bigger failings. After the race, I waded through the crowd and congratulated the boys on a poised win. We had not shown our best engagement. We had won ugly. None of that mattered. I was on a quest to find Tim Meincke. Long experience had taught me that I should not talk to an athlete after a race if I had only negative feedback. I knew this logically, but I found him anyway. He knew it was coming. As we walked back up the hill, I let my displeasure be known. It wasn't the fact that he had a bad race. Of course I wanted a better finish. He did, too. Of course I wanted him to be more patient. His race plan could be fixed. What bothered me was the small moment, a fleeting three seconds or so, when opposing runners had been streaming by, but he had reacted only when Zambrano moved alongside.

This small action betrayed a bigger violation. Tim had given more to defend his spot, but not for his team. The end part of his race had violated our team's spirit, a possible exposure of a bigger weakness. Individual agendas were not going to take us anywhere. We had already canceled all the college visits and rejected all talk of individual accolades. The commitment to the team had become utter. On paper, it looked like we won.

In the team huddle afterward it felt different. We had been selfish. I asked each man to critique his race and told them I was proud of our win, but disappointed that we had not run our best. Meincke apologized and swore that he would perform better with Zambrano next time around. Peter stared blankly ahead, unable to explain his late-race fade. Johnson simply stated that he felt sluggish. Tony and Zambrano glowed with confidence after career-best times, but put those thoughts back inside in keeping with the team agenda. Speaking last, Marcus said that we had been flat, but still won. In his eyes that was a huge positive. He asked a rhetorical question: "What can we do to these teams when we hit the taper and our peak?" Recalling the high from the week before, the rest gave knowing nods.

We had won the Palatine Invite for only the second time, but the positive going forward was that none felt we had run our best. I shuddered to think how good we could be when they fought better for one another. Getting on the bus to head home, I just hoped that I could help them time it right. If we ran our best when it mattered the most, the rest of the state would be running for second place.

RIVALRIES

Photo by Cindi Johnson

The team celebrates its tenth consecutive MSL West title and sixty-first consecutive dual meet win amid the fading twilight at Schaumburg's Hoover Park.

With the Palatine Invite safely behind us, the team settled in for the post-season. The first major test would come in the middle of October at the Mid-Suburban League championship meet. For the full team, this meet was the culmination. From then on only twelve men would be eligible to run in the state series—the IHSA Regional, Sectional, and State meets. The competition for those twelve spots would only increase as the training loads decreased and the emotions ran high toward the peak. For the frosh-soph and the junior varsity, the MSL championship was the state meet. Our goal all along had been to sweep all three levels. We had accomplished that feat the year before and were eager to stamp our authority on our local rivals yet again.

In many ways, cross country competition in the MSL is the most respectful blood sport I could ever imagine. It is rare to see outright conflict or disrespect among conference rivals. Instead, the rivalries seethe under the surface. They animate training and racing. Rivalries enhance desire, pure and simple, and few conferences have done more than the MSL to ensure that local racing is fiery and passionate. Each year the twelve-team Mid-Suburban League divides into East and West divisions and runs a series of dual meets to determine two regular-season divisional champions. All twelve schools then meet in mid-October for the true championship race.

For much of our history, Palatine has been a bridesmaid in the MSL. This isn't necessarily bad. Between 1970 and 2000, we qualified to the state title race sixteen times, yet won only one conference title. Thankfully, greatness is relative. You could barely make top ten individually and still be an All-State runner and a college scholarship athlete. You could never win a conference or division title, yet end up on the state podium as one of the three best teams in the state.

The purest competitions we engage in during the cross country season are our dual meets. Most conferences have given up on this suddenly archaic form of competition, choosing to "train through" or "tempo run" with their best guys. Most varsity runners will never seriously contest a dual meet in their careers. Even in the MSL we sometimes question why we beat up on one another. But each year, these weekly Thursday meets provide the most important barometer of our team's status. In a dual meet there is nowhere to hide. No other teams offset weaknesses or push back a rival's fifth man. MSL dual meet racing, especially when conducted between two equally hungry teams, is a poetic expression of everything good about cross country.

One of my favorite memories as a coach comes from a dual meet from 2006. We had established a lengthy winning streak in MSL duals and faced our MSL West rival Schaumburg to determine our regular-season title. Schaumburg sported a couple of future All-Staters in seniors Mike Spain and Jon Roberts while we matched them with our star duo of junior Mat Smoody and senior Sagar Patel. In most conferences this meet would be all about evasion, excuses, training, and relaxation. In the MSL, meets like this are bloody affairs fought with a passion that few teams would bother to bring to an invite. We ended up winning by a score of 27–28. The meet hung in the balance into the last meters. Thinking we had lost and utterly disappointed, I walked up and congratulated Coach Jim Macnider as the race was finishing. Unbeknownst to me, Kevin O'Brien rallied from a big deficit to slip by Schaumburg's Jim Link at the chute. That move switched 2 points and the result of the meet.

When I walked up to talk with my guys, I noticed the times. They were staggering. Our entire squad had exceeded their Palatine Invite times from the previous week. Mike Spain ran 14:18, a time that put him in the company of men who had qualified for the Foot Locker National meet. For the first time ever, four Palatine men broke 15:00 in the same race (the course was a bit short of three miles back then). I remember being stupefied. To win a dual meet in the MSL, my guys ran the fastest average time in school history. To win a dual meet.

Later that year, Schaumburg won a third-place state trophy at our expense as we settled for a relatively disappointing sixth-place finish. We won the first five rounds, but Schaumburg won the fight. It still stings five years later. The sting isn't from the fact that we ran poorly in the state meet. It's from the fact that Schaumburg upstaged us. I still have the same feeling about Conant and Prospect beating us in the 2008 state finals. We were beaten fair and square. We've lost to numerous programs in the state meet and other invites over the years, but those losses don't linger like a long-festering wound.

That is what rivalries do. They last. They are parts of a larger narrative, a history of competitions and personalities that persist beyond the length of any one season. Rivalries are the epic histories of the competitive world. They help each team unlock the myths and legends that infuse the present with great prescience. In a true rivalry one team is often up while another is down, but both parties have cause to look back and remember better times. The motive to usurp one's rival is everlasting yet grounded in the wind. The windy ebb and flow ensures that results in the distance always infuse the present.

Each rivalry has its own flavor as well. It could be couched within animosity between the coaches, a clash of personalities among the athletes, or mutual respect among all involved. It could be fired by the recent memories of bitter defeats. However it goes, rivalry is what drives high school athletics. To get off the bus at Ron Beese Park in Barrington is to know you have a fight on your hands. If you ever dare run at Prospect, be ready to tangle with Stokie's boys on that infernally complicated course at their school. Coach Stokes and his guys love it and couldn't care less if you don't. To get off the bus at Hoover Elementary School for a race at Schaumburg's home course is an experience all high school runners should have. The Schaumburg boys do nearly all their work on that course. They know every inch and contour of that deadly three-loop layout. Of course, the same holds true on our home turf at Deer Grove East. Rivalries have advantages. They have well-worn stories, famous turns, tried-and-true tactics, and outsized motivations. They matter, and the results last.

It was within this context that we took the first step on our journey toward the IHSA State meet. Throughout the 2011 season, we had faced nary a challenge in our dual meets. For the first time ever, we won meets before we got off the bus. Usually staunch rivals such as Fremd and Barrington chose not to race their best athletes or to run at tempo pace rather than race. We prepared for each meet with the same intensity as usual, but our tactical discussions had gone to waste. Conant's boys had given us a bigger fight in early September, but had been unable to muster enough depth to give us a scare. Since we had easily dispatched Elk Grove in that same race, our record stood at 4–0 heading into the final local meet of the season, a double dual between Schaumburg and Hoffman Estates at Hoover Park.

On the line was a remarkable dual meet win streak that had begun in

The Palatine pack groups together "like a fist" en route to a big win over crosstown rivals Fremd.

the final meet of my first year at Palatine. On a rather dreary and rainy day at Busse Woods, we dispatched Conant to finish the 2001 season with a 3–3 record. Ever since that race, we had not lost. If we won at Schaumburg we would run our consecutive dual meet win streak to sixty-one straight, spanning ten years and ten MSL West titles. It's not the equivalent of Christian Brothers Academy's streak in New Jersey (some 315 meets and counting), but the streak symbolizes excellence. It means that each class has held its own against the image of its forebears. It also means that many successive classes of young men have bought into the same spirit. When we race, we race. There are no distinctions between dual meets and invites.

The MSL record for consecutive wins was set by Fremd in the 1970s

233

at sixty-six meets. Tom Johnson and Chuck Elliott, two of our All-Time Greats, helped end that streak on the old Palatine Hills course in the fall of 1977. Fittingly enough, if we could finish this MSL season with two wins, we would have to defeat a resurgent Fremd team in 2012 to break the record. Despite the history in the making, this final triangular had another and much easier storyline. Schaumburg was good as usual and even better on their home course. They also entered the meet at 4–0 and looking to brawl. Coach Macnider had retired at the end of the 2010 season, but one of his greatest runners, former state champion Scott Lilley, ensured that this respectful but heated rivalry had lost none of its luster.

The day before the meet we prepared with our normal "chalk talk." Like a basketball coach, I draw up all the matchups on the board and discuss the strengths and weaknesses of the opposing team's athletes. I prepare years in advance by constantly making mental notes on how individual athletes in our conference race. Who is tough? Who possesses good closing speed? Who holds weak track PRs, but has a reputation for running well in cross country? Which athletes succeed off a fast pace? Would we be better served to lead the race or follow? Should we sit and kick or string it out? What matchups could we exploit? How could we best use our depth, our sixth through tenth runners, to impact the scoring? How would the terrain of the course play to our advantage? As I pulled the guys into the team room, they saw the scouting report on the chalkboard:

- Evan Prizy (Jr)—9:28 3200 PR, great closing speed, potential All-Stater
- Tyler Anderson (Sr)—9:28 3200 PR, strength runner, weak record against our guys
- Juan Barajas (Jr)—15:25 CC PR, emerging contender, relies on toughness, lacks experience
- Pat Swiech (Sr)—4:27 miler, weaker at cross country than track, susceptible to a fast pace
- Depth = questionable, they have four solids and hope for a fifth

For our varsity top five, these were not just times on a board. They were memories of long-ago conflicts. The developmental races that led them forward to this point were forged in the heat of frosh-soph competitions. Prizy had used his finishing speed to break our guys time after time the previous track season, while both Swiech and Anderson had been constant rivals.

We set up a simple plan. We were going to try to run the fastest opening mile in Hoover Park history. We talked not just of winning. We wanted to dominate a great team on their home course and put times inside their vaunted top ten list. In his course record run, Schaumburg's Pat Lesiewicz had opened just over 5:00 on the 5K course en route to a 15:44 clocking. Only five or six guys had ever broken 16:00, and few had ever opened faster than 5:00 for the mile. Our plan was to do exactly that, but with four guys rather than one. Prizy would outkick every man on our team if the early pace was not suicidal. We wanted him to choose early on whether he would go with us. If he stayed in contact, our guys would lose. We had to make him bleed from gun to finish. Anderson was a different story. He had run 9:28 for 3200 meters the previous spring, but had never quite matched that promise as a cross country runner. His skinny, willowy frame seemed less conducive to the physicality of cross country. With rain in the forecast overnight, we wanted him to hurt early and often. We figured that this strategy would also put Swiech in over his head and force him to either go out too fast or allow a giant gap to form.

The rest became a simple numbers game. We wanted to reduce the front pack to six by the mile mark—four from Palatine and two from Schaumburg. If we did that, then Meincke, Zambrano, Noah Brown, and our top JV guys would take care of their number five runner. After collapsing so badly in the last mile at the Palatine Invite, this dual also marked a significant revision to Tim Meincke's racing strategy. There, he had moved in the mid-race, but his shift had been furious and emotional. By the end of the second mile, he was finished. The goal now was to take that move and string it out over the last two miles of the race. Doing so involved unplugging many of the instruments that Meincke regarded as his strengths—his impulsivity, his competitiveness, his zeal for the team. We wanted calm. We wanted mature pacing. We wanted relaxation and flow. It had become clear that Tim Meincke would never finish a race at his potential if he ran too hard too early. His mind and body didn't fit that style. We had six weeks to build a race style that contradicted every fiber of Monkey's being.

That progression started on a cold and windy day at Hoover Park. Overnight rains soaked the course and effectively ended any hopes of running a fast overall time. The Hoover Park course is simple yet deceptively difficult. It is run on a one-mile loop around the grade school's perimeter, so anything that happens on the course happens three times. Each puddle and sloppy turn was repeated too many times for the race to be fast. Still, we looked one another in the eye in our varsity huddle and decided to stick to the race plan. We were going to hit the mile at 5:00 no matter what. We had already won a key psychological battle by carrying our number one state ranking into the race. What were they going to do, let us go off the front and expect us to fade? It was a trap. They either went with us early or bet all their chips on the prospect of running us down from behind on a cold, muddy, and windy day.

After watching our F/S score a first through seventh whitewash of both Hoffman Estates and Schaumburg, the boys strode confidently to the line and began their final strides. The spark had returned to their eyes. Marcus had his pre-race strut going in full effect. Tony and Peter both wore the grim-faced resolve that they slapped on for the biggest of meets. After months of training and "working on" racing, this one had some finality. An MSL West division champion would be crowned. There was no longer any room to try something new. It was time to execute our race plan like cold-blooded competitors.

Right from the gun, we got the most welcome sight. Schaumburg decided to take it to us. Both Prizy and Anderson bolted off the line and drove the race through a blistering first quarter mile. We could not have been more lucky. I screamed at the lead four to relax and then blast the pace from the half mile to the mile. Swiech quickly fell behind, and the math started to work in our favor. The plan could not have been any simpler or more difficult to accept. We were going to run all-out to the mile and then depend on our fitness and team-oriented running to wear them down.

It worked. Despite the soggy turf and gigantic puddles, we ran the first mile in 5:01. From then on, the race proceeded at 5:30 pace, but it was never been about time anyway. Like all MSL meets this was about pride and struggle. By halfway the race was left to the strong. Red-faced and struggling, Prizy could no longer hang on, but neither could Marcus or Timmy J. They settled back into their own battle while Tony, Peter, and a resurgent Anderson battled at the front. Each lap of the Hoover Park course involves a steady but debilitating climb up what most Illinoisans would refer to as a "hill." In reality there is a brief fifteen-meter climb up onto the back playing fields. The real nasty part of the course lies in the gentle incline that begins near the chute and climbs all the way to the farthest corner away from it. Here the athletes run away from the line. They often pay for their early speed as the gentle incline takes its steady toll over the course of three laps. By the middle of the race, most find themselves engaged in a death march, out of oxygen and slowing down to recover.

The only man not stuck in the muck and mire was Tim Meincke. He ran a race in direct opposition to his teammates. At the half-mile mark, he was nowhere near anyone. Slowly but surely, he picked his way through the field, first jumping inside Schaumburg's top seven and then slowly working up toward their scorers. More important, he wore the pose of a champion. He ran tall with bouncy slack in his jaw. His cheeks bounced in rhythm to his long stride. His eyes gazed straight ahead and showed no mark of pain. The men ahead were targets, and he moved forward gracefully in full flow. After months of injury and too much mileage, this was the first glimpse. By the last lap he not only had caught the Schaumburg fourth and fifth men, but was also barreling down the course toward Garcia and Johnson.

Up the hill the last time Tony and Peter broke Anderson, and the rout was on. Marcus cleaned up Prizy with a similar surge, and then Johnson and Meincke piled in together within seconds of each other. For the first time all season we glimpsed what our team could look like when all pistons were firing. All five men finished within thirty seconds. Even better, Meincke had shone like a champion. He had been methodical and cool under pressure.

Afterward, we gave respectful handshakes and made cordial talk. Fellow MSL athletes and coaches are more brethren than enemies. I bantered with Scott about some of his young runners and told Hoffman Estates' new coach, Brendan Mariano, how impressive his top sophomore had looked in the varsity race. We waited until the cool-down to crow about the victory among ourselves. Outwardly we behaved with great class and respect. But on the bus, in the team room, or on a road run, we would celebrate.

As usual after a dual meet, I repeated my favorite question: "And what do you get for winning tonight?"

Their bemused response: "Thirty minutes." Despite running to victory, this one was still part of the process. We were still hitting seventy miles a week. The math didn't work with a five-mile day. So after taking a picture with another undefeated senior class against the backdrop of the fading October sunlight, we strapped on our trainers and headed back out into the mud for extra time. The Schaumburg guys joined in for part of it, but after a while it was just us. We hopped a mud puddle and headed out the side gate into one of the neighborhoods adjacent to Hoover Park. Now we had a chance to let loose. We made fun of the looks on some of the Schaumburg guys' faces when we slammed the pace into high gear up the hill the first time. We talked of future years and how beautiful our seven frosh-soph athletes looked in their dominant win. Mostly we passed the time by telling jokes and trying not to get lost while running in the dark.

The meet had been a big win, but the time together felt like a win as well. As we jogged on, thirty muddy figures against the night, coaches and athletes alike, our fraternity felt sealed. The many months of time spent in hardship had now reached their logical conclusion. We had climbed the first step on the road to the top. More important, we were tight. Whether we won or lost in the remaining weeks, the tightness would remain. It was an eternal bet against the ephemeral nature of the competitions. As we skidded onward underneath the streetlights, I knew then that nothing could get in our way. There could be no disappointments. The only thing that could possibly go wrong was that it would be over. So we jogged on, content in our cloistered mass, laughing and joking, alive together under the stars.

CONFERENCE

Photo by MaryAnn Graham

The full team celebrates a dominant sweep of the varsity, junior varsity, and freshman-sophomore levels at the Mid-Suburban League conference meet.

Joe Newton, the famed York High School coach, once wrote that each cross country season came down to two goals: win the state meet and win your conference. I wholeheartedly agree. The first goal is the ambitious one. Everyone wants to reach the pinnacle of their sport. The second goal is more emotional. The difference between the two is akin to the division between winning a national political election and getting elected to city council. The former is the prestigious one, the line on the résumé, the capstone on the headstone. The latter is the one that matters in the lives of real people. Just as most governing happens on the local level, so does most competition.

Most high school athletes will never compete in a state final. But all of them, regardless of ability, are part of conference competition. Not all will play varsity in their conference, but they sure know what it means to get after a crosstown rival. So while it is well and good to venerate Olympic athletes or watch the NFL on television, most Americans understand sports best through the prism of the local—through the Friday-night lights, the crosstown hoops classics, and the mano a mano battles waged on tracks and courses across America. In these communities the stars are flesh and blood rather than mythic demi-gods. They have grandmothers and girlfriends and moms and dads who sit in the stands. They give unsure quotes to local beat reporters and hang out at bad fast-food restaurants after games with their peers.

Even better, most local stars exist side by side with good friends who will never see the playing field or the varsity lineup. The star of the baseball team may have gone to the same grade school with the four-year benchwarmer. The star gymnast may be just another kid who doesn't understand complex polynomials and leans on her smart friends for help. Local sports demolish the mythologies of sport even as they build them. The fastest kid in the state might just be another geek with acne. When sports lack the separation occasioned by TV and the marketing genius of shoe companies, they provide a species of emotional captivation that "big time" national sports can never replicate. The developing young athlete is still a species among us rather than a species apart.

Cross country offers a unique glimpse into elite athletics because few sports offer an environment where the best consistently mingle with the worst. Even at the highest levels, cross country and track are sports where the casual fan can reach out and touch the athletes. Go watch any major marathon and you can stand inches away from Haile Gebrselassie or Ryan Hall. Even better, you may be in the same race, albeit miles apart. Try getting that close to Lebron James or Michael Jordan. In a normal practice, the worst freshman on the team participates in the same training program as the college scholarship athletes. When we take attendance each day the Fab Five stretch right alongside everyone else. Our program's no-names—Devin Hein, Jon Young, Cullen Kilcoyne, Jordan Garcia, and countless others—do the day to day just as fiercely and diligently as their more talented peers. We train together at 6 AM all summer. We labor through killer core workouts together. We do the same intervals on the same course. We labor through the same weekly long runs. The paces differ, but the team is always together—fastest to slowest, youngest to oldest.

The MSL conference meet thus becomes the pinnacle of our season. Only twelve men would escape the weekend with spots on the post-season roster. The rest were officially done, but we had decided back in January that this was not how our team would work. If winning a state championship took every single man, then we were going to practice together to the end. The MSL championship with its three races—freshmen-sophomore, varsity, and junior varsity—was the first shot in our collective salvo at greatness.

The legacy of success established by our young men in this meet is unparalleled in our conference's history. We have won the last eight MSL titles on the varsity level. Our goal each year is even more ambitious. We want to win all six races: three individual titles and three team titles. We have only accomplished this goal twice, but each year it is our expectation. In 2010 we pulled off the trifecta by winning all three team titles, and the intentions as the boys arose to another beautiful fall day were the same.

I always stand outside the athletic doors at Palatine and watch them stride in. As they arrived for our 7 AM team meeting, their faces and body language showed that there was no more horsing around. For most, the training was over. It was time to cash the checks from the long summer and fall. They came with the grave look of competition in their eyes. The somber quiet wrote itself across our meeting spot in front of the cross country bulletin board. Guys listened to their headphones and put in their spikes. Nary a sound shattered the mood. In an age when teenagers too often need stimulation and noise, I reveled in the stillness, the quiet, and the all-engrossing concentration. We had been through many race days throughout the fall, but for most this would be the last one.

Some of the young men sitting by the board were fighting desperately for one of the twelve post-season spots. Our juniors especially had the tall task of proving their fitness and racing acumen under the most intense pressure of the season. Joe Mars, Zach Stella, Brian Smith, and Andrew Clingerman were all excellent runners. All four had run the mountain in Colorado and braved the rains in early August. On any other team in the MSL, a few or all four would run varsity. Because they ran for Palatine, they would race one another in the junior varsity race to prove they belonged on the state team. Our prodigy, freshman Graham Brown, was also a threat to earn a spot. He and the five emergent sophomores would contest the frosh-soph race earlier in the day on the same course. The spots would be determined by who could run fastest, regardless of grade. Everyone had worked hard. All were loyal. With no politics, the race was all.

For our varsity seven, the MSL meet was the first gauge of our championship fitness. No longer were we running two meets a week. Recent workouts had gone well. The week prior, Tony, Marcus, Peter, and Timmy J had shattered Glenn Morris's Morning Loop record of 27:20 for five miles. To set that record Glenn had barely nudged out Steve Finley, who went on to win the Illinois state championship in cross country that season. Now we had nearly an entire team of men dialed in at that level. Tony and Marcus ran a staggering 26:10 as all four broke 27:00. Even I demolished my personal best, finishing in 27:58. The meaning of the workout was not lost on anyone. Steve and Glenn were two of the best I had ever coached.

Rankings-wise, we still held the top spot in the state in both the ITC-CCA coaches poll and the DyestatIL rankings. The MSL was stacked as usual. Buffalo Grove had given Neuqua Valley a run for their money two weeks prior, while we knew from experience that both Barrington and Schaumburg were talented and ambitious. Our other great rival, the Prospect Knights, had been lying in the weeds all season. We had not faced them, but we knew they would be ready. Even after winning eight consecutive MSL titles, even after going through the regular season with only one loss, we still approached the meet with humility. The talent in our league—both the athletes and the coaches—demanded it.

Even Johnny Burke, our fabled bus driver, had on his game face en route. All the coaches and veterans could gauge the quality of the meet by listening to Johnny's swearing en route. If he was relatively mild-mannered, it was probably the early season. If he told us to "look at this broad" or called someone a "jackass" for doing a basic driving maneuver, we knew that we were in business. An old Chicagoan, Johnny is our attitude. I always leave for the meets hoping that someone will cut him off or give him inept directions about how to park the bus. When he brings his attitude, it translates to the boys. Tim Larson, captain of our 2003 state trophy team, made the varsity team yellow shirts that read, OUR BUS DRIVER CAN BEAT UP YOUR BUS DRIVER.

Johnny's was even simpler. It read, I AM THE BUS DRIVER WHO CAN BEAT UP YOUR BUS DRIVER. Tim bought it about three sizes too small to fit over Johnny's belly, but the point was taken. On each of our four state trophies since 2003, his name appears as "Bus Driver" right alongside the athletes and coaches. Big meet days would not be the same without Johnny swearing in his cigarette-stained voice. He has a few more gray hairs in his goatee each year, but that old Chicago toughness is still there.

As we pulled into the Busse Woods Forest Preserve, Johnny started railing right away on the parking scheme that Elk Grove had instituted. By the time he finally parked, everyone in the front half of the bus was rolling with laughter and ready to get off the bus and beat a parking attendant. As each boy exited, Johnny gave him a fist bump and that steely glare. No words. I loved seeing our freshmen get off the bus at their first MSL meet with a snap in their stride and a quizzical look about the crazy bus driver.

The Busse Woods course felt like an old friend. Each boy who stepped off the bus knew our method for attacking the course. We carefully developed race plans for each of the three races, and the boys were expected to follow them to the letter. The course is a simple mind-grinder—three one-mile loops with significant elevation changes within each loop. A man needs to be strong in both mind and body to succeed at Busse. The start is in an open field, but narrows down quickly to head up a gentle incline. Past the half mile, it proceeds downhill, slightly at first and then with a long downhill right near the thousand-meter mark. Once a runner hits this downhill, he heads with momentum and gusto down into the teeth of the crowd. To see the downhill descent and then the sharp right-hand turn at the bottom of the hill is awe inspiring. Each time the leaders hit the bottom, they are met with the MSL roar.

For a sport burdened with difficult scoring (try telling who is winning at any given time), no television exposure, and a lack of mainstream cachet, cross country surprisingly flourishes at the high school level. The northwest and west suburbs of Chicago are some of the nation's hotbeds for distance running. When you see the couple thousand people that jam Busse Woods for an MSL meet or a sectional qualifier, you see running at its purest level. That roar at the bottom comes each of the three times the runners come around. The key to running well at Busse is what the athletes do when the roar is not there.

One time each loop, the race heads back up the opening hill in near silence. The muddy section uphill toward the back corner is like running in a tunnel. Just the runner, his opponents, his thoughts, and the course. All extrinsic motivators vanish. No coaches, no teammates, no parents. This section of quiet, when the screams melt into the ether, is Palatine's money time. We gauge our entire race around furious uphill attacks in the middle portions of the race. A strong move uphill in the second mile shakes the tree. Another in the third mile is a declaration of championship status. By that time the men and boys have long been separated. Anyone can charge down a hill into the waiting arms of the crowd. But how many can charge through the silence to the top?

After catching up with my coaching friends and glad-handing parents and alums, our day began with the freshman-sophomore race. I had been convinced since the previous fall that a win in this race would be one of the great achievements of my career. Lacking a star, our five sophomore stalwarts had become—by necessity—a collective greater than the sum of their parts. Now joined to the emerging stardom of freshman Graham Brown, they delivered an unlikely title. We placed our top seven in the top twenty-three of the race. Weakened by illness, Graham placed second, while five of his teammates landed together in the teens. A year after looking like the weak links in a chain of greatness, they showed that we were around to stay. The winning margin was not trivial. We scored 55 points to easily outdistance the under-level teams from Barrington (115), Fremd (119), and Buffalo Grove (126).

As usual our preparation paid off. We had succumbed to a yearlong vision of improvement and found ourselves at the top of the frosh-soph heap for the seventh time in nine years. Other teams, most notably Hersey and Fremd, would have beaten us had they run all their best athletes in the under-level race, but we had served notice. If they wanted to beat us on the varsity level, the journey would still go through Palatine.

The buzz in our camp before the varsity race centered on the collective will of our sophomores and the outspoken effort of Dean Kolar. Conservative and thoughtful by nature, Dean had just embraced his irrational side. When all the odds said he did not belong, he thrust himself into the thick of the lead pack. It was a feeling easily understood by our varsity athletes. Meincke and Garcia were infamous for abandoning rational thought during races in favor of "the big shift." Such passionate outbursts had led to both triumph and failure during their careers. I had been forced to harness them and pull in the reins. Both men sat astride the fine line between the creative freelancing genius and the impulsive risk-taking fool. Frosh-soph races were easy places to bet on impulse and learn what it had to teach. Varsity races were for known quantities. With years of work on the line, we had to trust each man to run the race plan that guaranteed the best result.

Our varsity warmed up on the Busse Woods bike path before taking to the open field across the parking lot from the course to do their strides. As perennial favorites we were used to the stares and attention, but even I noticed an enhanced focus on our guys. For the first time we entered the post-season as the state meet favorites. In some leagues such a status might be cause for supplication. In the MSL we intimidated no one. Each man in the varsity race knew he could define a high point in his career or for his program by knocking us off. No one is invincible in the MSL. We run against one another for too long and across too many seasons for any one man or program to lord over the rest. The upsets are too frequent. The young men watching us do our strides knew our track record. Many of them had also beaten our guys in individual track races over the years. If they could accrue enough individual wins, then their team would win the MSL title.

As we strode to the line, we had one last surprise. We'd decided back in January to design post-season uniforms that harked back to the 1970s. Coach Joe Johnson had started the powerful legacy of Palatine cross country, and we wanted to run with that legacy in mind, especially in a year devoted to his memory. The early Palatine distance stars—All-Time Greats like Mark Visk, Fred Miller, Brian Barnett, Tom Johnson, Chuck Bell, and Chuck Elliott—had worn the simplest of uniforms. Red jersey over red shorts. Giant block *P* in white in the middle of the jersey with white lines above and below. The day before, we finally received our uniforms in the mail. As I handed them out to the varsity seven, it was like flipping an emotional switch.

I also asked Tom Johnson to speak to the team the night prior to the MSL races. Tom had been All-State in both 1976 and 1977 and was surely the best cross country runner in school history by both time and acclaim. Others had challenged his feats, but Tom's track record of great races had been unmatched by anyone since. He told us stories of those early great teams, and we instantly knew that we were unified with the great teams of the past. Tom's teams ran tons of miles and killer interval workouts on the track, too. Those early teams had also experienced ups and downs, difficult workouts and team triumphs. Mostly, he talked about the enduring memory of running for Joe Johnson. Joe had invested his life in the Palatine program, building it bit by bit throughout his illustrious career. Tom had been a junior on the first team that Joe ever qualified to state. Now here we were thirty-five years later trying to win the program its first state title. The uniforms were a tangible reminder of that invisible but ever-present legacy.

Watching our guys take off their sweats and strip down into those new uniforms was also a reminder that the end of our journey was near. There was no more time to refine our physiology. We would run the races with the engines that we had built. As I talked to the team in our huddle before the race, we focused on the usual mantras. Execute the plan. Focus on the means. Achieve the result. We dropped a resounding, "Pack on three, one, two, three, PACK!" that echoed across Busse Woods Lake, and then returned to the box to await the gun.

After winning eight consecutive MSL titles, I tend to lose perspective on the varsity race. I assume that we are going to win. I expect it. Our goals are selfish, acquisitive, and competitive. To remain on top, we don't want any weakness exposed. We do not want one single athlete to know what it means to win a varsity MSL cross country title. The goal thus becomes more than winning the race. It's about psychological domination.

I positioned my finger on the start button of my wristwatch and hoped that our guys would not take our past MSL success as an indicator of a promised future. As the gun flashed, the starting line erupted with action. A few lesser athletes, those with a storehouse of chutzpah rather than sound physiology, stormed to the front. The usual contenders were there as well—the defending champion Peterson from Barrington, Atchison from Buffalo Grove, Prizy and Anderson from Schaumburg, a trio of Prospect Knights.

Quickly Gregorio and Tomkiewicz worked their way into the lead pack and settled. Tony had finished only two seconds in arrears of Peterson the year before so he knew the score. He wanted others to work the pace early so he could jump it when the moment was right. Peter was in uncharted territory, but the regular season told him he belonged. He truly believed he would win. Just behind them, Garcia and Johnson grouped side by side. A born rhythm runner, Marcus could eat a field alive from behind if he gauged his start smartly. The weeks prior had been trying ones for Johnson, and I hoped that he could stick with Marcus. Throughout the season he had shown flashes of his top-end form, but had stagnated in the middle of races. I hoped Timmy J—a big meet player—would shake out of his torpor and make an attack up inside the top ten. Behind them, Meincke and Zambrano executed a far different plan. They started well behind the others and depended on their rhythm and cold calculation of pace to move gently up through the race. We hoped they would still be charging as the race entered its final desperate moments.

Marcus Garcia and Tim Johnson pack up en route to a varsity MSL title and All-Conference finishes.

As the race wound around to the mile, the team race was in hand, but Tony and Peter struggled to stay in contact with the leaders. For years Gregorio and Peterson had owned Jereme Atchison. But this was a new and improved Atchison. At the mile he jacked the pace and jumped the field. Both of our front-runners were slow to react, like they thought it was a joke. It wasn't. After training with York for the entire summer,

Atchison had discovered greater strength and a newfound ability to shift gears. His incessant surging destroyed the rhythm of the front end. Only Peterson, a cool and collected customer, was able to smoothly match Atchison's fury. Moving with his normal grace, Peterson saw those moves and rode the lead in anticipation of his own winning stroke. Both Tony and Peter looked rattled.

Not only had Atchison pulled something new out of his bag of tricks, but Prospect's Michael Leet was busy declaring himself a contender. We had watched Leet's varsity emergence with stupefaction all season long. The son of high school national champion Janet Leet, Michael had shown nothing resembling this type of form throughout high school. But here he was pushing pace off our front-runners. I saw the flicker of arrogance in Tony's eyes and reminded him to stay poised. The race was going sideways to his expectations, and he needed to deal with it.

As they headed up the hill past the mile, the pairing of Garcia and Johnson dissolved. A strength runner, Marcus found his rhythm and began demolishing the Busse Woods layout. The biggest danger on this three-loop course was stagnation. It was easy to lose focus and quickly drop places, but Marcus had done so many thirteen-milers with progressing tempo finishes that they had become part of his DNA. He found his gear and flowed from behind toward the front of the race.

The problem was Johnson. Timmy J possessed a skill set entirely different from Marcus. He could run long distance, but something about the slow creep of three-mile racing hurt him. Just past halfway, I noticed the hunch in his shoulders, the cocking of his head to the side. Marcus abruptly looked back down the hill and motioned for him to come forward, but the string had snapped. Johnson let him go and cast himself adrift. Untethered from his partner, he would founder in the wind for the rest of the race. With Timmy J backsliding, we could still win, but any hope of a dominating statement was over. At his best he could be an All-State runner, but his race left nothing but worry for all involved.

Luckily for the team, Tim Meincke and Christian Zambrano worked their race plan to perfection. The year before, Monkey had shifted like a madman at the mile and worked his way up into the top fifteen. From the two-mile in, he had suffered like a beaten man, scratching and clawing to stay inside the top twenty-five and earn All-Conference honors. He ran with mad furor, but failed to close. Now he and Zambrano ran loosely together as they moved up through the field at a gradual clip. Just as in his breakout race at Schaumburg, Meincke found his stride. Nothing in his race would beget poetry. There were no romantic charges to the front. The boy of impulse had been replaced by the fully poised man. Into the last mile he rolled the field and set his sights on Timmy J's back. Teammates since junior high and friends for even longer, TNT (their freshmen nickname) found each other in the deep race and carried us to victory.

As I jogged to the line, I knew we had won. Our seventh man, Noah Brown, finished just outside the top thirty, and six of our guys finished All-Conference. It had been a winning effort, but far from a statement. No one in the MSL or around the state would look at our front-runners or our five-man split and think, *There's no way Palatine is going to lose.* Every week was going to be a fight. As the runners exited the chute area, I finally got the rough count: Tony third, Peter sixth, Marcus tenth, Timmy J fifteenth, Monkey sixteenth, Zambrano twenty-second. Fifty points. We had scored less points in other years, and I silently wondered whether we had it in us to be dominant. Outwardly, I celebrated. Inwardly, I feared we might not have what it took to win a state title. Was Johnson tough enough to deliver? He had placed tenth in this race the year before, and most of the men in front of him had graduated. Why hadn't he improved? After running nine hundred miles over the summer, why wasn't he dominating?

Tony's reaction mirrored my own. He looked flat-out disgusted. The move at the mile mark shook his confidence to the core. The year before, he ran Peterson to the line and within an inch of a conference title. In this race he had been a well-beaten third, passed up by Atchison and challenged by both Leet and his own teammate. I could see the doubt creep into his eyes. He, too, had worked harder than ever. I could see him wondering why the work had not paid off. Had we run so much and come so far only to get worse? He seemed evasive and stressed. I wondered whether there was something more eating at him.

Even the usually unflappable Garcia looked sullen. He had expected to hammer through the middle of the race and run himself into the top five. The plan had not worked. He got to the edge of the top ten before hitting a major gap and stagnating. Either he did not have the will to move or tenth place was where he belonged. He had expected more.

While not somber, the mood was far from jovial. We had scored 50 points and defeated Buffalo Grove (74) and Schaumburg (88) by fairly handy margins. The individual results told a different story. Buffalo Grove had beaten us through four men. If they could get one more guy to fig-ure it out, it might be them on the top of the podium at state. Even worse, Buffalo Grove was a newcomer on the state scene. If they earned a bid to the state finals, it would be their first trip in school history. If they were beating our front four, what would perennial rivals York and Neuqua Val-ley do? As they left on their cool-down, I could read the unspoken anxi-ety in their faces and they could read it in mine. We had just won the Mid-Suburban League title for the ninth consecutive year, and the guys sauntered out to the bike trail with nothing but questions. The creeping doubt of that post-race huddle would threaten to consume the team.

After a clear but unsatisfying win in the varsity, I quickly shifted gears to what is always my favorite race of the day, the junior varsity. Most pro-grams view this as a race for the cast-offs and the also-rans. At Palatine it is serious business. Not only does it help to decide spots on our state ros-ter, but it is also the final exam for my yearly projects. As a runner, I had lacked talent and been wholly unspectacular. I became a varsity athlete because I worked at it, day by day, year by year until I became competi-tive. As such, my coaching struggle had always been how to understand elite athletes. Nothing about having talent made any sense. I never under-stood ease of motion, or grace, or freakish aerobic ability. What I under-stood was how to make runners. The men with the lack of foot speed, the weak mechanics, or the so-so mental game were my boys. I understood

The junior varsity team smiles for the camera after winning their level
and taking twelve of the top twenty-five All-Conference spots.

them and inhabited their triumphs and tribulations in ways I never could
with the best of the best. Every year, the MSL junior varsity race was a triumph of my guys. And this particular year had been my masterpiece at
the JV level. Our goal was to skunk the MSL—a perfect score of 15
points—by taking the top five spots.

The late parts of that JV MSL race are among my fondest memories
of the season. Our main group splintered in the middle of the race, but
the connection endured long enough to drive us to a dominant win. We
placed twelve men inside the top twenty-five—1, 2, 3, 5, 8, 10, 11, 17,
19, 23, 24, 25—for a paltry team total of 19 points. Even better, only one
of our guys in the top ten was a senior. Right under the noses of our rivals,
we had shown what was coming next. We had an entire second team, a
wave of juniors ready to go.

We would have more than we needed to continue our winning streak
the next season. But the major questions still remained. As we gathered
our conference awards, the team had been dominant. As I accepted con-

gratulations from fans and rivals, I did so amid silent fears. Logically, the varsity win had been definitive, but I watched the awards and worried. I could not put my finger on the bother. For the first time, I sensed it all slipping away. I finally felt the weight of the aspiration. Johnson had been dropped and badly. Was he even a top-fifty guy in the state anymore? Gregorio and Tomkiewicz had been badly dropped by competitors I thought they could beat. Would we have the front-runners that it took? Garcia had lost force in the middle of the race. If he was only tenth here, could he be All-State? Meincke had flourished, but was he running well or was Johnson running badly?

My outward calm belied the inward storm. All along I'd believed that we were a team of destiny. I'd assumed that it would work out. After fumbling through the conference meet, the entire enterprise became shrouded in doubt. I tried to fake it as the team posed for its annual conference meet photo, but climbing onto the bus I was scared. As Johnny drove the team on its usual route home through Arlington Heights, I looked sullenly out the window and worried what was wrong with my boys.

TWO CALLS

From left, Brian Smith, Peter Tomkiewicz, Tim Meincke, Marcus Garcia, Graham Brown, Anthony Gregorio, and Tim Johnson cap a tough week with a strong win in the IHSA Regional.

The post-season began in earnest the Monday after everyone's conference meets. It marked a decided shift in tone and a movement toward the final crescendo. Seven teams from each regional would qualify to the next week's sectional. Most teams would qualify easily before racing for a spot on the starting line at Detweiller Park on the first Saturday in November. Only the top five teams from each sectional would survive to contest the state final. At Palatine the goals differ. Winners of all but three IHSA Regional and Sectional titles in the past eight years, our boys know that

257

solid racing will earn us advancement to the state meet. We had mastered advancement. What none of us could know was what effort we would be prepared to give when we got there.

After a less-than-dominant effort in the MSL meet, two Sunday phone calls quickly gave clarity to my unspoken feeling of dread. That afternoon, Steve Johnson gave me a call to try and figure out why his son was not performing. He had seen the training schedule I laid out for the regional week and didn't like it. Unlike most parents, Steve had been a championship-caliber runner, setting the school record for two miles at Hersey and running collegiately at Wake Forest. Normally, I would not accept such a critique, but Steve and I had worked together throughout the past two years. He knew our program well. He also knew his son better than I. The conversation centered on mileage. I was asking the guys to head back up to sixty-five miles a week before beginning a three-week series of drops for the IHSA Sectional, the IHSA State, and the NXN Midwest Regional races. With less competition in the regional, I figured we would train through and come out the other end okay. Steve felt that the miles were eating Tim alive and asked for less mileage and more track work.

For Steve the matter was one of physiology. Tim has a lot of fast-twitch muscle and responds well to interval training. I had leveraged that fact against my need to keep the team tight. I was hoping to bring the team to a collective emotional liftoff that would outweigh any one individual's training regimen. I probably should have changed his workouts, but I dug in. The team agenda was the center. I made some small adjustments, but the entire conversation skirted the edges of my biggest fear. I worried that Tim Johnson simply did not have what it took to be a champion runner. He was sweet and gentle. He was polite and went to church each week. He genuinely cared about other people and his teammates. He didn't swear or talk bad about other people. In short, he was the nicest young man I had ever met. Therein lay the problem. I had watched Tim Johnson run races for four years, and the conclusion was inescapable. He lacked the nastiness to be a killer.

I hung up the phone and sat on my basement couch to collect my thoughts. Above my television in the basement are four photos of state champions: Steve Finley winning the 2005 state cross country meet, Mat Smoody breaking the tape in 2007 and 2008 to win the state 800 meter title, and Alec Bollman guns blazing in the air after claiming the 2010 state 1600 meter title. I looked to those pictures for advice. What was I doing wrong? Each of those state champions had a piece of nastiness inside that Tim lacked. Finley's piece of nasty was his outsized ego. Even when he had been beaten multiple times, he entered every race thinking he would win. He always believed he could pull the rabbit out of the hat, as if accrued evidence of failure didn't bother him. Smoody possessed the qualities of a showman. He liked the bright glare of success in the big moments. He raced not just to win, but to do it with aplomb. In 2008, much to my chagrin, he threw his arms out wide at the finish line in a taunting gesture, a body language declaration that said, *You thought you were going to beat this?* Bollman's piece of nasty was a direct descendant of both. He was equal parts egomaniac and showman.

Tim Johnson simply did not possess those traits. Actually, I liked him better because he lacked them. At times all three state champions had been difficult to deal with, insufferable, or just downright cocky. Tim and I had no such problems. I loved his humility and grace. The best word to describe him was *gentle*. That was the problem. I looked around my basement at the team pictures on the walls. I saw Glenn Morris winning the sectional cross country race while wearing only one shoe. I looked at my picture of Jimmy Mac's All-State cross country finish. I saw the torrents of pain across his face, the flogging action of his arms. I looked at Kevin O'Brien receiving his All-State medal and remembered how much unspoken pain he endured to run each day. That grit had served him well. Steve's questions also clouded my thinking. If I was losing control of Tim Johnson, was there a bigger mutiny afoot? Steve's call crushed my confidence just when I had been busy assaulting it on my own. I sat in the basement for the next two hours, my family gone at the grocery store, and worried that I had ruined it. If we lost, it would all be my fault.

As difficult as that first conversation was, it did little to prepare me for what came next. Later that night Anthony Gregorio's mom called me. She was in tears. After coming home earlier that day, she'd found Tony sitting in her kitchen with his dad. Back in the beginning of the season, Tony's doctor found a heart murmur during his routine physical. Thinking little of it, they scheduled a doctor's appointment the week of conference to have a cardiologist take a closer look. The results had just come back, and they weren't good.

All week before the MSL race, I sensed something amiss in Anthony Gregorio's world. He seemed distracted and distant. I chalked it up to school stress or just normal anxiety regarding the post-season. I had been dead wrong. The cardiologist turned up a defect in one of the valves of his heart. The murmur the doctor heard was the result of backflow from one chamber of the heart to the next. A normally functioning valve ensures that blood exits one chamber and moves along to the next with each heartbeat. A faulty valve allows some of the blood to leak back into the previous chamber.

As Maria cried on the phone, I feared for Tony's life. Then I feared for the group. I feared a lot of things, and that was the worst part of it. Nothing definitive had been found other than the leaky valve. No one knew whether Tony should continue running. No one knew whether he could function normally. We lacked information outside of what we observed. From my vantage point Tony was asymptomatic and had embarked on one of the most ambitious training regimes of my career. Barring one week when he had been sick, Tony had just completed twenty straight training weeks above seventy miles. Nothing in the anecdotal data told us that he was sick. Justifiably scared, his father told him he had to stop running. Maria, furious at that declaration and scared in her own right, got off the phone to hash it out and promised that Tony would call me back.

This second call was a body blow. The talk with Steve Johnson had been about philosophy of training and athletic performance. This call was about Tony's life. It was also about the dreams of the group. Everything centered on this young man—his toughness, his experience, his ability to perform in the clutch. In one instant everything we had worked for seemingly vanished. After telling my wife the story, I retired to my office to research the heart. As I sat there quietly reading, searching in vain for some knowledge that would give me solace, I thought mostly about heart. Tony Gregorio was our heart.

Almost every activity a distance runner performs relates to heart power. It is simply not an activity one should perform with a flawed heart muscle. As I stared at the computer screen, I saw images of collapse and ruin. A couple of weeks prior, I had watched the ESPN *30 for 30* documentary about the 1990 Loyola Marymount basketball team. The story of that season revolved around the collapse and death of Hank Gathers. Gathers had famously reduced his medication because it made him feel tired. In a game on March 4, 1990, Gathers threw down a massive dunk, retreated to mid-court, and then abruptly collapsed. He died on the court in full view of the crowd.

Logically I knew this was not the case with my athlete. Gathers had died from hypertrophic cardiomyopathy, a disease where the muscle of the heart is thickened without cause. Tony's valve issue was minute and unrelated. Later in life he could have a procedure performed to fix or replace the faulty valve. Still, my thoughts went back to images too frightening to fathom. Tony running in the regional race, suddenly staggering, falling, and never getting up. All because we wanted to win a race. It suddenly seemed so silly.

As I sat there and thought the worst, I started to cry. No coach should ever put an athlete at risk. Watching Hank Gathers lie on that court in a gym full of thousands of silent fans would knock anyone's socks off. There is a brief silent image in that documentary of Gathers's mother with her head to the hardwood, beating the floor in vain. The hubris of the moment was inescapable. They had known the risks and risked it anyway. I determined right then and there to make the safest call.

Later that night, Tony called me back. It was not an easy conversation. He was scared, defiant, and incredulous. His emotions were all over the place. I saw immediately the burden he had been carrying. During the buildup to conference, the fear had swallowed him whole. The call from the doctor turned some of those fears into reality. He just couldn't understand why he felt so good when a doctor was telling him that something was wrong. The medical test belied all the athletic tests he had passed. How could a man with a faulty heart be so strong in matters of the heart?

After talking with Tony, I switched over and talked with his mother. My emotions collided into one another at full speed. We had come too far for something to derail a team on the precipice. We had put too much time into this. We had to find a way. More rationally, this was about Tony's well-being. This was about more than sports. As we talked, I knew that the best course of action was to recuse myself. I was simply too biased to offer advice about what to do. I urged Maria to consult with the cardiologist, her husband, and Tony. Whatever they decided was going to be final. Just because everything on the outside looked okay did not mean that I should push him to run. They needed to decide. The rest of us would live on.

Threaded throughout the conversation were bigger questions relating to identity and quality of life. Tony had thrown himself into this headfirst for so long that he had little knowledge where Tony "the person" began and Tony "the runner" ended. At some point the quest had taken over, a creeping compulsion whose weight could not be measured until dropped overboard. To jump ship now might simply lead to a drowning of a different sort. When considering whether he could let it all go, I finally saw the mania of the pursuit. I felt the weight of it, saw it in its largest relief, perhaps for the first time. Tony wanted to be a state champion, a scholarship athlete, and so much more. We all wanted to win. What did all that pursuing mean if we never ran the race to its conclusion? After hanging up the phone, I wondered about my priorities. I wondered if I had spent too much time and energy chasing an inconsequentiality. If this didn't work out, what would I have left?

I wish I could say that I slept soundly that night, that I felt reassured by deferring the decision to the family and the doctor. But that decision did not allow for sleep. I lay there deep into the night—2 AM, 3 AM, 4 AM, time moving gently by—and invented futures with subfutures and branched-off realities. I saw us competing in his honor. I saw us winning. I saw him running well. I saw him collapse in pain. I saw myself retiring and giving it all up, a concession to the sick power of obsession and my own lost identity. The potential tragedies lay all around. We would be undone by the very obsession that had brought us so far.

After only two hours of fitful sleep, I arose more of a mess than the night before. None of the guys on the team besides Tim Meincke knew what was going on. We had shielded them from the distraction, but the team would have to know now. Our hallmark phrase when we got to the post-season was simple: "No distractions." We hewed closely to routine and focused on perfecting the small details. I went to morning practice that day with a sense of dread along with a delicate attention to managing the tone. I couldn't let them see the fullness of my fears. Neither could Tony.

We were scheduled to run our normal five-mile tempo run on the Morning Loop. The large groupings of the regular season were all gone. This run was just for the top twelve and the coaches. As they straggled in through the morning darkness, I was filled with a sense of foreboding. The day before had been like the dawning of some dark star, a force of unfettered darkness and evil intentions. Oblivious to the broader issues, the rest tramped in with the normal feelings. It was starting to get cold in the morning, they had not caught enough sleep, it was just a training week, advancing from the regional was largely a formality. They expected little more than a hard run and a hearty breakfast. Each year, I gave the same speech on this date. No distractions. We had worked too long and too hard to be distracted by anything—grades, Halloween, girls, jobs. From this point on, with three weeks to go, everything else would be on hold. Then I paused briefly and announced that there was one more issue.

I remember their half-listening teenage heads snapping to attention. Standing by the stairs to the gym near our board, Tony's eyes burrowed holes in the floor. Small to begin with, he looked crushed under the weight. Everyone sensed that this was one of those moments akin to when your girlfriend says, "We need to talk." So I just let it out in plain language. Tony's doctor had found a murmur in his heart. He and his family were going to a cardiologist for a final opinion later in the week. Every man in the top twelve should be ready to run. Every man inside the top seven would need to step up and carry more weight. I remember watching the mix of horror and fear come across Marcus Garcia's face. Meincke already knew the news, but that had not prepared him for his teammates' reactions. Peter just stared blankly ahead. They were stunned. Everyone was thinking the same thing I had the night before: *There is no way we win this thing without Tony.*

From then on we proceeded as if he would not run. I had talked further with his mom the night before, and she had cleared him to run in practice as they awaited the doctor's decision. Like me, she felt that the anecdotal evidence of his health outweighed some test from a lab. She asked me to watch him for any hints of distress. Inside, my nerves jumped. Distress? We were about to blast a five-mile road run at speeds most humans would never touch. On Tuesday we would run an all-out 1600 meter time trial as a preface to the main workout. Distress? Distress was the only dish we served! Distance training is a constant cycle of distress and adaptation, a search for the edge within a series of intentionally painful acts. After distress, we cope. But there is no other way. Tony had flourished because he could master distress better than most. More than the rest, he flogged himself with a vindictive urge born from being told he was never quite good enough. Always too short, too slow, and too weak, running had shown him how his love for pain could make him a champion.

So we did what we do best. We left the demons in the school hallway and hammered the loop. Out on the Morning Loop at 6 AM there is no room for rational thought or calm consideration. There is only brutal pace. No more. No less. In the isolated bubble of the Loop, we lived on impulse alone. The world might be trying to end our journey before its completion, but we could still fight one more time the way we knew best—through our fanatical dedication to the run. Locked into his element, Tony knocked out a 28:15 five-miler like everything was normal. The other four seniors did the same. As soon as the run ended, the doubts returned. They would hang in the air the entire week.

Our afternoon practice began with the unveiling of the top twelve. The twelve had been together since June, and every one of them had run the mountain. The top seven spots went to the six seniors plus one junior—Gregorio, Tomkiewicz, Garcia, Johnson, Meincke, Noah Brown, and Zambrano. Backing them were four more juniors, Stella, Smith, Mars, and Clingerman. The last spot was one for the future—Graham Brown. Despite running his weakest race of the year at the MSL meet, Prodigy had served notice that he would be in the center from now on. In his mind, he should be running on the post-season team now. Ironically enough, the events of the week would afford him an opportunity a year earlier than planned.

The rest of regional week unfolded like a surreal blur. After being named to the top twelve, Joe Mars went through the motions and looked as if he couldn't care less. With eyes downcast, he ran dead last in the workouts and betrayed an indifference that had been hidden throughout a solid season. To make matters worse, Noah Brown turned up sick on Monday and could barely function heading into the Tuesday track workout.

Tuesday's workout started well enough. The five senior stars crushed a 1600 meter time trial, recording the fastest average time in school history. Tomkiewicz kicked past Johnson in the last two hundred meters to win in 4:24. The rest pounded in right behind: Meincke 4:25, Johnson 4:25, Gregorio 4:26, Garcia 4:27. Even the alternates responded with blistering personal bests as five more guys dropped under 4:40. The team proved that it was sharp and had the fitness. Whether we had the rest of what it took was still up in the air.

Later in the workout, I noticed Marcus Garcia screaming at Zach Stella. After the time trial, we had entered the meat of the workout, a sharp set of twelve four-hundred-meter repetitions with only one hundred meters of jogging rest. Stella and Mars quickly dropped off the pace, and

I could see the varsity seething. When Stella stepped across the line after running an eighty-six-second lap, Garcia snapped. As I walked up, he and Gregorio were screaming at Zach, asking for more effort. He responded by walking out of the workout and out of the practice. I was incredulous. Mercurial by nature, he had flirted with the varsity top seven for much of the year before crashing and burning under the pressure. Quitting a workout at this point in the season revealed bigger issues. I had just named him to the state team, giving him a coveted spot, and he paid it back by quitting on his teammates. After watching he and Mars mail in the workout, I wondered which part would crumble next.

I got my answer the next day when Peter Tomkiewicz failed to show up for practice. We had a half day of school, and practice was scheduled for 12:30 PM. When I called roll, the ringing silence hit the ground with a thud when I got to Peter's name. A day after two juniors had melted down and Noah had shown up sick, our best runner was absent without leave. Garcia and Gregorio looked at each other with incredulous stares. I just looked at Coach Sheehan and set my temper to a fast boil. I sent them out on a run and pondered the next move. Peter magically materialized halfway through the run and finished with the group, but the damage had been done. When they walked through the athletic doors, I was waiting: "Team room. *Now*." They put their tails between their legs and trudged in.

I ordered Peter to the front of the room. As he lumbered to the front with his long gawky motion, I picked up a desk, turned it around, and slammed it to the floor. I screamed for him to "Sit down!" For a moment I let the quiet air breathe all around him. Sitting there, slumped in shame, he stared intently at the desk's smooth surface in order to avoid his team's rough judgment. But really, no one could escape the blame. We had gotten to the brink of everything we ever wanted and fallen apart. Indifference. Sloppiness. Shattered unity. Sickness. A broken heart. The pieces lay scattered throughout the silent team room.

I started with the juniors. On Monday I had asked for no distractions. Stella and Mars had done the opposite. Both had enacted psychic dramas that drained the team's focus. Peter had broken team rules. The buck had to stop here. When in doubt, I did what was best. I was honest. I told them of my fears. I laid out the drama of the two phone calls. At first I showed them the anger. Then I showed them my vulnerability. In the end the message was clear. We could either fall apart under the pressure or run to win.

Getting through the rest of the week was not easy. Our juniors called a grade-level meeting of their own and got themselves straight. Although they were mostly passengers on this journey, next year would be their turn. They needed to learn from the experience. There could be no flaking out in workouts or halfway gestures next year. As usual Andrew Clingerman took the reins and brought them to practice on Wednesday with some purpose.

Gregorio was a different matter. His appointment to have the cardiologist read his EKG was slated for Thursday during the day. The wait throughout that day was interminable. I remember seeing Monkey, Timmy J, and Marcus in the hallway that day and trading concerned looks. Finally, Tony arrived just before practice and gave us the news we needed. Excepting the leaky valve, his heart was fine. Someday he would need elective surgery to prevent deterioration as he aged, but the cardiologist cleared him for full activity. At that announcement a massive weight crept off everyone's shoulders and immediately lightened the mood.

Despite the good news, everyone still looked drained. Regional week tends to have that effect, but this slump was more pronounced. Even worse, Christian Zambrano missed Friday-morning practice. We were all heading toward the last mile of the Morning Loop when I noticed that Christian was missing. I was so sure that all of the varsity were present that I had neglected to take my normal attendance. We had already decided to replace Noah Brown with Graham Brown until Noah's sickness went away, but Christian's absence put me in a bad spot. The entire first half of the week had been an admonition to keep focus, reduce distractions, and get the details right. I decided immediately to replace him.

As we finished, I asked Stella and Mars whether they were ready to run. Neither stepped forth with any veracity. So I looked around and picked the best exemplar I could find, Brian Smith. Smitty had labored through sixty- to seventy-mile weeks for the better part of a year. His incessant base-building had been focused on the long term, but had cost him during the mid-season races. He was the right choice. He exemplified everything I taught about standards of conduct and work ethic.

As we entered the school driveway and gave our normal kicks down the sidewalk to the light pole that marked the finish, I saw Christian standing alone in front of the athletic doors. His eyes were downcast, and I could see that he had been crying. He knew the score.

I gave it to him simple, "You picked the wrong day to miss practice. Smitty is in. You can earn your spot back next week." His eyes immediately welled with tears. Difficult as it was to bench a loyal man, we both knew that the week's events demanded it. As we walked out to the track to run our strides on the turf football field, he ambled off alone to complete his run. It was his first unexcused absence in three years of cross country practice.

Wearing their 1970s throwback uniforms, Peter Tomkiewicz, Anthony Gregorio, Marcus Garcia, and Tim Johnson hunt the early lead.

To the outside observer our dominant run in the next day's regional may have indicated that all was well. With state-ranked powers Barrington and Lake Zurich in the field, the race was far from easy, but neither team possessed the depth to give us a run for the team title. We placed 3, 4, 6, 8, 12 for an easy win in a tough field, but our weaknesses showed. Our front-runners had not been up to the task. Garcia remained stuck in the gap between greatness and solid team runner. He lost contact with the leaders early and ran the entire race by himself. Even more distressing, Johnson failed to stay with him once again and drifted backward throughout the second half of the race. His racing continued to mystify all involved. Meincke ran solid, but our two substitutes, Smith and Graham Brown, ran like rookies. From then on both would be mired on the bench.

As the boys lined up in front of our home pavilion at Deer Grove East to accept our ninth regional trophy in ten years, I couldn't get over the gap between the surface reality and the actuality. All the parents and fans saw the smiles on their faces, the gleaming trophy that would be put up inside Palatine High School, the large margin of victory. All I saw were the tiny imperfections. In two weeks we would have to face York and Neuqua Valley for the state title. Both programs had won national titles in cross country within the past decade. To beat both in the same day would require a degree of excellence that we had not demonstrated in some time. In Illinois cross country there is no margin for error. We had two weeks to make it work. If we ran the same race in two weeks' time, the trip home from state would be a long van ride indeed.

SECTIONAL

The bunched field heads down the first decline into the teeth of the crowd at the Schaumburg Sectional.

The IHSA Sectional week inaugurates the real soul of the cross country season. Although a few teams are eliminated in the regional round, the late-autumn winds finally blow the breezes of finality during sectional week. As usual, the Schaumburg Sectional at Busse Woods reared its mythical head and sneered. Year in and year out, there was no tougher test. The Busse Woods course had claimed many worthy teams and individuals over the years, ensnaring runners in its devilish loops. In the immortal words of Buffalo Grove coach Jamie Klotz, "It's easier to get into heaven than it is to get out of the Schaumburg Sectional." Those who survived the crucible would be ready to compete with the best the following week.

My first memories of this race were not fond. In 2001 we tied for fifth in the regional, advancing to the state-qualifying meet by a single point. Without a prayer of finishing in the top five and qualifying to state, we ran impetuously at the front of the race for as long as we could. Our desperation saw us in the lead at the half-mile mark and sixteenth at the finish. I later realized that the mature teams, Barrington in this case, hung back early and then let it loose in the second half of the race. They won that year and taught me a big lesson. Precision, teamwork, and fitness were the cold keys to success. You couldn't just want to get to the state meet. You had to be ready.

We went away over the next year and ran hundreds upon hundreds of miles through track, the summer, and the season. There were triumphs along the way, a state ranking inside the top ten along with MSL West and regional titles. Our outward confidence was stark. Inside, I remember being racked with fear. The 2002 sectional race included no fewer than ten ranked teams. Of course, the rankings mattered little. Creating a winning race on that day was all that mattered. Surviving the Schaumburg Sectional had nothing to do with reputation or the regular season. It was simply one race that had to be executed perfectly on one given day. A bit full of ourselves and confident on the surface, we melted in the heat of the fire. We finished eighth place and missed qualifying by 18 points. I walked away devastated. All our work meant little in the face of that one race.

My emotions swung out of control. I was angry at the athletes. I was angry at the state for its unfair sectional layouts. The next week at state, the teams from the Schaumburg Sectional placed second, fourth, fifth, sixth, and eleventh. We would have qualified out of every other sectional. The Monday after the state meet I met with Fred Miller to decide what we would do next. We had two choices. We could complain about the situation, or we could get better. That conversation shaped everything our program would become. We looked each other in the eye and said, "Well, if it takes being in the top ten in the state each year to advance, then that is what we are going to do." The next year we won the sectional and tied for second in the state meet.

One of the tri-captains of that team, Tim Larson, was on the varsity throughout the entire three-year process. He flamed out when the team got sixteenth. He ran like a warrior and hung his head in disappointment when the team placed eighth. His senior year he placed seventh and was the first man to grab the sectional championship plaque. It was only the second time in school history that we had won and the first time since 1980. My dad told me when I came to Palatine that the most important way to build a champion team was to find one champion athlete. Tim had been that champion, and he and I had remained close ever since. No man bled the Palatine colors quite like Tim Larson. He was a loyalty extremist, an original zealot.

It was important to inculcate in the boys a clear sense of the program's stature. I wanted them to know that the pursuit of a state championship bonded them to thousands of other young men who had aspired to the same. To that end, I introduced a series of guest speakers who each explained to the current team what the program had meant in their lives.

J. P. Falardeau, captain of the 1997 team, came back the night before the Palatine Invite and spoke about how cross country had taught him to overcome adversity. A veteran navy pilot who had flown many missions over Iraq, J. P. had them on a string. He told them how the team had given him the discipline and fortitude to overcome difficulty as an athlete, as a person, and—most important—as a combat pilot. Tom Johnson spoke the night before the MSL conference meet. He told us what it had been like to run for Joe Johnson in the program's infancy. He gave the boys advice on how to deal with pressure and focus on the task at hand. Dave Gregory spoke to us the previous spring. Fresh from working in China, Dave told us how each guy on the team could matter and contribute. Jon Chermak spoke to our varsity the night before the regional. One of the fiercest competitors ever to wear our uniform, Jon talked about what it meant to perform in big races. He talked about the attitude that a champion carried into each race. Every one of these men had given a piece of himself to the program and created it for us.

As I herded the boys into my basement the night before the sectional, I hoped that Tim would be a rallying voice. A solid performance in the regional notwithstanding, the team still seemed disinterested and lackadaisical. Just that morning, both Peter and Marcus had overslept their alarms and missed the start of morning practice. They eventually showed, but I continued to seethe at our lack of focus. We were healthy. We were fit. But somewhere in that mix we were missing the magic. To perform at a magical level, the individuals have to become greater than the sum of their parts. Such synergy was impossible to create without everyone's full engagement. Our flaws were emotional rather than physical. Somewhere en route to the final chapter of the story, our sense of trust had suffered.

Tim understood the synergy principle better than any athlete I ever coached. His team, the one that started our recent run of success, achieved at a higher level than talent should have allowed. In the last half mile of the state meet, they found the magic and ran with an elevated spirit. That year we beat teams who were faster than us because we flourished as a unit. My fear now was that the reverse would happen. We were the fastest team, but I wasn't sure we were the best. As the boys told jokes in my basement and shot hoops on my kids' indoor basketball hoop, Tim and I gathered with my wife and Coach Sheehan in my kitchen. I laid out my concerns and then turned it over to him.

Tim had a special connection to the team not just because he had run with us throughout the summer. He had also hired Tim Meincke and Anthony Gregorio as employees at Running Unlimited, our local running store. In many ways he had raised these young boys into men alongside me. Comfortable for once to listen, I parked myself in the corner, right beneath the plaque on my wall that contained the pictures of the 2003 varsity holding the state trophy in their hands. The boys were surrounded by the plaques I had made to honor previous trophy teams from 2003, 2004, 2005, and 2007. It is our tradition to take a picture of each man in the top twelve holding the state trophy. I then have those pictures framed alongside our state meet patch, the team picture, and my state medal. As the boys sat to listen, the ghosts of past successes hovered over them as both tormentors and saviors. The spot I had reserved for the first state championship plaque, the wall at the bottom of the basement stairs, was white and empty.

Larson opened by complimenting the boys on their season. He shared with them the memories he had written with his teammates. James Macatangay and Mike Nigliaccio, two of our volunteer coaches, had also been on the 2003 team. We told them about the beginnings of our journey together. Much to their disbelief, we told them about the first time we all broke 30:00 on the Morning Loop. Tony and Marcus laughed at us, remembering their 26:10 clocking from a few weeks before. We told them about all of our quirky habits and the utter belief we had found in one another. For a solid three years we built a championship ethos by running all-out over the last half mile of every run. This strategy had gone by the wayside as the program developed, but we all agreed that those manic finishes had been the key component in our charge to a state trophy.

The second half of his talk shifted tone. He stood up from his chair in front of my television and related a lesson he had learned from his days running at North Central College for Al Carius. At North Central the specters of fourteen national championship teams in Division III cross country lord over each new varsity group. The proud alumni are always rallied in support, but quick to compare the current team with successful groups from the past. Tim saw this support as both a blessing a curse. He told us that no man can live up to the incredible memories of someone else. Counter to our impulse to honor those who came before, he told us to be selfish. He told the boys, "This is your time. Be selfish. Run for each other and forget about all of us alums." Trying to please everybody was the biggest impediment to success. His advice was counterintuitive. After all he was an alum, speaking as a representative of past success. An eerie sense of quiet descended. The pause caused the hairs on my arms to stand at attention. I looked across the room and saw Marcus's nostrils flare as he gazed at Tim with rapt attention. Point taken.

The next morning came on chilly as usual, but sunny and bright. As we boarded the bus, we all grasped the coming finality. Training was about increments and delays. To train was to work hard and wait. Then, when the peak came, you rode the wave and let loose. The trick in a qualifier was to run well enough to advance, but not so well that it became the peak. The hardest lessons of my coaching career had come when my athletes rose to the qualifying occasion only to be tapped out for the state meet.

Watching the guys warm up, I felt their confidence. Marcus ensured that we had a tinge of cockiness. He gave us the requisite swagger. The plan for the day was simple—group up with your running mates, be patient early, hit in the middle, hang on late. Once again I implored Johnson to stick with Marcus. Rather than pressuring him, I reminded him of his power to inspire. Always an enigma to his teammates, Johnson did have one powerful article of faith on his side. His teammates believed, as did I, that he always performed in the clutch. Save the ghastly result from the previous year's track sectional, we were all right to believe it. Quiet and unassuming, Johnson often ran like he didn't want to offend anyone by showing what he had. Only in the big ones, through some species of strange necromancy, did he summon the giant lurking within.

As I jogged away after giving the final instructions, I found my parents and brother in the crowd. They asked me if the boys were ready, and I told them, "We'd have to give it away in order not to win." Then the gun fired, and we started to give it away. As I had the year before, I cautioned them about the early fliers and counseled a patient and building race. Our start was more slow than patient. Had Meincke and Zambrano looked behind them at the two-hundred-meter mark, they would have seen only the ghosts and the crowd. I found out later that Gregorio fell exiting the box and the team had to hold up to avoid trampling him. He and Peter squirted through most of the crowd and got in position, but everyone else was well adrift.

To make matters worse, our old rivals from Prospect had found their pride. Two weeks before, they had delivered a weak performance at the MSL meet, a lackluster race that belied their true potential. It was obvious that Coach Stokes had lit their collective fires. They got out and rolled

Peter Tomkiewicz and Anthony Gregorio ride the shoulder of Barrington rival Erik Peterson early on in the IHSA Sectional race.

Marcus Garcia and Tim Johnson race side by side through the mile mark.

277

Photo by Cindi Johnson

Tim Meincke and Christian Zambrano work together in perfect harmony.

with great purpose. By the half-mile I was left to wonder just what we were doing, whether our overconfidence was our downfall. Still, our guys found their partners, absorbed the rough opening, and started to work.

We did not rally to pound the field. Somewhere deep in the race our acquired poise came to bear. When the race slowed at halfway, Peter tempted fate and took the lead. He took a risk and ended up fading to sixth late in the race. Tony hung on per usual. Still visibly frazzled and unfocused from his recent health ordeal, he snuck inside the top ten. Unbeknownst to Johnson, I had ordered Marcus to run with him through the first half of the race. It still didn't work. Marcus couldn't move up enough in the last half while Johnson faded anyway. At the beginning of the summer, we harbored hopes that Timmy J would be our lead runner. Now he managed only twenty-second in the state qualifier. Even worse, the aborted start and the frantic move through the field slayed Tim Meincke. From the two-mile mark on, he gave spots away freely and willingly. He finished just inside the top fifty. We had hoped that he would be top fifty in the state meet. Only a daring kick from

Zambrano staved off Prospect's charge. He kicked with his soul on fire in the finishing stretch to nail Prospect's fourth and fifth scorers. It was a hero finish on a day when the usual heroes abdicated the role.

I felt stunned in the aftermath. We won, but barely. The final margin of victory—13 points—felt like a sliver. Even worse, the run shook our confidence. Prospect had delivered as usual, but they had certainly not shown the ability to run with the best teams in the state. As the boys filtered back from the finish corral, each one betrayed a shaky face. The mood was grim. I collected the cards and tried to offer congratulations on a key win, but they could fill the hollow space in my voice with their fears. When I asked them to gather their things and meet me under the "tree," they all knew what that meant.

We put on our sweats and walked away from the team camps toward a quickly fading tree just opposite the bike path. As I turned around and faced them under its bright yellow leaves, I searched for the right path. It couldn't be fear. It couldn't be anger. It had to become an advantage for us to have run this race. As the seven assembled with the five alternates and coaches flanking them, I went down the line, asking each man to grade his race and point to possible improvements. Peter embraced his risky moment and said he'd be ready to finish it off next week. Marcus knew that I had stalled his race for Johnson, but refused to use that as a crutch. He pointed to his mid-race stagnation as a weakness. Gregorio simply stared a hole in the ground. He put on his pout face, the one that could fill me with rage in a blink, the one I had worked long and hard to destroy. It spanked of self-pity. It also caused the weak races he detested. When he wore his pity on his sleeve, it hurt all of us. He grumbled something about a C, and I moved on. Meincke and Johnson simply had nothing to say. Both knew the score and vowed to do better.

For two weeks our season had teetered on the brink. Call it indifference. Call it overconfidence. Call it boredom. I'm not sure what caused it, but when I looked around the semicircle I knew what I said next would have to end it. So as I began to speak, I asked them to zoom back to one year ago. We had stood underneath the same tree, with the same feelings, a narrow loser to Lake Zurich in a failed come-from-behind attempt. In both races we had run not to lose. The solution was simple, but difficult to embrace. We would have to run the exact same race we had run the year before. The wins of the regular season had cemented our favorite status. The problem was that carrying the burden had diminished our ability. We had to run to win.

I implored them to simply go for it. We had to run the race we could execute best. We would have to send our guys right to the front of the state meet and bleed all the way from gun to finish line. We might fade again. We might cough up the ball entirely. But at least we would go down fighting like men and fading in style. Around the circle, the boys started to nod. Garcia knew that he could hit it from the start, guns blazing until he ran out of ammunition. Tony knew that he could bet on his toughness. That was a hell of a lot better than what had just happened. We had never been a team that flourished when coming from behind. We had to run free and let expectations be damned. Tim Meincke captured it all in a phrase: "Let's call it Jackass 2: Not quite, but yes."

Photo by Cindi Johnson

From the left, Marcus Garcia, Noah Brown, Anthony Gregorio, Christian Zambrano, Tim Meincke, Tim Johnson, and Peter Tomkiewicz pose arm in arm after a tight win in the Schaumburg Sectional.

PRELUDE

The morning of the state final, I rose early from a ragged sleep. Darkness still leaked through the window, intermixed with the pale orange of the streetlights. My eyes fixed on the ceiling as my heart beat at an unnaturally quick rate. My wife snoozed gently next to me as I got up to wake the boys.

In my preparation I left no superstitions behind. Every article of clothing was chosen to make me feel lucky. Dressing in the raw pre-dawn darkness I pulled on my Palatine race jersey, the throwback we had designed especially to honor Joe Johnson. The jersey was a surprise for the boys, part of the script. Next I put on the Joe Johnson T-shirt. If we were going to do this today, it was going to be in his spirit. The twin images on the front said it all. On the left, Joe in his early years, full of life and a passion for running. On the right, Joe in his later years, still full of the same vitality.

Fred Miller and the alums had packed the shirt's back with Joe's favorite sayings, but we only needed one: GUTS AND DESIRE. Over that I pulled on our team shirt, expertly drawn by Emanuel Rosales and anointed with the words, ONE WAY —> UPHILL ONLY. We had grabbed the phrase from the sign at the bottom of the mountain we ran in Colorado. We were going to need the spirit of that run in the final sprint. Next came the new lucky hat. For every other championship, even the birth of my children, I had worn a faded-out, salt-stained disaster of a Cal Berkeley hat. The boys had convinced me to switch to the sun-scorched Colorado Buffaloes hat I had punished through our brutal summer of training.

Only one room of athletes was awake, but the rest swung quickly into action. I meandered down to the hotel lobby to await their arrival. Breakfast at the Spring Hill Suites is often like breakfast at Wimbledon. The hotel's continental breakfast often draws the best in the state into close proximity. I got some apple juice and wished Edwardsville's Garrett Sweatt well in his bid to win, remembering how Steve Finley, Ryan Craven, and Kevin Havel had all eaten breakfast with one another, remembering how Lukas Verzbicas nonchalantly texted as he slouched through his breakfast. The boys straggled into the lobby finally, and we were surprised to see Johnson arrive early. I made some crack about how he could finally understand what it was like to be the rest of us before we gathered everyone and headed outside.

It is a running joke in our camp that the most important run of the weekend is the ten-minute morning jog. Forget the state meet. The goal was to hit 10:00.00 exactly on the pre-race jog. All-State alum Kevin O'Brien had done it once, and Timmy J replicated the feat the previous spring at the state track meet. Tensions ran high. The boys synchronized their watches and headed off into the new dawn chill for an easy shake-out run. Ten minutes later they arrived back in the main lot, weaving around as they tried to burn up the last few seconds before the clock hit ten flat. Johnson gave it a go, but was only able to clock a 9:59.98. Not quite championship-level execution, but a noble result. We walked in for breakfast and let the waiting begin.

Ever since Illinois moved the Class AAA boys meet back to 2 PM, the wait had become interminable. How much Discovery Channel and *Sportscenter* can anyone really watch? The boys were probably climbing the walls, but I had the good fortune to have my family around. Walking back upstairs, I was surprised by my father-in-law and sister-in-law, who had come down to support the boys and me. We chatted for a minute before I decided to take Madeline and Christopher down for breakfast. Christopher spilled his apple juice all over everything and ran around in his pajamas with his hair sticking straight up. Mads, in her difficult five-year-old way, refused to eat anything but Frosted Flakes. Of course, the hotel was out. She threw a fit because Lucky Charms just were not good enough. If I needed any more convincing that the race did not matter in the grand scheme, they certainly provided it. Throughout much of the day they would frolic in the woods at Detweiller Park, oblivious to the races going on all around them.

Later my wife came down and took the two older children swimming while I went upstairs to watch the baby and prepare for the team meeting. Joshua Jeffrey (J. J.) was born on August 24, right before cross country season, and he continued to expand at an exponential rate throughout the fall, reaching a critical mass of fifteen pounds just before the state meet. I laid him on our bed in his light blue lion sleeper and started to walk around and fret. He fussed so I gave up on getting overly excited and lay down next to him. His pudgy face turned toward me as he flashed a quizzical expression. I looked into his deep dark blue eyes. He paused for just a second and then laughed, sticking his tongue out and rolling it around as he curved his lips. I ran my hands along his cheeks and then flung them out to his sides as far as I could, telling him that J. J. is soooo big! No state title can compare to a happy and healthy baby.

My wife finally arrived back in the room with my two soaked and happy children, and I knew then it was time to go. We made our goodbyes and I headed down to Coach Hajik's room to have one final meeting with the team. All season long I had thought about how to manage the emotions of these final moments. More than once during the summer, I brought myself to tears driving around Palatine, thinking of living the moments I was about to live. Then, I could fill my entire chest with blood and quicken my pulse with just a few seconds of thought. And that was in July. Now it was time to go, and the finality hit me. I walked in and saw that Coach Sheehan had laid out all the race numbers on the table. I grabbed a chair in the corner and watched the boys pile in.

Mark Magnussen had sent an email the previous day talking about the incredible speech Joe Johnson gave to the boys the night before the 1980 state meet. He told me that none of the boys thought they could win, that they spent most of their trip screwing around and acting crazy. But after Joe spoke, they walked out knowing they were going to win. The next day Mark Magnussen led the state meet coming out of the back loop, and the Palatine boys won their first-ever state trophy. I promised that I would read his message to the boys, but I also denied its implied challenge. I was certainly no Joe Johnson, and the hour was running late for fire-and-brimstone speeches. So I quieted the room down with Tony seated straight across from me and Marcus seated behind me near the door. I dutifully read the email, but then remembered what Tim Larson had told us the week before. Sometimes the most important part of being a champion was the pure selfishness of it. He had encouraged us to listen respectfully to alums, but then put them out of mind and focus on our hopes and dreams.

I read Mark's message before abruptly shifting gears. Later, I regretted how I started, but the sentiment kept with Larson's message. I told the boys to forget Mags and forget about Joe and his great speech. This was our time. I was not going to give that speech because I was not that man, and they were not that team. What I did have for them was my heart, and I tried to speak to them in the same way that I wrote to them before the big meets of their careers. For years I have written the boys notes on big meet days, reminders of race strategy and how much pride I have in who they are. I had decided to tell them face-to-face what they all meant to me, but I suddenly had no words. It wasn't the first or last time I had cried in a team meeting. This one was different, though. Tears flooded in, reducing my words of love and encouragement down to gasps and small staccato phrases. I looked straight across the room at Tony and saw how much all of this meant to him, all the trials and tribulations, all the dreams and defeats and victories, all of it. Peter stood to my left staring at the floor, tears rolling gently down his cheeks. Our time had come.

I attempted to talk to each of them in turn. For Zambrano, I reminded him of my pride in his perseverance. His first three seasons at Palatine had been ruined by Osgood-Schlatter disease. Not ruined because he ran poorly, but because he could never love running for what it was really worth. His persistence meant the world to me. For Noah I recalled the choice he had made to quit soccer and pursue running with his full heart and soul. No one had ever put in more work at Palatine—eleven hundred miles' worth over the summer—than Noah Brown. I told him those miles would be available to him when it mattered most.

Now it came to the Fab Five, the boys I had helped raise into men. The entire year had been an exercise of collective will toward this day. We had spent more time together than we had with anyone but our families. For Timmy J, I reminded him of the power he held to inspire. I reminded him of his first great run, when he won the Palatine Invite freshman race. I reminded him of the incredible race he had run to advance to state track as a sophomore. I reminded him of his audacity the previous November, when he had come through after a season crushed by mono. Lastly, I reminded him of the past spring, when he put his best racing behind three other men and anchored them to All-State honors. Gentle by nature, he needed no further chiding from me. He needed to see his inspirational force through my eyes in order to believe its truth.

I turned next to Marcus. He sat, eyes on the floor, just behind me. I attempted a moment of levity, but my care for the young man extended too far to joke my way through what I had to say. Who knows how Marcus Garcia would have turned out if he had not found running. I made a quick crack about him being a pot-smoking bass player in a great local band, but that belittled my real intent. Marcus had given this season everything, bending his furious individual spirit time after time for the good of the group. He had committed utterly. I told him what an honor it would be to see him running at the front of the state meet later that day. After last year's late fade, I let him know that he would be a hero this time around. His dark eyebrows could not hide the tears, and I was glad for it. Everything we had done and were about to do mattered to Marcus in a fundamental way. Our relationship had moved far beyond athletics. I was glad for that, too.

Next up was Peter. I simply let him know how proud I was of his transformation into a champion athlete. The year before I hoped that Peter could make a serviceable fifth man. He had done much better than that. His ascension sparked the team to unimaginable heights. All through the summer I met with Peter at night for the extra miles, the ones that nobody knew about. As I conveyed my pride, my voice deteriorated, but my mind saw it all so clearly—the ten-mile runs late on humid summer nights, the debilitation of twenty-mile days, the hundred-mile weeks. His season validated everything I had ever known about distance running. The battles often aren't won by the talented. Most often they are won by the survivors and the lunatics. Peter's preparation had invoked elements of both, and he ran now with the urgency of a man with something to prove. I had never before witnessed such a stunning change. Along the way he and I had forged a forever bond.

Now it really got tough. Unlike the first three, I knew what I wanted to say to Monkey and Tony. The winning of a state title had been a consuming passion of mine for so long that I sometimes forgot why I wanted it. I just knew that I wanted to win. When I looked at Tim Meincke, I understood why. All summer long, all season long he had dominated my thoughts, as if I could scheme and plot a young man toward a performance that I had sculpted in my mind to utter perfection. Over and over again I saw him finishing like a maniac up the final hill in the state meet. From just a figment of my imagination, I had carefully willed that finish into being. I thought endlessly of the psychology and physiology that could bring that pre-established memory into being. Now that we had arrived at his moment of truth, I still had my doubts. Choking on my words I told him what I felt to be true. Watching him finish in the state meet and win us a state championship was going to be the greatest thing I ever did as a coach. It was still just a potentiality, but I wanted him to hear it as fact. I thanked him for the memory before it ever happened.

Then it was time for Tony. He cried throughout the entire meeting, same as I. Not small weeping cries. Choke tears. The kind that seize your throat and constrict your breathing. Looking at him in that moment, I had to stop. A heavy pause filled the room. Just two weeks before, I had lain in my bed and questioned the universe. I stared into my ceiling for hours that night, ticking away the minutes, wondering why God would take away Tony's heart as we neared the final hour. Was it hubris? A cruel coincidence? Had we chased too long and hard after an inconsequentiality? These questions had no answers. As I looked at him, all I could squeak out through my labored exhalations was how I never believed that God would take away our heart. Tony was the rock upon which the team was built. It didn't work without him. I had refused to concede that something could be wrong. I loved him too much to have to take it away from him, but I would have. That might have killed him just the same. Thankfully, he had been cleared. It had not been easy, and I could see the burden written all over his face. For years this had been our common quest. Now, at the end of the journey, I lost the voice to tell him what he meant to me, what the entire road we had run together meant. I hope he saw the answers in my face.

With that, we adjourned to our rooms for one final hour of waiting. We would leave at 10:30 AM to catch the girls race. I think everyone exhaled a deep sigh of relief when the appointed hour came and we headed to Detweiller Park to see just what the universe had in store for us. As I stashed our gear in the van and slammed the door shut tight, everything felt in place. The team meeting had produced more tears than fire, but our emotional resolve had reached a fevered pitch.

We arrived at the course in caravan and headed directly to the golf course on the opposite side of Highway 29. Once safely parked we performed our normal runner ritual. We pissed together in the weeds. I think our brazenness probably offended Liz Sheehan, and I must admit that fifteen people clad in red sweats casually contemplating the dying weeds and the Illinois River must have been an odd sight. Better a final team piss than spending our time in line for the porta-potties.

I released the boys for forty-five minutes of socializing with friends and families while I went off to watch the Class AA boys race and find my family. With my wife and kids happily lunching at Chuck E. Cheese, I was free to enjoy the day. Usually I do my best coaching in these moments. My continued presence around the athletes would just cause more nervousness. In such moments less can be more, a lesson I had learned through long experience and one too many "inspiring" speeches. I found my mom and brother sitting in their normal spots near the finish line. The feeling was the same as it had been all year, an unspoken acknowledgment that this one felt right. My mother had been to almost every state meet since 1980 and had ridden shotgun on more than a few rides where the hopes exceeded the results. She had been at my dad's side through all of the ups and downs of a career spent coaching young people. I think she enjoyed following my teams because win or lose, she wouldn't have to come home to a distracted husband and another crushed dream. Retirement for both meant that there were no more trips back to the drawing board.

She and Chad asked me if I was ready, and I gave the obligatory response. My confidence was high. Sometimes outward confidence betrays inner doubt. This time I meant it. I had never been more sure of an intuitive truth. I told Chad directly, "We are going to run our best and we are going to win." He was a cross country junkie at heart, and I let him in on the race plan. I told him it was a basic Moline plan from the 1980s. We were going to send our first four right to the front and expect them to hang on. Tim Meincke had given the plan its name the previous week after the sectional, "Jackass 2: Not quite, but yes." The title was an homage to our desperate attempt at victory from the year before, and a slight admission that the "not quite" part applied cardinally to him. While the front four had the psychic ease of committing to a fast early pace, Monkey was expected to exercise discipline and come from behind. The year had taught him a valuable lesson. Romantic charges made good poetry, but often led to bankrupt results. After all, the Light Brigade never rode back out of the valley of death. Romanticized or not, 135th place was still 135th place. It would not do on this day.

I wandered back toward the line and found Marcus and Tony outside the ropes watching the Class AA race. We kept our eyes on defending state champs Belvidere North, keen to do some scouting and see what type of match they might offer the next week at the Nike Midwest Regional meet. At that contest there would be no classes. Just the best from four states. After watching Decatur Macarthur's Michael Clevenger overtake Belvidere North's junior star Tyler Yunk to win the state title, it became clear that North's power had lessened. They won Class AA, but had fifth-man problems. A man over 16:00 for three miles would translate to a huge score the next week. While easy to contemplate the near future, we quickly snapped back to reality. It was time to begin our pre-race routine.

Our team encampment is the site of an ad hoc alumni reunion each year as well as the headquarters of our parents. The only people you usually won't find there are the men about to race. As we walked into the crowd, the excitement from our fans was palpable. The fan bus had arrived with the rest of the team, and they huddled around the varsity, offering final words of encouragement and their considerable enthusiasm. Each year we cater in Jimmy John's for everyone, but my stomach had no room for food. Watching the growing fray of well-wishers, I extricated the team and sent them to our spot of solace across the highway. Other than the coaches and me, no one would see them until after the race. Before proceeding, we rehearsed the warm-up instructions once again. Jog at 12:55 for 15 minutes, 10 minutes for stretching, 5 minutes to cross over to the starting line, 10 minutes to check in, 5 more minutes of jogging, 10 minutes for strides, and then the final huddle. The regimen had been well honed over a series of years, and they would follow it to the letter. We wanted them to bask in the warmth of routine.

Coach Sheehan and I left them and headed to the north end of the field to ready ourselves for the start of the Class AAA girls race. The previous two years our girls had been state champions and state runners-up. This year, injuries to key personnel had crushed our depth and left us with four great runners and the search for a fifth. Coach Parks had spent most of the season pulling out the final few strands of his hair and searching in vain for one more runner. After Cassidy McPherson passed out in the stretch drive of the sectional, they had qualified only by virtue of tying for fifth place. Their entire season had rested on an old IHSA rule decreeing that ties for advancement to state would not be broken with the sixth-man rule. Parks and the girls had been lucky to land a box on the starting line, but that luck had landed them in Box 37, the end of the line.

In any normal year I would have been living and dying with our girls coaches, but I had a divided rooting interest. One of my dad's greatest runners, Rob Harvey, coaches the girls at Wheaton Warrenville South, and they were one of the favorites. In 1989 Rob had anchored my dad's state championship 4 x 800 meter relay. The shaky and well-worn video of that triumph is at the core of my family's culture. For years my brother and I would watch it over and over, memorizing the yells from the crowd and my dad's frantic commentary as he watched one of his dreams come true. You can hear my pre-pubescent vocal cracks and the desperate cheers of my brother. As Rob runs the anchor leg, you can read my father's entire career in the shaking of his hand. He desperately manages to keep the lens focused as the excitement builds. On the backstretch, he wonders out loud, "Where's second place?" and then has to pan back to find it some fifty meters behind. At one hundred meters to go, he stands on the bleachers to catch the final surge to the finish. In the final ten meters his voice starts to crack. At the line the camera goes up in the air and all you see is sky. That was the only state champion he would ever coach.

Rob and I started talking in the summer about winning twin state championships for my dad. Each of us knew that our teams had what it took on paper. Rob's girls had placed third the year before to Schaumburg and Palatine, but they had only been 12 points from the win. I had adopted Palatine as the center of my professional life, but Rob is blood to me. I wanted our girls to do well, but as I stood in the nervous moments before the gun it was with long wishes in my heart for my friend. Rob had been the hero of my youth. His dreams were the same as mine. Neither of us had been able to give my dad a state cross country title as athletes, but we were both determined to give him one as coaches.

The girls race unfolded beneath the same beautiful blue sky as ours would in just a few short minutes. Right away I saw the orange uniforms of the Wheaton South girls charge to the lead. They were serious underdogs to New Trier, who had been ranked in the top five nationally all season, but that was no matter. They hammered down the opening incline with little regard for intelligent pace. As they passed me at the quarter-mile mark, I could see the intensity in their eyes, senior captain Lauren Mordini heading the group. All season long Rob had bemoaned their lack of intensity. Pundits had expected them to dominate, but the emergence of New Trier had thrown his girls into a purgatory of doubt. Now they had thrown caution to the wind. I ran to the half-mile mark full of inspiration. Rob had given them reason to believe, and they ran in the same spirit that we had run at Moline. The entire exercise unfolded as an homage to my father. He taught all of us to love unchecked aggression, to bet big on one another, our team, and our school. These lessons from across the years had not fallen on deaf ears.

Heading into the back loop just past the mile, his girls kept hammering near the front with absolute faith in their mission. I had seen enough. Each year I watch the girls race to see if I can discern any clues about the day, the atmosphere, the tactics. This one answered my riddle. So I watched the rest of the race, running around with Coach Parks and watching as the Palatine girls sank under the weight of expectations. Even before the race was over, I could read the despondency on his face and in his body language. Two years before, I wore the same disappointed look as he walked off the stage with the state championship trophy. Their season had been trying, but our girls would be back for more. They had won seven previous state titles for a reason.

I trotted up the course and took in the finish as best I could, but the time for spectating had drawn to a close. Rob's girls had not won the race, but they had run their best when it mattered the most and placed second in the state. As I jogged over toward the golf course to find my boys, I thanked him silently. We might not give the old man a two-for-two, but we could still give him one. After being motioned by the police officer, I headed across the highway. Our plan was the right one, and it would work if we could only summon the magic at the end of the race.

STATE

I found the boys stretching behind the shuttered clubhouse, enjoying the calm weather and blue skies of another gorgeous November day. I had feared that some manner of weather might derail us. Unseasonably warm weather, rain, or snow would be equalizing factors that we could ill afford when we had the fastest five-man group. The torrential downpour that hit on Thursday night had muddied the course, but it was not sloppy by any means. We were not going to have a mudder. It would be a thoroughbred race. The temperatures also cooperated. Our guys wore their winter sweats as an obligatory gesture, but the thermometer had long since passed sixty degrees. I stormed into the stretching circle with the intent of bringing some fire. Rob's girls had ratified my thinking. We would not wait one second and run even splits like York used to do. We would not set conservative splits to the mile and two-mile before obliterating the finish like Neuqua Valley would do. I had been taught to race one way since I was a child. We were going to seize the race by the balls and twist. If York and Neuqua Valley wanted to win, they would have to come from behind and take it. I pulled them into a quick huddle for one final recitation of the race plan.

By then they could see the elevation of my normal self into race mode. In their own ways each followed suit. The year before we had ridden our style of race, and it had bucked us. The challenge would be to ride that same horse and believe that we could stay on. Just as we had done at the top of the mountain in Colorado, we linked arms into a circle. We had waited the better part of a year for this moment, and I could read the mix of urgency, fear, and excitement in their faces. Marcus's nostrils flared gently as they always did when he concentrated, and Tony had on his fight face. Stoic as usual, Peter and Timmy J had the steel in their cheeks. Monkey looked ready. By that time each man in the huddle, from the five senior leaders, to Noah and Zambrano, to the alternates, to the coaches, could have recited the race plan verbatim. It had been ingrained down to the level of muscle memory. We had run this race many times on the track or on the closely mowed course at Deer Grove East. Now we would get to run it with the last defining element—the full force of our emotion. Our practice sessions had missed that adrenaline, but more important they lacked the love and care we had so carefully stored up for one another. The memories we created had not just been something to remember. Those memories were going to get us to the finish line.

I talked to them in a tone of careful recitation. The most important thing was to focus on process rather than outcomes. Each man had heard this same idea before every big race. Still, I went over the race keys. First four—Gregorio, Tomkiewicz, Johnson, Garcia—right to the front of the race. No rightward drift to join the crowd. Run the tangent directly to the first turn. Forget about the field collapsing down. If you run straight, you will beat most to the turn. Meincke, Noah, and Z—group up like a fist and measure your start, quick but relaxed. Stay poised as the field collapses. Be aware, stay on your feet. Once clear of the turn, move gently to the outside. Everyone runs down the right side of the running lane. Run a couple of meters farther, hook up with your running groups. We'll be the only ones out there. Then stay relaxed and hit your splits to the half mile: 2:14 for the lead four, 2:20 for the back three. Clear the trees and run the shortest distance up the inside line. At the top, hard turn at the tree. Then another hard turn by the highway. Build momentum on the downhill. Launch at the mile, up on the balls of your feet. Hard turn at the woods. Ten quick steps. Then a chance to gain ground. Hard turn into the bridge and a hard turn out. The Triangle is full of turns; use each one as a pickup. No stagnating. On balls of feet, going forward. At the exit of the loop, hard turn out. Then stay together in the run-up to the two-mile. Hardest part of the race. Run the inside line, relax your arms and cheeks, stay in rhythm, commit to your partner. All five scorers under

10:00. And that is where I stopped. We had no plan for the last mile.

With that we began our silent walk. We passed the obligatory high fives and phrases of encouragement, but those were momentary interruptions. Everyone was locked in. We jogged across the highway, hit the field, and realized that it was showtime. For much of the year, this race had been a myth. Now here it was, complete with its usual trappings—the York band, the frantic energy of high school fans, the congregated well-wishers, the best of the best staring at us as we crossed the field to our box.

Scheduled thirty minutes before the race, the check-in procedure both interrupted our focus and showed the depth of each man's nervousness. The alternates, the men who would run this race next year, had it easy. Clinger, Mars, Stella, Smitty, and Prodigy simply had to carry the gear and assist their teammates as they donned the required race regalia—hip numbers, race bibs on the front and the back, timing chips on each shoe. Each of the racers had to remove himself from the impending action to suddenly focus on the mundane. Zambrano's fingers shook as he tried to manipulate the twist-ties and affix his timing chip to his spike. Gregorio struggled to iron out his hip numbers and get them to stick. Earlier in the season such trifles would have caused nary a concern. Now sixteen people, coaches and athletes, labored at the interruption. We had come to run a race, not fiddle with stickers and twist-ties. Finally assured that we met uniform compliance, we embarked on the final team jog of the season.

We wound our way through the crowds and thickets of teams warming up and headed toward the woods at the course's north end. I struggled to keep it light. We made fun of overzealous nerds in the crowd, talked some smack to our frosh-soph lining the finish stretch, and generally tried to do anything but think of the race. We jogged lightly. The day was perfect. Across the thousands of miles of preparation, we had jogged together countless times. But everyone knew this was the last one. It would never be so pure and directed again. Sure, there was track season and the same cast of characters, but track suffered from bifurcation. Even then, they would all be heading toward separate events before graduating and embarking on separate lives. As we reached the end of the course we rang in our final jog of the year with another collective ritual: a group piss. As we invaded the woods to find a spot, a female official ran over and started screaming at us, chiding us for our lack of decorum. A few of our guys chuckled, probably remembering runs that saw far greater breaches of decorum, runner emergencies that left the victim with a couple less socks and a story about that one time, on a trail in Deer Grove West . . . We jogged away, laughing at her admonitions, realizing that she thought all of us coaches were athletes in our own rights. Marcus looked at me and told me I still had it. I guess it pays to be skinny.

We took the hairpin turn back toward the start, and the thousands of fans and the assembled field came back into sight. We headed up the final straight one last time before ducking under the ropes and beginning our pre-race sprints. Standing silently, I watched and left each man to his rituals. Marcus made sure to add three or four quick struts to each stride before shifting into gear. Johnson held onto Clingerman's shoulder and did his leg swings. Meincke came downhill right at me in full stride, finding his rhythm. His cheeks bounced with relaxation. United as running partners, Gregorio and Tomkiewicz sought in vain to touch their speed. Striding next to each other with their freshly shaven heads, they looked more like a comedy duo than a pair of highly trained athletes. Peter towered over his diminutive teammate. He looked determined, a man ready to put his long limbs to effective use. One year ago, Peter had found his rhythm. It had occurred suddenly, like a thunderclap. Ever since, he had become a paragon of efficiency. Having lost my watch earlier in the week, I asked Coach Hajik for the time: 1:50 PM. Ten minutes to race. I called them to me.

Once again we situated ourselves in a circle. I put a sign on our bulletin board the Monday prior to state that read FULL CIRCLE. Above it was a photo of the state team from the year before, grinning madly and posing with our fake "fourth-place trophy." They give no trophy for fourth, but you could see the elation on our faces anyway. Only Tim Meincke refused to smile, glumly hanging out in the back and staring into the camera with dead eyes. Now from my position in the middle I looked him in the face first. We had situated ourselves into this same circle at the top of Old Fall River Road those many months ago in Colorado. There, under the beauty of a blue sky on a crisp morning, we vowed to persevere through all obstacles. And here we were, all those months later, standing on the precipice.

Coach Quick's hand in the air signals the countdown to the final "PACK" chant of the 2011 season.

I had saved one final surprise. I stood in the middle and took off my long-sleeved team shirt, the one that read ONE WAY —> UPHILL ONLY, and let them see my race jersey. I then ripped off my warm-up pants to show the racing shorts I had carefully hidden underneath. For weeks I had rehabbed my foot to be able to run around at the state meet, and I told them that there was no way they were running this race without me. I had not trained eighty miles a week through the summer to be left out of the best part. I took my disgusting, salted Colorado hat and threw it on backward. Marcus grinned. I had already covered the race plan before we crossed the road, but I had one last thing to say. There would be no plan for the last mile. They had to want it. I told them the mantra they had heard hundreds of times. In the end of a race, it's all about guts and desire. Somewhere along the way a challenger would emerge. Beating that man would mean the difference between winning and losing, between ecstasy and a long ride home. I told them then that one other thing was missing from that saying. Love. They had to love one another enough to take the pain. Making sacrifices out on the edge was a function of nothing else. A man would hurt to win a race for himself, but he would pulverize himself to win for a teammate.

We had built that bond of hurt in practice after practice, through six-hundred-meter finishes too numerous to count. The entire exercise pointed toward this situation. I reminded them that kick time came at the candy-striped pole at six hundred meters to go. I would be standing there urging them into the homestretch. One shift at six hundred. Then another shift at three hundred meters out, through the zigzag, to the arms, and then to the house. I told them that generations of Palatine men had reached that incline, given their all, kicked as hard as they could, but never found a way to kick down the door. I told them that all those men would be there in spirit. Each man would have his boot on the door. But only they could kick it down. I put my right hand into the middle of the circle and my left into the air. Each man threw a hand into the pile. One last ritual. I counted it out with my left hand and let them hear it in my voice: "Pack on three, one, two, three, PACK!" The twelve athletes and the coaches spoke it with one voice, and its echo bounced with vigor across the crowd.

With that I released them to the line. It was up to them now. They carried my dreams, but really it was all about them anyway. They had ceased to run for me long ago, and I wouldn't have had it any other way. Now dressed awkwardly in my racing gear, I headed down the course with my coaches—Sheehan, Hajik, Macatangay, Vargas, and Nigliaccio—to go through the nervous five minutes that preceded every state meet. Content to let it all play out, I parked myself on the grass and lounged. The course was full of our alums, and I was glad to talk with John Lancaster and his buddies from North Central. John had run on two state trophy teams at Palatine. He knew what this one meant to me and to his two teammates, Jimmy Mac and Niggles, who had coached with me. Jon Chermak, another All-Time Great, had made the trip. A veteran of our 1993 trophy team, Jon wanted to see a Palatine win just as bad as anybody.

Just before the call to the gun, I jogged over and gave one last handshake to Jamie Klotz. He had his men from Buffalo Grove on a dream run of their own. After barely qualifying out of the sectional, they were enjoying their first trip to the state finals. Jamie's lead runner, Jereme Atchison, was a favorite to win the individual title. I looked stealthily into his devil eyes and gave him our usual look. It was time to bang.

Staring up the field toward the line, I thought briefly of some advice I always gave the boys. Don't forget to pause and take it all in. The colors of autumn, the beauty of a race at full gallop, the view from atop the hill at Busse Woods, the panoramic shot from the bottom of the course at state, the aesthetics of mutual pain, the value in deciding one's worth through a race. Briefly I searched across all the years to the memories of my youth. Holding my mother's hand and watching a young woman pass out right in front of me at the 1984 state meet, vomit clinging to her left cheek as she crawled toward the line. Moline's Mike Leemans running the race of his life in the 1992 finals only to fall in the mud at three hundred meters to go, pick himself up, and then streak to the line like a ghost half encased in mud. Another of my dad's dreams shattered so close to the end.

I thought of the men I had brought to this race, Kevin O'Brien thundering up the inside line to bring us to the state podium in 2005; Paul Kwak, the little Korean that could, doing the same in 2007. Steve Finley. Mat Smoody. Glenn Morris. Champions all. Each year I had lived and died with the young men of Palatine in our various attempts to scale this mountain. Sitting there on that beautiful sunbaked field, it felt like everything we had ever done, everything we had ever worked for, had been a clear preface to this exact moment. I had no doubt whatsoever. We were going to win. Lost in thought, I suddenly looked up as the race exploded into motion.

Each year the IHSA apportions starting boxes randomly by the place a team finishes in the sectional meet. We knew that we would have a tall task if we won the Schaumburg Sectional because its winner was slated for Box 5. Unlike last year the entire field would crash down at the first turn. Fortunately, the inside box also played into our hands. We were going to start so fast that no one would be near us. Three hundred meters in I sighted my lead quartet. Both Marcus and Tony drove their arms slightly quicker than usual, but remained poised. Tomkiewicz simply gobbled up ground, a picture of easy motion, cheeks bouncing, eyes locked straight ahead. A speed man to begin with, Johnson did it all in rhythm. The conditions and the course played to his strengths. By the quarter-mile mark, they had cleared the field and the rest of their teammates. From that point on we would win or lose on our terms. When they hit the candy-striped pole at the first turn there was hardly a soul to be seen.

I lost our back three in the thundering herd of the main field and hoped they had gotten off okay. After the field passed, I sprinted toward

Anthony Gregorio, Peter Tomkiewicz, Marcus Garcia, and Tim Johnson head straight to the front of the 2011 IHSA State meet.

Photo by MaryAnn Graham

the half-mile mark, eager to fill my intuition with hard information. Usually the feel I get in the early stages predicts the coming reality. As the field made its way down the entry road, I could see the thicket of red safely abreast the front of the race. Unlike the manic dual between Verzbicas and Driggs the year before, there was no front-runner willing to drive the pace. As they hit the zigzag, I found Tony, Peter, and Marcus running like a fist, tight enough to tap each other on the shoulder, right on the lead. Unlike the year before, there was no panicked courage. This time they belonged. Johnson held the group in his peripheral vision as he, too, tagged in near the front. All four hit the half-mile in 2:12, a scorching early pace. Then the wait. It may have only been three seconds, maybe five, maybe eight, but the field flowed by as I struggled to find my back trio. They came through running together in perfect rhythm, hooked up but far adrift. This was the risk we had chosen. It would be up to Tim Meincke to lead Zambrano and Noah home through the dense field.

I watched them roll up the inside line in rhythm and then bolt for the entrance to the back loop. Ever since my childhood, I have loved the wild intensity of the Illinois state cross country meet. Fans celebrate at football stadiums, and roar to their feet at big plays in basketball games. I do those things, too. But cross country fandom is full-body. Each year thousands of people—coaches, parents, fans, friends, teammates—turn the center of Detweiller Park into a manic inferno of energy. To really watch a cross country race requires a physical commitment, a point-to-point drive to see the race and be in it, too. Each year, I watch the race from the same points. It is a ritual with a spark of religiosity. In those moments I feel whole. I share my wholeness with hundreds and hundreds of others who get it, too. After sprinting across the field and avoiding my share of full-speed collisions, I ensconced myself on the rope line next to a young girl, probably ten years old, and became part of the surreal tableau of her moment. Here I was, thirty-five years old and panting, wearing my race uniform and backward hat, drooping all over the ropes and shouting to my assistant coaches. I warned her that a grown man would be going crazy in her ear in about two minutes.

As the race made its way toward the back loop's entrance, I loved our audacity. It was one thing to be expected to do well. It was something entirely different to do it. As the leaders hit the turn, Tony and Peter tailed right behind. They had competed with and held their own against the top men all year long. Tony had run against Barrington's Erik Peterson and Buffalo Grove's Jereme Atchison since he was a freshman. They belonged, and they knew it. Just off them, running in the mid-teens, Marcus and Timmy J ran stride for stride in the wake of York's first runner, Scott Milling. The difference from the year before was staggering. My eyes welled with tears just watching them take the turn, ten quick strides exactly as they'd been taught, and head with their poise into the stormy depths of the race. All season long Johnson had floundered in the mid-race, confounding expectations. I had railed. I had yelled. I had encouraged. Nothing had worked. Still, I maintained focus on one beautiful shred of hope. Tim Johnson always ran well in big races. And there he was, hammering and hanging on to his teammate.

Photo by MaryAnn Graham

Marcus Garcia and Tim Johnson shadow York's Scott Milling into the back loop of the Detweiller Park course.

With the first four in the All-State mix, I turned to find the man of the hour. At moments during the season Monkey had cracked under the implied burden of his position. At first I had scared him with reminders of what I knew all along: The whole state meet would come down to his performance. I never wanted to let him into the full weight of the pressure, but I gave him more glimpses than he could handle. At the Palatine Invite and the IHSA Sectional, he had folded, unable to carry the load. Zambrano stepped up each time to plug the gap, but as the field approached and I finally found Monkey, I saw that the safety blanket had disappeared. Zambrano was nowhere to be found. Noah had faded even farther back. For the rest of the race, he would carry the burden alone.

As he approached, running on the outside of the running lane, I recalled his manic charge from the year before. He had run with such naïveté, such belief in his body, a man with an unshakable faith in his infinite power. Discovering his finite limits had been a blow. We had celebrated the romantic heroism of his charge after the race, but I saw something more when I looked back at the pictures of that time. He looked reserved and thoughtful. His quiescence betrayed how much that innocence had faded. This year we had focused on dull reality rather than spirit. The lessons had been about maturity, reserve, patience, and rhythm. The intensity of his youth had been the easiest weapon to fire. All the rest felt like grown-up business, toys to play with but nothing you would want to master. At times I wondered whether the process of molding him into a better runner would dull his spirit and numb his love of the game.

Watching him pass five feet in front of me, I knew that I was wrong. Tim Meincke had the fire. He had possessed it ever since I saw his first outbursts of speed in junior high. Now he was a man. He ran on the balls of his feet, arms driving rhythmically, as he passed people. Instead of moving in bursts, he flowed. Smooth. Calm. Collected. His body language filled me with confidence. His eyes gave me even more. They smoked with purpose.

I broke from the rope line and headed for the halfway point in the back loop. I had spent the four weeks before the state meet rehabbing my foot after destroying my plantar fascia in the Prairie State Marathon. The work and rest paid off. I was able to book it to the back corner of the course to get my first look at the team race. I loved what I saw. Peter's grip on the top ten appeared unshakable. His stare encapsulated all of those long runs, and more than ever I felt his smoldering burn. Peter had never made friends easily or been a socialite. He was no Marcus. In moments such as these, ones that prioritized competitive spirit, he took a lifetime of grudges and channeled them into the stewardship of his pain. Here, in the far reaches of elite competition, he had found a place to declare his worth. By this time Gregorio had been dropped and looked to be struggling. In prior years such a setback would have driven him awry. He would have panicked and searched vainly for more speed, swinging his head to and fro, dipping his chin to his chest. I got in his ear, yelling for rhythm, rhythm, rhythm. In such moments a man meets the paradox of speed. The more you reach for it, the less you find. The less you struggle, the more it flows. His fade into the teens concerned me, but in the end it was Tony. He would fight until the end.

As he passed, I looked farther back and found true beauty. Marcus and Timmy J ran in concert, both in All-State positions, confidently joined at the hip. The months of training had given them the belief they could finish here. All the miles had also given them the unshakable body language of champions. By then I knew we were putting it on the rest of the field. I saw four Palatine guys bookending York's first man. Neuqua Valley's top two were safely challenging the same four, but the rest of their scorers looked to be well back. Our driving early pace had been a bet in two ways. One, we believed we had the most fitness. Two, we believed that we had the most experience. We wanted to force the younger runners from each team, most of whom were running in the state final for the first time, to come from behind and beat us. Did they have the emotional wherewithal to take the first punches and then come back to knock us out? After seeing Meincke continue his careful move, I bolted down the road to give our guys the message I had counted on from the start. We were winning. And we were winning big.

I stormed through the ropes just before Leland Later made his turn around the hairpin and headed to the two-mile mark. The New Trier senior had shocked many with his drastic improvement. We had seen him run twice already and knew that Later was legit. I wondered as he coasted by whether I was seeing the winning move. As he passed, I ducked under the ropes so I could look each of my runners in the eye. I wanted to give them a message they could not deduce from inside the race. I got to Peter first. "We're winning! Up big! Our race! Our race!" Up and down the line, the same thing. Gregorio, "Our race!" Garcia and Johnson, "Our race!" Just as he had one year earlier, Marcus gave me the *We got this* look. I saw him pick it up once again, going to his arms for another surge. I had seen that move hundreds of times in runs where Marcus destroyed us all. I hoped it had the same effect here.

The irony of the moment, of course, was that we were not winning at all. I knew that we were beating York and Neuqua Valley, but looking back at the splits, I realized I had missed O'Fallon, the silent assassin in the field. Jon Burnett's boys program had been ascending for some years, and they had also survived a narrow miss the year before, returning with a bevy of top runners and an aching thirst to find the top of the podium. The halfway splits later revealed that they were up by 4 points.

The climb to the two-mile mark at Detweiller breaks the wills of many men. From that point on only the strong remain. The pretenders vanish out the back of the race, never to be seen again. With my front four safely by and fighting hard, our fate depended on Meincke. I found him, still passing people and under control, but stuck in the mid-nineties with a little over a mile to go. I gave him the same message as the other guys—that we were winning—but knew just as clearly that words mattered little. He had never been able to finish. No manner of cajoling could make that happen. I watched him run away, powerless to change anything that happened from then on.

For the first time since the gun, I stopped to take it all in. The race had entered its frenzied final phase, striking out with its own momentum to arrive finally at a tangible reality. No more myths. Just a sheet of paper that spelled out winners and losers as concrete fact. I watched the action boil at the top of the course as I jogged over to my final spot. For years I had worked the tangent across the main field by the two-and-a-half-mile mark. I would sneak down under the hastily assembled rope line, get down on my knees, and plead. This time, I just let it all go. There was nothing for me to do except let it play out. So I relaxed. Dressed in my race gear I strolled down to a new place, away from the frenzy of the crowd. We had questioned many old assumptions about training and racing to get to this point. I might as well see the state meet from a new view. I jogged off toward the tree that marked six hundred meters to go.

Safely planted next to the appointed marker, I looked down the course and finally found the race again. Leland Later had blown it wide open, seizing control earlier than anticipated. I saw Jamie Klotz leaning over the rope line screaming frantic devil yells in Atchison's ear as he battled for second in the state. I reentered the battle myself, searching vainly for my guys, snapped back into my reality of need. All the training had been intended to give them the magic in the last mile. Did they have it? Would they stick? Magic only occurs in a cross country race when the emotional truths exceed the physical toll of the act itself. Just like emotion, magic is not quantifiable. It offers an aura that fends off physical reality. For a group of runners it is the vehicle of transcendence.

I found Peter first. Nothing the leaders did had shaken him. He was glued onto the back end of the top ten, running relaxed and tall. He battled side by side with Neuqua Valley's Mark Derrick. The year before Neuqua Valley manned their late charge behind Derrick, who had been shorn of his shoe early in the race. Now he and Peter went toe-to-toe, stride-to-stride down the back tangent. Still hanging behind Peter, Tony grasped his spot like a man clinging to his life. His chin swayed furiously up and down as he chewed his tongue and gasped for more oxygen, more oxygen. I had seen this body language hundreds of times and knew it did not bode well. More than anyone, though, Tony can marinate in pain. He absorbs its sharp stabs willfully. In the deep mania of a race he gorges himself on it. Long practice had made such devotion to difficulty a neces-

Peter Tomkiewicz charges toward the finish line and an eleventh-place All-State finish.

sity, and I hoped he could last to the line. I counted him at twentieth, the same place he finished the year before.

Just behind Tony, I found Johnson. I knew then the magic was in full effect. Timmy J was ahead of Marcus and driving the pace. They hung together in the tenuous bargain that teammates make when they punish themselves for each other. Johnson's eyes filled with electricity. Too often he wore a mask of defeat, drilling his eyes into the ground. In such moments he looked all too conciliatory. But when he ran well—with the verve and spirit I'd glimpsed for years—those eyes came off the ground and bored holes in the spines of the men he was tracking. He was in the mid-thirties and moving. Marcus trailed just behind, fully ablaze and driving. They looked like combination meteorites at the heated moment of plunging to earth. The flight had been a long one, and they were now gathering heat and speed for the final plunge. I gave them the victory call: "Our race! Put it in the chute! Put it in the chute!"

307

That left Meincke. It was clear from the halfway point that Zambrano and Noah were cooked. I have no idea what Monkey did while I stood powerless at the bottom of the course. But all of a sudden he was there. Exactly where he was supposed to be. And he was firing on all cylinders. By rough count I had him in the late sixties. I knew then, like a jolt of electricity to the heart, that the race was ours. Later facts would prove how close it really was, but I had dreamed about this moment for far too long. Getting Tim Meincke to run this race had become a silent obsession, a living and breathing part of myself for so long that I just lost it. Seeing him run up tall, with authority and absolute conviction, was a piece of aesthetics far beyond what I imagined it could be. How Michelangelo must have wept when he saw the fully realized David revealed from the stone.

I burst into tears even as I urged him on. All year long I told them a lie to cover up the pressure. All I cared about was that we ran our best when it mattered most. Now, in the heat of the moment, I realized that it was not a lie at all. What is coaching but a search for the best our charges have to give? Few people live their lives honestly enough to say they ever witness what they fully can do. But in that brief span—the space of four minutes perhaps—Tim Meincke solved some basic dilemma about himself, demolished some powerfully constructed road-block with all the might at his disposal. There he was. And I wept, suddenly and without seeming provocation, just as I had when I saw my daughter for the first time.

Frantic now with the bloodlust of competition in my throat, I sprinted up the course to catch them one final time before the finishing hill. I caught Peter and Tony around 350 meters to go and gave each a reminder of what we had worked on so long. Six hundred meters to go, one shift. Three hundred meters to go, second shift and to the house. At that point Marcus pulled alongside Johnson and the pair hit the zigzag side by side with the hammer down. We had asked them to commit fully from there to the line, had taught them through repetitive repeats without oxygen that three hundred meters was the distance they could go at full tilt even

Tim Meincke finishes off a come-from-behind effort to seal Palatine's first-ever boys state cross country championship.

Photo by VIP Photography

after they thought they could go no more. Monkey went by me ripping, and I took off in a dead sprint to the line. I did not see Peter, Tony, Marcus, or Timmy J finish in real time. I only saw their finishes in the pictures after the race. But I did follow Tim Meincke. I saw the whole thing.

I sprinted straight up the middle of Detweiller Park, screaming like a madman, watching him blow people away and run us to a state title. Step by step I ran with him, he inside the ropes, me some fifty meters away running behind the crowd jabbing my fist in the air and yelling, "To the hoooouuse! To the hooooouuse! Put it in the chuuuute!" His knees lifted like pistons and the arms came to full drive. Wearing his usual mask of pain (dubbed the Gremlin by his teammates), Tim Meincke got on his toes and found a brand-new piece of himself. The beauty lay within the revelation. He didn't pass twenty men or anything like that. Probably just five or six. But in the end, that made the difference. Unbeknownst to either of us, somewhere within the last hundred meters he passed O'Fallon's fifth runner and put us on top for good.

I stopped my mad sprint fifty meters away and watched him cross the finish line, posed with my hands in the air. I gazed to the sky as the tears rolled down my face, knowing that win or lose we had done our best. Nothing could feel any better. Meincke's race moved me in a way that no performance ever had. It bridged the gap between monomania and reality, between the specter of need I wore each day and the purity of a young person's discovery of who he could truly be.

As I reached the coach's box, the race still streamed to its conclusion. I had already seen the vital facts and looked for my dad to figure out what they meant. Unable to find him, I gave some high fives to our managers filming the finish and went behind the stands to seek him out. I didn't have to look far. He came running out with a sheet of paper in his hand, showing me our places and our raw score at 157 points. He counted us at 11, 20, 29, 30, and 67. I looked in his eyes and knew that we had won. Not logically of course. I just knew that whatever we had just done was what winning is. The feeling was going to stay true whether the reality was true or not. Like author Tim O'Brien says, sometimes the story-truth is more real than the happening-truth.

We stopped then for a moment, and I gave my dad a hug. No one but the two of us will know what that meant. On some level a sport is an incredibly silly thing into which to invest so much time. Any good coach knows, though, that relationships with young people are not silly. Good coaches know that helping young people to set goals, work hard, love one another, and reach for their fullest potential is not silly. Doing something that unites fathers and sons is not silly. My dad and I had been after this moment our entire lives. To share our best race with him was the sweet-

Jeff and Chris Quick share a father–son hug thirty years in the making after learning that the Palatine team has won the state championship.

est victory I could imagine. For years we had shared the phone calls, the advice, the war stories, the successes, the failures of the coaching life. I used to think that coaching was something I did for myself and for my kids. But in that moment I saw its real truth. It created a space for my dad and me to be together. As we hugged, the tears streamed without hesitation. It was a hug with real tightness, the kind you give when you want the extra ounces of energy to show the person the vital heat of your love. It's the kind of hug I give Mads when I put her to bed, or when I carry Christopher up the stairs and he tells me, "Daddy, I'm still a little guy." Those hugs have extra ounces. It was a forever moment.

As I stood there frozen in tears, my mom and brother came out to meet us as well. My mom has been an impassioned coach's wife for her entire life. We hugged, and I knew how much this meant to her, how proud she was. My mom had been gifted with two sons, one who could ostensibly do it all and another who could not. When I became a teacher, I always felt that she wanted more for me, some grander potential. It had been hard to give up a PhD scholarship to Northwestern thirteen years before and call her on the phone to tell her that I wanted to devote my life to coaching. Now at the pinnacle, I knew she understood. She had the wisdom to let me give it all away so that I could be myself. Her eyes showed her pride, and I leaned down and kissed her red cheeks and tasted the tears.

Then I looked at Chad. Now I was already crying, but the look in my brother's face is one I will remember forever. Chad spent 108 days in the hospital after he was born prematurely, and his entire life had been a miracle ever since. Chad is simply the toughest person I know and lives his life through athletics. He wept mercilessly. No one can guess what it meant for him to witness a state title. All of this makes sports seem too outsized and serious, but you would have to meet my family to understand. In our family this was the shape that dreams took.

My wife and kids walked out next, and it was great to know that my kids couldn't have cared less. Mads and Christopher spent much of the day playing in the woods with their aunt Kelly; the true highlight had been going to Chuck E. Cheese for lunch before the meet. Meredith was carrying J. J. in the BabyBjörn and clearly knew how much this meant. The day I gave up my fellowship to Northwestern to become a coach was also the day I told my mom that I was coming home to marry the girl I had been dating. Thirteen years later we held our three kids and hugged. She puts up with track season and long absences on the weekends and a distracted husband more than she should. My absences had made all of this possible, and I am not sure that I can ever repay the sacrifices she makes so that I can be myself. I'm not sure someone you love can ever give you a bigger gift.

With the family celebrations done, I had to find my boys. I staggered through the crowd, searching in vain. Finally, I saw a giant cluster of Palatine people behind the starting line. I busted into a sprint and came crashing into our huddle at full speed. We laughed and cried and celebrated even though we did not know the result. We had run our best race. It was gratifying to know that our pursuit of that goal was something they believed in all along.

Now I needed to see a victory confirmed. Each year the IHSA performs a video review of each race to determine the scoring. The timing chips record each athlete's finishing time, but they cannot be trusted to get the order of finish correct because the torso, not the foot, determines the score. The scoring delay doubles as a suspense device. As usual I wandered and listened to rumors, gathered information, milled around, composed myself, twiddled my thumbs, relied on innuendo and hopeful feelings, and searched for affirmation. As I wandered, I suddenly remembered that I had charged Tyler Squeo with taking video at the finish line with his iPhone. I jogged back to our team area and searched him out in the celebrating crowd. Coach Sheehan and I pulled him to the side and double-checked my dad's count. He had been nearly dead-on. We had beaten York and Neuqua Valley, much as we suspected. What we had missed were the five young men from O'Fallon.

In the last half mile of the race, O'Fallon's junior star Alex Riba found his speed and closed like a madman. He ran the race of his life to finish second. Tony had caught Patrick Perrier, their super sophomore, on the way up the hill, but just barely. I thought Marcus and Johnson, finishing in the exact same second in twenty-eighth and twenty-ninth places, would seal the deal, but the video did not lie. Two O'Fallon guys had finished right on their heels. As we looked frantically through the unsteady video, we knew it would come down to fifth men. We found Meincke passing an athlete in navy blue right before the line, but could not be sure that was an O'Fallon runner. Even if it was, the race would come down to points you could count on your hands. Single digits. As more of our varsity watched the finish, a hush fell over the previously celebratory camp. Nerves reignited. We had run our best and that celebration had been justified. A year before we had celebrated just the same, but the results told a different truth.

One of the most dramatic scenes each year is enacted at the finish boards inside the officials' area. Fenced off from the public, only coaches and officials are allowed entry. All of the results from the five earlier races had already been posted. I awaited the dramatic moment when the door of the officials' trailer would open, and the head official would stride out with the results board held aloft. Each year he walks through the crowd and then hooks the top of his board to the standard. He then flips it down for the big revelation. Dreams and disappointments are made each year in that moment. In 2007 I had squatted down low in the cluttered throng and seen Palatine come up third. I saw nothing else. I bolted out and celebrated with glee. More often, the moment revealed disappointment. A year ago the board had dropped, and we were fourth. The finality stunned me to the core, and the walk back to our camp had been methodical and disappointing. We all put on the brave faces, but they couldn't hide the sting.

This time around I sat with my dad on a picnic table and slowly put myself back together. Sweatpants. Long-sleeved shirt. Jacket. I pulled off my Colorado hat and ran my hands through my sweaty, greasy hair. Inside I kept rationalizing the unknowable. It felt too perfect. I'm not usually wrong about a race. I know a winner when I see one. They had gotten us by 9 points on first man, but surely we had gotten enough points back on the other four. Had there been individuals in the mix who would put them ahead? Where was their damn fifth man? Had Meincke passed him? Did we miss him in the video? I entered a universe of hope and doubt, helpless to change what had already happened. For years, good or ill, I would look at these results the same way I did all others. You can count up the fragments of seconds when you might have improved. You can move a guy here or there. You can plug an injured guy into the lineup or put him in his usual spot. But the irrefutable fact is that they never change. Ever. This was the tablet, the stone in which I traded.

As I punished myself with nerves, I looked toward the trailer and saw Mike Newman and Bob Geiger walking toward me. They wore the look of inside info in their eyes. Mike writes for Dyestat.com, and he and I had bonded throughout the season over our mutual love of cross country. He had run on a state runner-up and a state champion for York in the late 1970s, and he had returned to Illinois the previous summer to throw himself into cross country coverage. I went over to meet them, and he gave it to me simple: "You guys won."

"No way. I don't believe you. Show me. I want to see results." To my surprise, he had them. Palatine 114, O'Fallon 120. A 6-point winner. Six points. Probably a second or less on each of my five scorers had made all the difference. Mike asked me for an interview, but I just smiled and demurred, telling him we'd talk before the end of the day. I looked at Sheehan, who stood just over my shoulder, and told him we had to go find the boys. We took off, side by side, in a dead sprint out of the coaching corral and toward our team camp. He and I had run many miles together and harbored this big dream for a long time. We exchanged low fives and put it in full gear. In my hands I carried my coach's pass and a half-drunk bottle of water. When I reached our camp, I flung both in the air and let it out. "We won, boys, only by 6 points, but it is our time!"

Ecstasy. Pandemonium. We celebrated right in the middle of the road, surrounded by our fans, alums, parents, and other random passersby. We celebrated with unfettered joy, with a lack of consciousness at the spectacle. Immediately I found Tony and gave him a hug. The tears streamed

Coach Quick and Marcus Garcia "hug it out" during the team's manic celebration.

Photo by MaryAnn Graham

from his eyes. All of the pent-up need and desire shattered right there in that moment, like a windowpane punched out from a great height crashing to earth with a sonorous gasp of beautiful destruction. Abandonment from reality never felt so good. We floated in one of the smallest spaces of our lives—minutes perhaps—unafraid to revel and not yet able to start remembering.

Sweet memory and nostalgia can never compare to the nervous grip of first experience. When we drove away later that afternoon, we would have lost "the freshest and the best of it forever." But in those pre-conscious moments, before the contemplation of what it all meant, before the suddenness of vanity and ego and pride, it just existed. To live those few moments with those boys was enough. As I stood there basking in it, letting our great joy swim over the assembled crowd, all I could do was weep and celebrate.

AFTERMATH

The 2011 Palatine seniors pose with hall of fame coach and Palatine legend Fred Miller.

The rest of the day floated by as if we were viewing a surreal picture in some far-flung museum. We stood there rapt with attention, staring at the picture, only to see that we were the subjects just now brought into focus. Backstage before the awards, we congratulated the other teams and traded stories with our fellow coaches and competitors. I shook hands with Paul Vandersteen and his Neuqua Valley boys, content to finally win a round in a fight that had lasted across the years. We congratulated Jon Burnett and the O'Fallon team on running the defining race in their program's history. Classy even in defeat, York's Chris May and Alex Mimlitz ducked under the ropes to shake my hand and congratulate the boys. York had placed fourth, but returned nearly their entire team. They would be the early favorites to win the state and title in 2012. Finally defeating York in the state final was lost amid the joyful celebration.

As the time approached to mount the podium, I reminded the boys of our deal. If we won we would celebrate without regret. Standing at the bottom of the stairs to the podium, awaiting the roll call of our names, I couldn't stop thinking that no one knew what it had taken. Only the guys behind me really knew. Even our alums, who had been privy to so many quests, could only graze the surface. We had ventured as deep into the well as we could. We stood there, ready to collect the spoils of victory, knowing that there had been nothing more we could have done. In itself, that was a reward.

As they called my name, I pumped my fists to the crowd and held my Joe Johnson shirt out for all to see. The rest of the boys had worn their team shirts, but it was my duty to honor Joe and everyone who came before. They all had to be up there with us. Sheehan came next, streaking across the stage, and we embraced in front of the crowd. It had been four years of tireless and ambitious pursuit. The boys came next, Marcus wrapped in his blanket and the rest clad in their red racing shorts and black long-sleeves. ONE WAY —> UPHILL ONLY indeed. For the second time in our journey, we had reached the top of the mountain.

The officials presented the trophy to Tony and Peter, and they held it aloft to the hundreds of fans and alums. It wasn't enough. It had been too many years of seeking to let it go at that. I came around from the back and took it from them next. Stepping out to center stage, I felt its tangible weight for the first time. The first-place trophy was taller and weightier than the ones I had been privileged to hold before. The glimmering gold runner at the top shone beautifully in the late-fall sunlight. I thrust the trophy above my head and paused just for a moment to take it all in. The rest of the team arrayed down below the stage, my junior varsity and frosh-soph, roared into full throat: "Palatine XC! Palatine XC! Palatine XC!" Steve's chant, one last time.

Coach Quick throws the state championship trophy aloft as the boys and coaches celebrate onstage.

To live that gorgeous aftermath, to spend our best day together in the sun with family and friends, was the most fitting triumph any of us could imagine. Behind the stage, we ringed the trophy and invited the families to take pictures with their sons. Tony, Timmy J, and Peter gave interviews off to the side. One by one, each of the boys stood with his parents and siblings and held that trophy in his hands. You could see the pride in their parents' eyes. Some of them realized that day for the first time what all the mania had been about. I was glad to see that recognition in their eyes, to watch each set of parents see their child's potential rendered into reality.

I also got to experience the moment with my own family. Mads joined me as I gave a raft of post-race interviews, and we all gathered for one of the best family photos of our lives. Baby J. J. wore his light blue lion sleeper, and the assembled crowd laughed as I propped him up next to the trophy for pictures. Sophia Parks and her daddy Joe had been winners her first time at the Illinois state meet, and now it was J. J.'s time to get a picture with Dad and the big trophy. Meredith, Madeline, and Christopher joined us soon after and the picture we took made the perfect Christmas card. Mads smiles coyly off to the side while I hold the baby. Christopher, long past exhaustion and ready to leave, cries uncontrollably. Meredith and I just laugh. I hoped somewhere in her forgiving and warm heart, my wife could see the value written across the boys' faces. She knew. We had walked too long down the road together for her not to believe in the journeytoo. As we hugged and celebrated, only she knew what it had really taken to arrive at that particular moment in time. The years of lateness. The distraction of my obsession. The nights and Saturday mornings spent alone with babies. I look at that picture now and see that she knew.

Photo by MaryAnn Graham

The Quick family celebrates a dream come true. From left, Chad Quick, Penny Quick, baby J. J., Chris Quick, and Jeff Quick. In the foreground, Meredith holds Madeline and Christopher as they touch the state championship trophy.

Just before leaving the park and heading back to our lives, I took one final picture. Rob Harvey and I had talked throughout the summer and fall about winning two state championships in the same day for my dad. He had been the primary influence in both of our lives, and to see him flanked by his three sons—two his own and one all but adopted—was a fitting tribute to the man who had shaped all our lives. Now flanked by the boys state champion trophy and the girls runner-up trophy, his influence became even more clear.

With the pictures done and the sun setting, we packed up our gear and prepared for the long haul home. Back in the van with just the top seven, we paused for a second, looked around at one another, and then burst into laughter. Marcus said it all: "Holy shit. We just won state!" Frenzied cheering. I had waited my entire life for this next moment. I scripted it somewhere around 1983 sitting in the gym at Peoria High School watching Elmhurst York win another state title. Just once I wanted to win it all and sing Queen's "We Are the Champions" like I meant it. At last, the team had found its song. Who else but Freddie Mercury could so brazenly capture what we were feeling?

So we cruised down the entry road to Detweiller Park windows down, volume full blast, and sang it from the bottoms of our souls. We shouted rather than sang, played air drums with reckless abandon, and belted out Brian May's guitar solo note by note as obnoxiously as we could. We crept slowly past the start–finish line, past the Long Green Line's picnic tables, past the zigzag and the point of no return, and into the history books for our moment in the sun. Many teams had won in the past. We certainly had not run a dominant team time or set any records. No matter. Our spirit would forever mingle with this fabled course, just one more set of ghosts to speak to someone else's dreams and best intentions. I looked in my rearview mirror and saw them all—Noah, Z, Tony, Peter, Timmy J, Monkey, and Marcus—singing with utter joy, smiles writ large on their faces.

Hitting Highway 29 and heading toward Palatine, we turned into an uncertain future. After this night, this ride home, nothing would ever be the same. We would never feel this tight again. So we lived. We saw Jamie Klotz and his Buffalo Grove boys at a Subway in Chillicothe and stopped to invade their bus. They, too, had run a race that would go down in their school's history books. Both Jereme Atchison and their team had placed fifth. Klotz and I traded friendly insults and gave each other a huge hug. We stopped in Lasalle-Peru to get gas and discovered that we now had groupies. A number of our previously desperate guys, Noah Brown foremost, struck up a conversation with some York girls at the gas station. After sweet-talking them for a while, Marcus and Tony figured out that one of them was Scott Milling's girlfriend. Milling had run to All-State honors for York earlier in the day, but their team had faded to a close fourth. The conversation might have added insult to injury so they cut it off.

At the Cracker Barrel in Ottawa, we carried the trophy inside and treated it like royalty. It got its own seat, menu, and table setting. Marcus wanted to order it a meal, but that would have been egregious, even for the state champions. Peter quietly stewed as he waited for his food. Even in victory, he couldn't escape thinking with his stomach. Halfway through the dinner, Marcus stood on a chair with a water glass and fork in hand. Clinking the glass like he was calling for a wedding toast, he announced, "Ladies and gentlemen of the Cracker Barrel, can I please have your attention." Our entire half of the restaurant fell silent, like they were about to witness a wedding proposal. When he had their full attention, he paused and then screamed, "We won state!" Everyone laughed and clapped, both at the absurdity of his pronouncement and at his joy. He sat down next to grumbling Peter and had a hearty laugh.

Later in the drive as the tone turned toward contemplation, Tony stated the obvious, "No one will ever know how hard we worked for this." Driving along with just the seven of them, I felt a similar kinship. We flashed back through all the hardships—the ninety-minute long runs, the thousand-mile summers, the mountain running, the 6 AM wake-up calls. What he left unsaid was the emotional work. The leaden burden of commitment had hung over everyone for the better part of two years.

We had shouldered the yoke together and pulled it along, but the slog had been long and tedious, at times overpowering even the most devout.

I realized then the depth of his devotion and how much of the load he had carried. The rest of the seniors had been incidental players in their youths. Tony had borne the varsity burden since sophomore year. With little talent to cruise on, he had no chance for joyriding. Just uphill slog, day by painful day, for the better part of three years. His devotion to the team had been utter. It had not been without cost. The night of the phone call, some three weeks prior, had shaken both of us to our cores. This unidirectional athletic pursuit had defined our parallel paths for so long that the only thing scarier than failing was having it all end. Even after the biggest win of our lives, both of us were concerned with the fallout.

The dark and intense quiet of a return voyage always promotes such contemplation. Mostly we staved off the thoughts of what would come next. Instead, we conjured up the memories and told the old stories. Some were so well worn that you could feel the ruts in their telling. We remembered Noah's nastiness and all the disgusting sweat that flicked off his elbows every time we ran hill repetitions at Riemer Reservoir. We remembered the entire summer before junior year when Marcus didn't shower. We tried to come up with our top ten list of Monkey-isms, but failed as usual. We talked about the old times when Peter sucked and no one liked him and he could only win races at St. Charles's course at LeRoy Oakes because that was where his mom lived. We remembered Clinger eating the gigantic bug in Colorado and all the times we made fun of Devo for his old-man ankles.

As we pulled onto the Palatine Road exit ramp and headed toward the school, we realized there would be no grand parades or welcoming committees. No screaming sirens or police escorts. So we made our own welcome. As soon as we turned onto Rohlwing Road, we once again rolled down the windows and cranked "We Are the Champions." We sang with our fullest hearts as I honked the horn over and over in accompaniment, long blasts, enough to make our presence known. Our arms flailed out the windows as Freddie's grand voice once again belted it out. As we passed the half-mile-to-go mark on the Morning Loop, I laid on the horn and let it ring all the way to the school.

In the school drive the boys threw off their T-shirts and race jerseys and pranced about barefoot in their "short shorts." Nearly naked, Meincke aimlessly ran victory laps around the parking lot. That sparked the rest to take the trophy out to the track for an actual victory lap. All seven of them padded about without a care in the world, lost in the beautiful trance of the moment.

Soon after, our cheerleaders returned from the football playoff game and informed us that our boys had suffered a tough defeat in their second-round play-off game. The loss momentarily blunted our outward shows of joy, but no one could contain their glee for long. They kept showing off the trophy and telling of their exploits, many of them content to hold court with a bevy of good-looking girls for just one day. Already the exploits enlarged as the narratives passed into legend. Only the sullen return of the football boys—many of whom were track teammates—put a damper on the proceedings. As soon as they entered the building, the party continued unabated.

Soon enough the realities of life—curfews, rides home, luggage—started to encroach and the spell was lifted. It had been an incomparable day, one none of us could ever relive or recapture. Inevitably, it had to end. As I drove the school van home, I strapped the state championship trophy in the shotgun seat and chauffeured it to its final resting place on my kitchen table. Exhausted from the long and emotional day, I contemplated going to bed. But I just couldn't do it. Across town at the Oak Alley Saloon, our normal post-meet watering hole, the party was just getting started. All the parents, ex-coaches, and alums would be there. They were the ones who knew how long it had been, the ones who had striven and come up short, the people whose legacy we struggled so hard to fulfill.

So I threw the trophy in the car, grabbed my wife, paid the babysitter, and took our Stanley Cup out on the town. We were tired from the long day, so there was no manic drinking. Just genial, old-time camaraderie and a tacit acknowledgment that we had indeed come full circle. It was too bad that Joe Johnson couldn't have seen us then. His spirit had wafted through the day's proceedings, and more than a few of his alums were there to hold that big trophy in their hands for the first time. By the next day, scores of alums from all eras of the program had written emails to the boys and me. On Monday morning I printed out every one and started taping them to the bulletin board. At first they covered just one pane. Then another. Then the basketball board, too. Then the walls above and below, until by Wednesday there was an entire wall of messages sending congratulations for a long task finally completed.

The next day, a photo of me holding the trophy aloft appeared on the front page of the *Daily Herald*. As I sat drinking my orange juice and eating a bowl of cereal, I still felt the internalized charge. So did the boys. By 10 AM, Marcus, Tony, and Monkey appeared on my doorstep and asked to take the trophy. I had already booked my time with our Stanley Cup. Now it was theirs. So they took it on a tour of Palatine, to their friends' houses, to their favorite haunts, and to all of the places where we had dumped so much sweat in the process of winning it. Their pictures told the whole story. The trophy stood atop the dirt hill at Riemer at dusk. It visited Napoli's pizza and Zach Gates's house and Tony's favorite porta-potty at the Palatine High School track. It visited the houses of girls they hoped to impress, current teammates, and alums long-graduated. Within two weeks, it would live inside a trophy case for eternity. The school would "own" it. But it was really ours, and no one could take it away.

What they carried, of course, was a symbol, a totem really. Trophies come cheap in an entitled culture where everyone has to be a winner and self-esteem is protected by blanketed parents who want to salve the wounds of life before their children ever have a chance to live. To those seven boys, this trophy represented the opposite. It had been won through dearest effort and great personal cost. They had risked greatly and failed countless times en route. Nothing in their cozy young lives had prepared them for the onslaught of realities during the journey. Injuries, boredom, diligence, and an overbearing responsibility to one another had been the cost. It stood as a testament to all the countercultural aspects of the elite running world. In a world that didn't get them or their cause, it was validation.

So it was no wonder that our state championship trophy, for a week at least, became a part of the team. It slept in Marcus's room, lived on Coach Sheehan's kitchen table, and sat shotgun on a Friday-night jaunt through Palatine. It impressed girls with its good looks and silent but deadly charms. Bigger than most of its brethren, its muscled aspect communicated a masculine power that belied the slightness of the runner adorning its top. It also knew it was good. After all, the plaque on the front declared 2011 CLASS AAA STATE CROSS COUNTRY CHAMPIONS. Later it would bear all of our names along with that of Johnny Burke, our faithful bus driver. It would take up residence at the end of the state championship trophy case—the nineteenth in school history, but only the third among boys teams.

Before our trophy sauntered off to a life at stud, it had to be unveiled. It is tradition at Palatine to hold an all-school assembly whenever an athletic team wins a state trophy. I had been privileged enough to speak in front of the school as head coach on two other occasions, and I always looked forward to the assemblies, whether it was my team being honored or not. For each of the athletic seasons—fall, winter, and spring—the school hosts a mandatory pep rally for the entire student body. Usually, these painful affairs spank of the worst feelings our students have to offer. Rude behavior and blanket indifference are the norm. The forced edge of the "pep rally" has the opposite effect, churning up resentment rather than school spirit.

The recognition assemblies always assume a different tone. Two years prior, when our Special Olympians won a state trophy in basketball, the entire school, students and staff alike, stood and wept as our athletes spoke and presented their trophy to the student body. Such moments allow Palatine to show its true heart. Ever since I interviewed for my job, I could feel it beating underneath its suburban surface. We have all the usual trappings of a moneyed school—a whiff of entitlement here or a faint friction between ethnicities there—that go along with a plethora of resources. But Palatine High School has heart. It's not just the wheelchair kids that populate our hallways, cruising down the especially wide halls in their power chairs or heading to class with their walkers amid their fellow students. It's not just our mentally handicapped kids communing with their more able-bodied students in dance clubs, school plays, or Best Buddies. It's not the inspirational stories of our poorest students rising up from nothing to find success, either.

No, the heart is in the vast confluence of so many different kinds of people under one roof. It's not always an easy mix. An edge of discontent always rides under the surface, perhaps an aching anger at those who have more means one day or conflict between rival ethnicities the next. There are days when it works. At its best, the school functions as a vehicle of empowerment. When it does, you can feel the inspiration in the air. Sixty-five times Palatine teams have reached for that inspiration in state competition and found their way onto the podium in their respective sports. Sometimes you wouldn't believe there was something special going on by walking down our hallways on a daily basis, but you would be wrong. I count the state trophies everywhere I go and rarely find a collection like ours. The magic we had developed and ridden to the state title was available because of the place itself. Like most Palatine students and teachers, we believed in the possibilities.

Sitting in my second-hour Advanced Placement English Language class, I realized that this was one speech I couldn't wing. I had written most of what I had to say in my head while lying in bed well before dawn, but I wanted to get it right. So I started to scrawl some basic notes while compiling a monster list of thank-yous. In my class we talk about rhetoric every day, about the infinity of choices an author or speaker has available when crafting a communication. As my students all knew, rhetoric was the "art of audience manipulation." In that spirit, I made them a small bet. If I couldn't bring the house down at Palatine by introducing my handicapped brother to the student body, then I didn't know Palatine High School.

Even though it was a Monday, my parents and Chad drove up to join the festivities. Chad gladly took a day off from his teaching assistant job at Rock Island High School to come and soak in the glory. As the gym filled to its fullest capacity after second hour, my family along with Meredith and the kids took up their places in the front row. At the last moment my wife grabbed our Flip video camera and decided to tape the whole thing. The video would serve as a portal for our alums and fans to join in the celebration.

Sometime before becoming a high school teacher, I discovered a basic truth about myself. I love to talk. My wife's old adage is to "never give a show-off a microphone," but I was going to take full advantage of the moment. I wanted the people assembled in that gym, from the youngest and most attention-challenged freshman to the most cynical old staff member, to feel just for a moment what the boys and I had experienced. As much as I could, I wanted them to understand how much we had sacrificed to achieve this shared dream. Most couldn't care less about running. Most probably had no idea how you scored a race. But everyone had a dream.

So rather than start with a boring list of thank-yous, I told them about our run up the mountain. I asked them to feel the stinging cold air and hear the rush of the water down the mountain. I let them in to our intentional suffering. They all had to know at least one ounce of what was necessary in order to touch their dreams. That ended up being the challenge everyone remembered. All had been privy to clichéd school discussions about "reaching for the stars" and "following their dreams," but too few had ever realized that the beauty of dream-making lay in the determined pursuit. Before giving thanks and introducing them to the boys, I challenged everyone in the gym—students, support staff, and teachers alike— to come by the main office and "touch our dream." The state trophy would take up residence there for two weeks, and I wanted them to feel its tangibility.

To that end I gave my camera to Marilyn Wolter and Marla Morrissey, the two ladies who work in the front of our main office, and asked them to take pictures. Over the course of two weeks, the pictures spoke to the chord we had struck inside the school. Teachers brought down entire classes and posed with it. My runners brought their friends and girlfriends. Random, unsure freshmen held it in their arms and felt its weight. Aged secretaries and custodians came by and touched their dreams one more time.

As I worked my way through the endless list of people who had made our dream possible, I knew that I wouldn't make it through the final people on the list without bursting into tears. It didn't bother me to cry in front of three thousand people. It felt good. Too often we hide the feelings that matter the most. Our success had surely flowed from a commitment to running, but the final margin, a scant 6 points, sprang from an unabashed love for one another. It is hard to get a group of young men to love one another so openly, but it is not impossible. Once such bonds are forged, they stick.

It is the same with marriage and family. We suffer, live, and grow together despite all the myriad setbacks of the journey. I made two choices on the same day in 1999 that changed my life. I decided to become a coach and marry my wife in the same instant. Ever since that fateful decision, my life had become whole. Meredith and I had walked many a mile together. We toured Europe, followed our favorite band around on road trips throughout the United States, and started a family together. Through it all she gave me the space to follow my dream. That's all I wanted. Just the space and time to do something that I knew had great value. So standing there in front of that gym not just with a state championship, but with eleven collected years of relationships and memories, was more than I could bear. Every runner I ever met, every nasty twelve-miler I ever hammered, every distracted dinner I spent half listening while dreaming of some far-off race had been possible because she loved me enough to support the endeavor. I couldn't say how much she meant. I just stood there blank-faced and cried.

Then I turned to my parents. Already straining to talk, I simply couldn't choke out the words. I looked and saw both of them in the front row, my dad holding baby J. J. and my mom drowning in tears, and knew I could never repay them. This moment would have to suffice. My mom had quit her job as an elementary school teacher to raise my brother. She also had taken the time to teach me about all the things I loved. I thanked her for showing me everything about what it meant to be a teacher. She showed me the value of patience and how to find meaning in even the most difficult students. In working with my brother she showed me that love and sacrifice mattered in education and that getting it right, no matter how long or difficult the journey, was always worth it.

My dad taught high school social studies and coached for thirty-five years. From the times I watched him teach to having him as a teacher in eighth grade, I saw just how much fun an adult could have when he filled his life with kids. When he was my coach, I learned the power of vulnerability and the beauty of forming honest connections with young people. I remembered how he used to talk to us, how we would grip the benches in the Moline locker room and let him wind our inner clocks. Then we would stand up and burst through the doors to practice like our lives depended on the outcome. I remembered standing against that wall in Peoria High School's gym the year we placed fifth in the state, my senior year with all my best friends, when we came up so woefully short. Thank God that story didn't end there. No, my dad knew that the great teams were about more than outcomes. They were about family, and the visits that mattered years down the line, the ones where athletes returned to sit on our couch, when they brought their fiancés by to meet the old coach, when they would hit bottom and find their fingers dialing the phone number to our house once again. The great teams lived their lives together long after the last run was complete. Because of him, I knew that this state championship was a crowning moment, but far from the last one. There would be college graduations, reconnections, personal tragedies, and reunions. What we had built would last. With a shattered voice, I thanked him for teaching me everything about what it meant to be a coach.

I saved Chad for last. As looked into the crowd, I saw students and staff weeping in the stands. I told them that this was the best part. I walked out to center court and asked Chad to come out and meet me. Slowly he kicked his power wheelchair into gear and started to drive. Sadly, he would never be able to understand the joy I found in running. He had spent his entire life observing something he would never be able to do. There were days, surely, where he bemoaned his fate and cursed that chair. But on most days, he chose to live, and watching others run had been the vicarious pursuit he enjoyed most. He lived his life through the dreams of others, and this one, the one we had just given him, was the crowning moment of his life. As he hit center court, I reached down and hugged him. I held him close and whispered in his ear how much I loved him.

Photo by Cindi Johnson

Chad Quick, the biggest cross country fan in Illinois, shows the number one and squeezes a dream come true.

331

The crowd rose spontaneously in a standing ovation. Usually people stand and clap out of obligation, but this one was the truth. As Chad drove over to hug each of my varsity boys, I saw the tears rolling down the eyes of nearly every teacher and student in the lower bleachers. Face red with tears, Chad worked his way down the line thanking and hugging my athletes. All the while, the crowd clapped and cried, from the seniors and wheelchair students sitting on the floor, to the administrators standing against the gym's walls, to the freshmen and sophomores in the upper bleachers. Only at Palatine.

As Chad drove back to his seat by my parents, I turned the microphone over to the boys and sat down. Tony reveled in how we had run not to lose and told all the guys on the team how proud he was of their efforts. True to his nature, Timmy J thanked all the people he loved. Monkey played it like we would clown around, but then won some teenage hearts by telling his mom and dad that he loved them. Marcus, of course, spoke last. He reached down inside the podium and pulled out the blanket one last time. He slowly unfolded it and then dropped it across the front of the podium. Once again, the blanket was all. A performer to the last, he told the crowd what an honor it was that they had all showed up to congratulate him on his state championship. His speech was the perfect capstone, full of random shout-outs to his friends and an earnest declaration of just how hard we had all worked.

As the students and staff headed back to class, we lingered for some final pictures. For me this was the end of the road. Starting the next day, the varsity would move into the club cross country season and meet without me to train for the Nike Midwest and National meets. Illinois rules prevented my coaching, so I turned over the reins to Fred Miller and Steve Johnson. It was bittersweet to miss out on the journey's end. After all, the title of our January goal poster had been "The Architecture of a National Championship." From then on I would have to settle for the title of architect rather than coach.

But walking around school later that day proved edifying enough. A couple hundred students and staff stopped in the main office to hold the state trophy and have their pictures taken. Random students stopped me in the hall to tell me how much the message had meant. Alums from my gifted program and AP classes gave me hugs and cried in the hallway. I quickly became known as "the guy who gave that speech." In teenage vernacular, that's a huge compliment.

The rest of the week was full of good feelings and congratulations. But the best part was the knowing glances I traded with the guys when we saw each other during the school day. I would see Peter walking down the hallway or Timmy J getting a drink and exchange a grin that spoke volumes. We had given the rest of the school a glimpse, but the full narrative rode deep within our memories. Slowly but surely, it was becoming internalized. It had been the grand framing experience of their young lives, creating a border for all the rest that would follow. Their pictures were yet to be fully revealed, but these years spent together would color everything that came after.

From the left, the 2011 Palatine boys coaching staff: Matt Sheehan, Chris Quick, Mark Hajik, Mike Nigliaccio, James Macatangay, and Chris Vargas.

Photo by Cindi Johnson

For me there would be more journeys. The cast of characters would change, but I would keep seeking the magic. These were not the first stolen glances I had traded with my athletes as we went through the mundane balance of our school days. The knowing closeness was deeper this time, the accolades more concrete, the view from the mountaintop clearer than ever before, but I knew this wouldn't be the final climb. There would be many more worthy men. In a journey without end, I finally understood that the successes and failures were but temporal occurrences, no more graven in the rock face than the wind. The only part that mattered was who you climbed with.

NIKE CROSS NATIONALS

Photo by Meredith Quick

Palatine XC Club coaches pose with the boys just after the finish of the Nike National race. From left, Coaches Fred Miller and Steve Johnson with Marcus Garcia, Peter Tomkiewicz, Anthony Gregorio, Tim Meincke, Tim Johnson, Christian Zambrano, Graham Brown, and Chris Quick.

With my season over, I slid awkwardly into the role of spectator. The weekend after our state-meet triumph, the boys traveled to Terre Haute, Indiana, to contest the Nike Midwest Regional. Only the top two teams were guaranteed spots in the national final. The teams that finished third and fourth went into a pool for the four at-large bids. After the emotional peak of the previous week, I half expected them to pack their bags and head home. Instead, they ran with pride and poise, scrounging for places late in the race, and finished third behind Columbus North from Indiana and York. Exhausted in both mind and body, they ran our worst race of the season, but did just enough to impress the selection committee. Two weeks later, Steve Johnson called to tell me the bid was official. Nike would be flying our boys to Portland, Oregon, to compete for the national title.

I awoke on the morning of the Nike Cross National meet like I do on every other race morning. The only thing missing on a dreary and overcast Oregon morning was my involvement. As I lay in the middle of my comfortable queen-sized bed while my wife and baby slept, I reflected on all the years of work it had taken to see my boys run on this stage. However they ran in the next couple of hours, I knew that I was at a career end point. Nothing from this point forward would ever be the same. This was the final day of the original energy, the final first. I knew then that we might get a chance to run in this meet again. We might win future state titles. It might get "better" in the concrete ways that people measure a life, a career, or success. But I knew lying there at 5:54 AM that nothing about this could ever be "better." Whatever happened would be the end of one road and the start of another.

Since the end of our high school season, Fred Miller and Steve Johnson had been enlisted as our coaches. Fred and I had coached together for eight years before his retirement, so I trusted him completely. He and Steve kept the boys cruising along smoothly during the training interim, and I knew from their reports that the boys were still fit. Sadly, I realized that I had lost contact. The morning of the race had none of the usual stomach quivers and nervous apprehension. I was simply an excited spectator. In some way, that seemed apropos. For eleven years I had been at the center of building a team capable of running in the national final. It was finally time to step back and watch the handiwork.

Originally, I planned to make an odd battle statement by running the five miles from the La Quinta to the Portland Meadows race course, but Meredith thought better of that and agreed to drop me off. I wanted to soak in the atmosphere. The baby and my wife wanted to relax and eat breakfast. Driving up Martin Luther King Jr. Boulevard, it was easy to see the ramshackle racetrack from a distance. Rob Harvey told me earlier that it reminded him of the old Quad City Downs, a rather seedy breeding ground for low-rent harness racers rather than the venue for a national meet. He was right.

I walked through the gates as one of the first arrivals and stepped across the muddy racetrack onto the sodded infield. The morning frost had firmed up the course and rendered the perennial mud less noticeable. I started to walk. There would be no fantastic sunrise as the dank clouds gripped the racecourse and a thin fog started to roll in. The early-morning silence rang across the grounds as Nike workers rushed to set up cameras and the finish area. I walked over the famous moguls en course, the "whoop-dee-doos" that broke up each runner's rhythm. I jumped the hay bales that the runners would encounter five times during the race. I frolicked without a care in the world, awaiting the imminent fireworks of championship racing. I could not coach, but I wanted to feel the lay of the course, inspect it while clad in its race regalia, soak in the iterations of terrain, the interplay of turns and footing, the tufts of grass and the viscosity of the frosted mud.

After walking a couple of circuits I sought out Noah Brown, who was running in the open race prior to the boys championship race. Much to his chagrin, we had replaced Noah for the NXN race in favor of Graham Brown. Graham was a budding star who needed experience, but Noah had contributed more time and effort than any other senior. The choice still bothered me. We flew him to Portland on the club's dime to give him the experience, but that was no matter. True competitors do not like a free ride. Still, he prepared well, and his race loomed at 9 AM. As I talked with him and stretched, I basked in reflected glory. Bill Aris and his Fayetteville-Manlius girls walked by, looking stern and focused. A dominating and tall man, Aris possesses a rigidity that transfers into the DNA of his athletes. He carried a long wooden stick, about the size of a relay baton. I wondered if it was a reminder of their famously oaken resolve or a prod for the girls. I looked one girl dead in her eye, and she peered back at me with a face of steel. The five-time defending champions had their game faces on.

The running community is so insular, and an event like NXN only reminds you of the tight borders of the niche. I headed into the merchandise tent to buy my brother a sweatshirt for Christmas and walked by Galen Rupp, clad in a pair of oversized mudders and a pink collared shirt. His navy-blue knit hat disguised a pair of ears that stuck out awkwardly from his blond head, and no one except a runner would recognize him as an American Olympian. On this morning Rupp played the part of distance icon much as if he were an extra in a movie set with a host of bigger stars. No one would have guessed that this particular man—this skinny nerd from Oregon—had some three months before set the American record in the 10,000 meters, a staggering 26:47 clocking that sent shock waves through the running world.

As I wondered what piece of merchandise I could buy to win my brother's heart, I saw the boys stride in with Miller and Johnson. They had just arrived from the athletes' hotel, and I was surprised at the distance between us. Here I was buying a souvenir program while they were the main event. They passed quickly en route to gather their race bibs and chips while I was left to scurry after to whisper good luck. I finally stopped them and got a picture, but it was clear that their thoughts were elsewhere. Initially I wondered whether they would be happy to be at this event, content to qualify and meet a few famous people. But Peter Tomkiewicz lacked his normal affability. It had been replaced with a piercing stare. Marcus carried his camera to document the sights and sounds, but even he was not agape at the scene. Whatever Miller and Johnson had done had worked. No one betrayed any inner nervousness.

With no official role I settled into a foreign place to watch a foreign race. Nothing about the event screamed *national championship*. Noah ran well early in the open race, putting himself into the top ten before fading and finishing sixteenth. As he ran I tried to map out how I would watch the succeeding races. Usually my emotions would be at a zenith, peaking in a fury of action and piercing vocal energy during the race. Instead, I was struck like a thunderclap by how small it all seemed. I felt more passion and intensity at a Mid-Suburban League conference meet. It felt like a destination wedding where all the crazy friends and not-so-kosher guests had been lopped off the guest list by virtue of their poverty.

The best teams in the nation might have been congregated, but I quickly realized that no cross country meet I had ever seen could compare to the Illinois state meet. The fervor and emotion, the drums and the crowd hum, the frantic running to and fro, the sheer powerful speed of the fabled venue, could not be replicated. We were about to run in the national meet against the best of the best, but it could not touch the soul of Detweiller Park. Running here was like preaching to a congregation of the wealthiest donors in the church. It was an esteemed crowd, but not an impassioned one.

As the race quietly approached I casually walked around taking pictures of the various signage and people-watched for stars. Olympian Matt Tegenkamp walked past, looking out of place and sullen in his puffy vest and pink collared shirt. Alberto Salazar wandered through the mud by the team camps, then abruptly reversed field and strode off in the other direction. Maybe he left his car keys somewhere. As Tony Reavis introduced the teams, Oregon Olympian Andrew Wheating gave each kid a jolt of his child-like energy. A smoke machine inundated the athletes. Our boys heard their names announced, grasped hands, and ran out toward the crowd. The rest of the teams followed suit.

A mild chill enveloped the starting line as the runners stripped down and prepared for some cross country pain. A steady fog rolled in, first in wisps, then in larger thickets, and the temperature dropped as the gloom descended. Luckily the course retained its rather firm footing, and the slight whispers of wind would do little to impede the runners. The year before this race had been run in ankle-deep mud, every step, for the entire five-thousand-meter course. Today was a fairer test, more track meet than slog, and our guys had to feel at home. Illinois is renowned for the "track on grass" nature of its flat courses, and our boys were prepared.

Our race plan was simple. Play to our strengths by attacking the first half mile with reckless abandon. I had seen plenty of teams from outside Illinois not be ready for the shock of a 2:15 first half mile. We had trained for this. Just prior to the start I saw Marcus Garcia stride out from our box looking like a boxer in his black Nike arm warmers. He wore a steely glare, and I loved the *damn the torpedoes* nature of his body language. Marcus breathes confidence when at his best, and it was clear that he had come to Portland Meadows with his strut intact.

All week long I had worried about Gregorio. On Wednesday he had barely been able to run a sub-5:00 mile. The weak track rep revealed not just his ongoing physical sickness, but the frail state of his psyche. Despondent in mind and body, he draped himself over a fence as the rest of the team joked around and recovered. Today the coaches were asking for a 4:45 opening mile. He had saddled up so many times for so many years that he had to be tired, but we were now asking for one final ride. One for the road.

As the starter called the assembled field back for their final instructions, I took my place along the pennants near the line. For both athlete and spectator, time slowed down. The crowd, previously engaged in small talk and energetic support, hushed on its own accord. While still jiggling in the frigid morning air, the boys found their stillness. Here they were assembled, the best teams and individuals in the nation. No more polls. No more prognostication. All paused to collect themselves, paused to consider the gross stillness that always precedes a championship race.

A cross country start is a space of contemplation, a tiny window within an enormous sublocation of time itself. Previously autonomous signals come to the fore—the silence before the gun, the pulse in the wrist, the anxious heart in its moments before exertion. I watched our boys stand tall, clad in their green-and-navy uniforms. The veneer of confidence fooled no one. The moment before action brings an exquisite banquet of anxiety. Many men on the line. Many in the crowd. Silent all. Pause . . . pause . . . pause . . . gun.

The starting line exploded with furious action. I thought I had seen fast before, but this race cooked right from the gun. Most starts include a quick burst and then a lenient time when all agree to settle in and let it play out. This one galloped from the start as the field rushed forward in a leftward-bending sway of quickened arm drive and rapid turnover. We had gotten the track meet we desired, and our boys charged right into the thick of it. We knew that the race would play out in the oddest of manners. After all, forty of the best individual runners in the nation had been included in the field, and most runners on the teams could not be expected to beat them. In effect you could run just inside the top fifty and be one of the top players.

From the gun Nick Ryan from Fayetteville-Manlius asserted control. Actually his race had less to do with control than with pure and desperate courage. Futsum Zeinasellassie from Indiana was the overwhelming favorite, but even he hung back from the suicidal early pace. Through the series of moguls Ryan built a fifty-meter gap on the field. As I saw the boys the first time, our race was developing just as planned. Tony and Peter hooked up. Marcus and Timmy J hooked up. Monkey and Zambrano hooked up. Often a race is more mystical than physical. Hooking up means more than just racing together. It means communicating via your body language and closeness your intent to race in unison. The best team race involves a bond among the racers that is equal parts mental sacrifice and physical performance. When it is going well, you feel it before you see it. We were on our best game.

Marcus later told me that he and Johnson passed the thousand-meter mark in a blistering 2:58, but the big board up in the grandstand did not register our team as part of the top five. Each runner wore a timing device on his shoe, and Nike posted the scores at each thousand-meter mark in real time. Still, I was thrilled with what I saw. Peter and Tony were hammering far up in the field. Over the hay bales the first time I blasted Timmy J right in the ear with an invocation to stick with Marcus. I saw the desire in his response. He picked up his arm drive, took ten quick steps through the mud, and reattached.

Back by the starting line, Zeinasellassie assumed control. He would run away from there to an easy victory. As I headed out to the north end of the course, I glanced up at the massive electronic scoreboard and there it was. Palatine in fourth at two thousand meters, right on the edge of the top three and the podium.

All year long our guys had run best when committed to one another and out in front early. All teams have a style. Ours is lead until you bleed. We weren't quite in the lead, but for newcomers on the national scene our presence was a shock. I had believed we had this performance in us all along. My reaction was immediate. Near the halfway point I got in each guy's ear, "Palatine fourth! Palatine fourth! We're way in it! Relaxed and fast. Relaxed and fast." Peter looked like a man on a mission. Denied his opportunity a year ago when Nike rescored the Midwest Regional race, he ran as if lit from within. Who knows how much the slight had impacted his development, but here he was, a calendar year after running his breakout race, leaning on the best runners in the nation. His body language, his rhythm, his bearing said it all. He belonged.

Behind him, Tony Gregorio started to fade, first slightly and then more pronounced. He was still only ten to fifteen places behind Peter, but showing hints of dissipation. He looked pale, almost blue with the addition of the foggy chill in the air, and his chin started to quiver in a slight betrayal of strain. He started to reach. Still, the three-thousand-meter score saw no change. We were twenty points out of third, hanging on with increasing desperation. Mud covered Timmy J's face and thighs as he desperately heaved himself over the hay bales. He and Marcus continued to run as a loosely melded duo, continually in each other's sight lines, but never together.

Then it came to Meincke. Zambrano and Prodigy had dropped off precipitously after the two-thousand-meter mark, and once again Tim Meincke was alone. The NXN organizers give each prospective fifth man a red armband, and Monkey wore his with pride as he rolled up through the field. He had spent much of the year as the question mark, the "area of concern," the unstated recipient of much pressure. And here he came over the moguls, running in confident rhythm, and moving. Once again my eyes filled with tears while watching him make his mark. Monkey's career had always been marked by inconsistency. Hell, for much of his life both athletically and academically, people had doubted him and defined him by his shortcomings. He existed usually as a variable rather than a constant, yet once again he answered the call.

Monkey's momentum stanched some of the bleeding, but by four thousand meters it was clear that our guys were suffering. The elastic finally snapped on Tim Johnson as he dropped ten, then fifteen meters adrift of Marcus. Marcus simply cast his eyes downward at his leaden thighs and the increasingly deteriorated sod of the course. He concentrated only on his rhythm and his suffering as runners drifted past one by one. More so than the others, Gregorio had reached his limit. Pale from weeks of a cough and general sickness, he hung on with fantastic desperation. Blood streamed down his left shin from a spike mark, and he limped on a badly sprained ankle suffered earlier in the race. My immediate reaction was that he would not finish. He was a study in obliteration, pulverized by his earlier drive to the front. I yelled at him to compose himself. The only response was a slight relaxation and a steady flow of competitors by him on either side. Toward the north end of the course he flogged himself over the last hay bales. He dug ounce by ounce, cell by cell, down deep into his limits. I had watched every race he ever ran in high school and had never seen him so bankrupt.

But in the end running is more than a cellular activity. It is more than a scientific process of biomechanics, sweat rates, ATP production, VO_2 max, and lactic acid removal. It is an act of will. As we ran into the final quarter mile of the final meet on the final day of our year together, we were not going to win the national title. We did sum up our will for one another one last time. I found a spot nestled just far enough away from the finish line to let them hear my voice. Over the final hay bales they struggled to maintain their positions. In each man I saw intense commitment, full effort, and inscrutable care.

Echoing Shakespeare, I thought once more into the breach, dear friends, once more. But running is not combat. There are no empires at stake. Running is the refined elegance of the body in motion, a vast quest to fight off dilapidation, an impulse to feel one's pure biological flow. It is an evacuation of the head, an abandonment of consciousness, an evocation of primal urges from our evolutionary memories. When you exercise the body, you exorcise the demons of thought on the altar of carnality.

The body in full motion is the poetry of the age. All year we sought this moment together. In the beginning the hopes were arranged around glory and the concrete of achievement, but those had slowly faded into what we all craved—the doing of the act together. To run hard is to eviscerate yourself. To run hard for a team is to put that evisceration into the service of another. At its best, whether the race is won or lost becomes immaterial. To fully realize your ability to sacrifice for another is a profit far greater than the vain acceptance of an award. When the self becomes the sacrificial lamb, we eat the glory of eternal effort.

So those last meters will remain undescribed. The boys finished fifth in the nation. Some passed, some were passed. Awaiting each man at the finish line was his reckoning with the result. Each would undoubtedly have time to think about what his race meant, whether it was a success or a failure in his eyes or the eyes of the world at large. But in the small moment of the act such a reckoning was not possible. So I prefer to end it here with the seven of them, and me, and the scene, and the competition, and the crowd, and the atmosphere, hanging in eternal tableau. The only failure in a race from the heart is that it ends.

So let's freeze time right there. Better yet, let's extrapolate that final space of time into infinity. Let me forever see the lift in Peter Tomkiewicz's knees as he drives up the last bump before sweeping to the finish. Let me see Tony Gregorio's eyes downcast in one final desperate churn, one last moment of seeking the powerful kick within. Let me see Marcus Garcia faded out, erased from the effort, limp, torn up, dragged straight to the bone with exhaustion. Let me see Tim Johnson one final time swinging his left arm across his body and summoning the speed from those muscled quads. And finally, let me see, forever, Tim Meincke with the pain in his eyes, staring straight ahead in a fit of relaxed desolation. If time stops then memories do not fade and the clamor for meaning never begins. If time stops it will just be us. The dreams. The effort. The joy. Years from now, down the passing of an age and up the slopes of another, we will all hang there in ethereal bliss stuck eternally inside one last moment together. In such a moment, the race never has to end, and we will be together forever.

EPILOGUE

Photo by Cindi Johnson

One year after their dream run, the Fab Five reunite at the 2012 Illinois state meet wearing their college gear. From left, Tim Meincke (Eastern Illinois University), Anthony Gregorio (University of Iowa), Peter Tomkiewicz (Grand Valley State University), Tim Johnson (University of Missouri), and Marcus Garcia (University of Illinois–Chicago).

With our season in the sun over, it was not easy to pick up the pieces. Neither the boys nor I had ever experienced something so satisfying. Winning the state championship and finishing fifth in the Nike National meet were experiences that both validated our work and strengthened our bond. The shared memories would last a lifetime, but it is in the nature of working with young people to move on. After a well-deserved break, the next order of business was track season. We began with high hopes, but it was a difficult season for all involved. Nothing they did, no time they ran, no race they won could compare to the ultimate prize we had shared. They soldiered on anyway.

Peter Tomkiewicz accepted a scholarship to Division II track and cross country powerhouse Grand Valley State midway through the track season. He went on to demolish his personal bests, running 4:20 for 1600 meters and anchoring our distance medley relay to a school record of 10:21.8. After barely qualifying to the state track meet in the 3200 meter run, he rallied the next week and became my first All-State runner in that event. In ninety-degree heat and humidity, he ran a gutsy race to win the slower section in a near-personal-best time of 9:19. He placed eighth in the state.

The above race never would have happened without Marcus Garcia. He actually trained over the winter months and came into track fit and hungry. Throughout the season, he charged hard as usual, one-stepping the field whenever possible. Along with Peter, he qualified to the state track meet in the 3200 meter run. In the final, he ran the greatest team race of his career, trading leads with his teammate until he couldn't take his turn anymore. Faithful until the end, he set Peter up for an All-State finish while hanging on one more time to finish fourteenth in the state (only four seconds from an All-State berth himself). After procrastinating on his college search, he signed a track and cross country scholarship with the University of Illinois–Chicago.

Tim Johnson continued to explore his potential as a track athlete, never quite reaching his individual goals, but once again demonstrating the speed of great service. His attempts to emerge as an elite miler never panned out to his satisfaction, but he did run a great race to redeem his sectional disappointment from junior year. He qualified to state track in both the 1600 meter run and the 4 x 800 meter relay. Running second leg, he once again led us into the state final, into the school record books, and onto the All-State podium. He and his teammates—converted sprinter Kendric Cornelius and juniors Christian Zambrano and Andrew Clingerman—placed ninth in the state. Earlier in the spring, Tim accepted a guaranteed walk-on spot at the University of Missouri.

After the emotional end to his cross country season, Anthony Gregorio prepared to close out his career as an All-State 3200 meter runner. It didn't work out. After running 9:21 during the indoor track season, he contracted mono in early April and missed nearly a month of training. He came back anyway, training as best he could with little prospect of making our invitational lineup much less qualifying to state. With Marcus and Peter dominating and mono rendering him exhausted, we knew there would be no reprise of his best. I put him in the MSL conference lineup anyway, more to save Peter's strength than anything else, but he responded. Five weeks after the mono diagnosis, he ran 9:26 to finish sixth in the conference. In many respects, it was the greatest race he ever ran, full of the faith and toughness that had made him an All-Time Great. After turning down numerous scholarship offers, he accepted academic aid and a guaranteed walk-on spot at the University of Iowa. His dream of competing in the Big Ten will come true beginning next fall.

Tim Meincke never again summoned the magic he found uphill at Detweiller to kick us to a state championship. He competed well at times, running 4:26 for 1600 meters and 1:58 in the 800 meters, but a late case of strep throat sapped his strength and kept him from winning the intra-team competition to make our 4 x 800 meter relay. It was no matter. In one of our last runs together during the week of the state track meet, I told him that those sixty seconds of running—from the zigzag at Detweiller to the finish line—were the most unforgettable moment of my life. He told me that he thinks about that finish every day. Me too. Tim decided to continue his track and cross country career as a walk-on at Eastern Illinois University.

As for me, I just keep on trucking. It took a long time to absorb that thrill of a lifetime. Living those few months after we won was like floating on an ethereal cloud, knowing that it would have to dissipate someday, but wishing the magic could last forever. I am used to it by now. I help raise them and love them and run with them for four years so that they can move on. My work is never really finished. There are more young men to meet and more journeys to enjoy. Like an individual, each team has its own personality and potentiality. Just as soon as I let one go, another avid group of strivers emerges with another story to write.

So I am just going to keep writing, living through our common dreams, and spinning more narrative from the ambitious days we spend together. Someday, there will be no more journey, no more quest, and I'll have to find other stories to tell. But for now, it's once again summer, and I'm spoiling to keep searching for that elusive magic. I don't feel it in the air each day. But if you live the life of the run hard enough and splay yourself across the altar of its pain long enough, the universe might just give you a glimpse. You once again will see "the pearl of great price." It's not attainable through money or reputation. It has to be sought faithfully and at great personal cost. But I know now its weight. I have held it in my hand and felt its smooth perfection. Someday I will hold it in my hands again and share it with the people I love. In such a moment, all of it—the striving and the heartache, the elation and the sorrow—will take tangible form, and I will feel once again what it is to live.

The athletes and coaches of the 2011 Class AAA Illinois state championship team. Top row (from left): Brian Smith, Peter Tomkiewicz, Zach Stella, Tim Johnson. Second row: Graham Brown, Noah Brown, Tim Meincke, Christian Zambrano, Andrew Clingerman. Third row: Coaches James Macatangay, Mike Nigliaccio, Chris Quick, Matt Sheehan, Mark Hajik, Chris Vargas. Foreground: Marcus Garcia, Joe Mars, Anthony Gregorio.

Photo by Cindi Johnson

ACKNOWLEDGMENTS

I am indebted to many people who either inspired or aided in the production of this book. The initial inspiration to write came from the members of my 2010–11 sophomore critical thinking–gifted class. I'd like to thank Jenny Ripka, Jenny Tucker, Emma Goodwin, Maddie Rasor, Bekah Van Wolvelear, Faith Hollander, Mike Nowicki, Connor McCall, Alex Brons, Nick Brucks, and Preslav Mantchev for creating an honest and emotionally satisfying learning environment. They inspired me to become a writer again.

Many of my colleagues and friends provided invaluable advice through the many drafts of this work. My teaching partner, Lynda Appino, deserves credit for encouraging me during the early phases of writing.

She provided the positive feedback I needed to see this through to completion. Karen Brookwell-Miller was my first mentor in the English Department at Palatine, and her reading of my first manuscript was invaluable. I'd also like to thank Dan Horyn, a dear friend from my University of Illinois days and a coaching colleague from Niles North High School. Dan and I spent four hours at a diner in Des Plaines going over his notes on the manuscript. Just two weeks later, he learned he had cancer, and he's been fighting it ever since. He continues to be a source of inspiration for me as a teacher, coach, and person.

My high school English teacher and mentor, Tim Curry, died during the writing of this book. I am forever indebted to him for fanning the flames when I was sixteen years old. He showed me that you can follow your passion for reading and writing and turn it into a career. My continued desire to teach Advanced Placement English owes everything to the example he set for so many of us during our years at Moline High School.

My parents were of course my first inspirations, and I can't say enough thanks to Jeff and Penny Quick for raising me and continuing to inspire me. My dad taught me how to be a coach, and my mom taught me to love reading and writing. Both of their imprints are all over this book. Thanks, Mom and Dad, for allowing me to spend so much of my childhood with my nose in a book and for actually encouraging me to study what I loved.

My brother, Chad, continues to be the long-standing inspiration for the life I hope to lead. He could spend so much time bemoaning what he cannot do, but instead focuses on helping young people. His work at Rock Island High School with their special education and ESL learners reflects an amazing spirit and a sincere commitment to kids. I try each day to meet his standards.

I would be remiss if I didn't thank the men and women whom I have coached with at Palatine High School. Other than my father, Fred Miller, Steve Currins, and Chaille Gleason have been the greatest mentors of my professional life. From the first time we spoke on the telephone in 2001, I knew I had found a kindred soul in Fred Miller. Our combined work as coaches set the table for the amazing events that make up this narrative. As for Steve, everyone who knows him understands the passion he has for cross country and track. I am honored to have learned as many of his tricks of the trade as I could. Chaille Gleason is one of the great jumps and hurdles coaches in the state. Watching her share her passion for track with kids has been an inspiration.

I also need to thank our current girls cross country coach, Joe Parks, and my current coaching staff. Joe and I decided that we would coach both of these programs all-out and together as long as we could. He and our girls team won their seventh state title in 2009, leading the way to our title on the guys side. For Matt Sheehan, I am indebted to all of your hard work and the energy you brought to help us stop winning second-place state trophies and finally win the big one. I would also like to thank Mark Hajik, Chris Vargas, Mike Nigliaccio, and James Macatangay for all the time they volunteered to help the boys.

I would be remiss if I didn't thank the boys for everything they have given me over the years. If I could, I would list each one of you from 2001 to now because you have all been worth my time, effort, and love. I spent years dreaming of coaching at a school like Palatine, and I am constantly surprised by the boundless energy and enthusiasm of the young men and women I have met through the cross country and track programs. Special thanks is due to Eric Blyth whose encouragement, book design skills, and friendship got this project off the ground. To the men of the 2011 Palatine cross country team, thank you for taking me on the defining journey of my adult life. You wrote this book for me. All I had to do was catch the best moments.

Lastly, I am forever in debt to the patience and love of my family. Coming home each night to Madeline, Christopher, and J. J. keeps my priorities straight and helps me realize that the daily ups and downs of teaching and coaching always take a backseat to three happy and healthy kids. The fact that all three of you love Daddy whether we win or lose means the world to me.

For Meredith, my wife and partner in crime, I owe you everything. The strongest part of love is giving of yourself to make someone else's life possible. I can never thank you enough for helping make all of my dreams come true as a husband, father, teacher, and coach. In the end, I'd be happy just to watch you age.